FROM ALICE TO HARRY POTTER:

CHILDREN'S FANTASY IN ENGLAND

Colin Manlove

From Alice to Harry Potter:

Children's Fantasy in England

Cybereditions

Cybereditions Corporation
Christchurch, New Zealand
www.cybereditions.com
cybereditions@cybereditions.com

Cybereditions welcomes comments from readers.
In particular we wish to be informed of any misprints
or errors in our books, so that we may correct them.

ISBN 1-877275-55-7

Printed in the United States of America

CONTENTS

FOR EVELYN

ACKNOWLEDGEMENTS

I am grateful to Macmillan Press for permission to use six pages from my *The Fantasy Literature of England* (1999) at the beginning of Chapter 2.

I should also like to pay tribute to the late Mrs Sheila Campbell of Edinburgh for the devoted secretarial work done for me over the past twenty-five years.

To my wife Evelyn, more thanks for her help than a dedication can convey.

C. M.
Edinburgh, February 2003

1 INTRODUCTION

In 1817 Robert Bloomfield, author of *The History of Little Davy's New Hat*, wrote 'The longer I live ... the more I am convinced of the importance of children's books.'[1] That similar statements are still being made two hundred years later shows us how much children's books have always had to prove in England. And it has been harder still for children's fantasy, since it supposedly goes against that hearty empiricism which has been as much the hallmark of the standard Englishman as once was his roast beef. Bloomfield, after all, was talking about 'realistic' children's books which could be made useful by being directed to the moral and social education of children. Towards the comic or fantastical others he harboured nothing but scorn, and directed parents to put them to the one use for which they were fitted, namely, lighting fires.

My broad intention in this book is to support Bloomfield's enthusiasm and answer his scorn, showing how excellent English children's fantasies often are as literature, and how ample the range of originality that has gone into their making. Indeed I want to show that they often have the amount of depth and literary skill we find in more evidently sophisticated texts. The issue has nothing to do with children's literature's popularity, which is a wayward thing that comes and goes, but with its cultural acceptance. Though this might seem a *fait accompli* in the growing numbers of courses in children's literature in universities, anyone who teaches it will know the veiled condescension with which it is regarded by colleagues who teach more 'academically respectable' texts. To remove the grounds for such condescension seems an essential goal.

Indeed in recent years just such a goal has been pursued through current literary theory, which has found strangely fertile soil in children's literature. Now such procedures as intertextual, 'new historical,' metafictional, reader-response, ideological or feminist readings can be applied to texts from Sarah Fielding's *The Governess* to J. K. Rowling's *Harry Potter*. But while these approaches have often benefited children's literature, they have also tended to confine themselves to particularly responsive examples of it: so that they have established something of a literary canon, the very thing to which they are theoretically opposed. This canon involves texts which are sufficiently complex or problematic to afford ready handholds for what are complex critical methodologies. Thus we find an odd crew of the acceptable, such as *Mopsa the Fairy*, *Charlotte's Web*, *The Mouse and his Child*, *Where the Wild Things Are*, *The Chocolate War* or *The Stinky Cheese Man*: but rarely if ever an account of the whole kind, nationally or internationally. Further, by using critical procedures that have current academic vogue, these approaches sometimes have the appearance of giving priority more to the theory than to the literature. Jack Zipes puts it this way: 'There is still a certain sentiment or ideological attitude that the work in the field is not as demanding and deserving of recognition as the work in other areas.'[2]

What I want to do here is try to make sense of the whole tradition of English children's fantasy, covering as many texts as possible. More specifically, this book will give a critical survey of English children's fantasy from about 1850 to the present day, placing all the texts in a current of development. Each chapter will consider a phase of the growth of the genre, whether as long as the Victorian period or as short as each decade from 1970 to 2000. Each of these periods marks a particular idiom or concern which all the works in it share, though there will be transitions and discriminations to be observed. The sequence of these different impulses will be shown to constitute an ongoing cultural and spiritual process behind the whole development of English children's fantasy. Thereafter there will be a consideration of how the various characteristics discussed make this fantasy peculiarly English. The whole subject has not yet received the attention it deserves.

Children's and young adult literature is the one area of writing where one age group writes for another. Children's literature is therefore written at a distance, by people who have to try to remember what it feels like to be a child, or try to construct a childhood to write at. The tendency either to talk down to the child, as in Victorian improvement literature, or to talk up to it, as in Wordsworth or the 'Golden Age' writers of the 1890s, is ever-present. We are insatiable evolutionists, seeing childhood either as a time of ignorance from which we have grown up, or else as a paradisal time from which we have declined. There have been those such as Jacqueline Rose or Karen Lesnik-Oberstein[3] who argue that this means there cannot really be a *children's* literature, and that what children are given is a series of images of themselves by adults. While there is much truth in this, it does neglect the points at which there is contact and genuine communication between adult writer and child reader, where as Peter Hollindale puts it, there is 'childhood intensity and urgency of storying' because 'childhood is alive in memory and present existence.'[4]

Some of the best books written for children are those in which the author seems to forget he or she is doing so, because adult and child worlds of discourse are so perfectly joined: Hollindale calls this 'childness'; authors speak of writing to the child in themselves. When Lewis Carroll talks in an adult voice about the wonders of childhood before and after the stories of Alice, and when he devotes *Sylvie and Bruno* to the glorification of a precocious infant, he is awkward and embarrassing: when he is preoccupied within his imagination in the *Alice* stories, the years have not dimmed his magnificence. His stories may be told to and for children (as to the Liddells in the boat in 1862) but when he tells them he too seems partly in a child's world. That too is the power of Hans Andersen's stories, or Kingsley's *The Water-Babies*, of Kipling's *Jungle Books* and E. Nesbit's magic tales; of the adventures of Masefield and Tolkien, of the best of C. S. Lewis's Narnia books; of Roald Dahl and Richard Adams and Diana Wynne Jones.

There is arguably no difference in status between the child and the adult; only ignorance separates them.[5] To a greater or lesser extent we are still children, only with different ends in view. (In Germany children now have equal rights with adults.) Indeed both Rose and Lesnik-Oberstein have said that the child continues in the repressed (and largely inaccessible) unconscious of the adult.[6] And in the same way there is not any final difference between children's and adult literature. Children's literature will often have less complexity of plot, less profundity of psychological analysis, and more simple pleasures and pains than are found in adult writing; and it will, usually, have the security of the happy ending; yet in its creations of new worlds, its explorations of alien points of view, its subtle investigations of language and metaphysics, and its continual spiritual penetration, it gives us a creative country as 'mature' as the adult's. In the 'Golden Age' of American children's literature from 1865 to 1914, there was often little felt distinction between adults' and children's literature, and *Little Women* and *Tom Sawyer* were reviewed beside *Moby Dick* and *The Marble Faun*. Children's literature was in a similar position in England from about 1890–1924; and throughout the nineteenth century, authors from Thackeray and Dickens to Wilde and Kipling wrote children's fantasy as well as their more 'adult' fiction.

Here, then, there will be less interest in children's fantasy specifically as children's, than simply as a certain kind of fantasy literature, to be set beside more 'adult' works such as William Morris's tales, Herbert Read's *The Green Child* or Mervyn Peake's *Titus Groan*. There really is no categorical difference here between Tolkien's *The Hobbit* and *The Lord of the Rings*, between C. S. Lewis's Narnia books and his *Out of the Silent Planet*, or between E. Nesbit's fairy-tale parodies and Terry Pratchett's Discworld novels. George MacDonald, whose adult fantasy *Phantastes* is no more 'advanced' than his children's book *The Princess and the Goblin*, once said, 'I do not write for children, but for the childlike, whether of five, or fifty, or seventy-five';[7] and many writers of children's fantasy would agree with him. The present-day fantasy writer Philip Pullman has put it in these terms: "'Down with children's books!'".[8]

What makes children's fantasy a genre at all, is – apart from the features we have noted already – that it usually has child characters, and that publishers market it for children. Until their recent financial empowerment, it has not generally been children who buy it, but adults for them: many children would often rather buy less approved objects. Librarians, teachers, publishers, prize-awarders and then parents: these are the people who have really constructed a canon of children's literature, from *Alice* to *Northern Lights*, a canon continually defied by children's more enthusiastic cultural attachments through the decades, from *Biggles* or Blyton to *Harry Potter* or R. L. Stine. For years, as writers themselves have recognised, the prizes may go to the finest books, but these are not often the ones most read by their supposed targets, unless they are middle class, intelligent, inquiring and, most commonly, female.

So we are talking about a largely invented genre, directed at children, but not always freely chosen by them. It is a genre that floats between two ages, often without really belonging to either. A child, reading it, might often learn more about an adult's re-creation of childhood than about the often hard-edged thing he or she knows. But despite its mongrel nature, children's literature, and in particular children's fantasy, is currently enormously popular, and remains a phenomenon to be seriously discussed.

So what, then is English children's fantasy? To answer this we will have to take the name piece by piece. Fantasy is one thing: children's fantasy narrows it; and English children's fantasy further. Even so we have to remember that adult constructs of children and childhood themselves have changed over the past century and a half,[9] that England is not the same thing it was in 1850, and that fantasy has developed forms and materials that were not possible in its inception.

So far as 'fantasy' is concerned, the definition is, as in my *The Fantasy Literature of England*, 'a fiction involving the supernatural or impossible.' 'Supernatural,' as said there, implies some form of magic or of supernatural being, from an angel to a fairy; 'impossible' means something we think cannot be, such as E. Nesbit's Psammead or the world of the *Pooh* books. This definition is open to challenge, but is a serviceable rule of thumb, and is broadly the one used to define fantasy in the encyclopedias and bibliographies. It is also the one adopted by the current leading writer on children's fantasy, Maria Nikolajeva, in her *The Magical Code: The Use of Magical Patterns in Fntasy for Children* (1988). However, there are numerous modes of fantasy. Sometimes it is comical, as in *Pooh*; sometimes it is nonsense, as in Lear; it can be social criticism in Wilde, Christian apologetics in C. S. Lewis, nostalgia in Kenneth Grahame, or political allegory in W. J. Corbett. The definition given here can only be a formal, not a vital one: more a corral than a characterisation.

Some further justification of it is needed in relation to other current definitions of fantasy. Perhaps the most influential has been Rosemary Jackson's view of fantasy as a 'literature of subversion,' which liberates the suppressed areas of the psyche and undermines repressive structures, from rational self-control to political tyranny. Jackson's definition is particularly illuminating in relation to 'dark' or gothic fantasy, but it wholly excludes the fantasies of such writers as

INTRODUCTION

George MacDonald, C. S. Lewis and J. R. R. Tolkien, which she sees as authoritarian and life-denying. Broadly Jackson's preference is for a fantasy of the unconscious rather than the conscious mind, and one that is radical rather than conservative. Another recent writer of a not dissimilar view is Joseph Monléon, who sees fantasy as a post-Romantic phenomenon exhibited in certain Spanish writers of the period 1780–1830. And so we might go on through the narrownesses – and sharpnesses - of focus in Tzvetan Todorov, Christine Brooke-Rose, T. E. Apter, Tobin Siebers, Neil Cornwell or Lucy Armitt, all of them discussing the same kinds of subversive text, commonly from nineteenth-century Europe, and all of them constructing definitions of fantasy out of a single class of animal rather than the whole zoo. No less narrow, however, are those on the other side, such as Tolkien or Lewis, who see fantasy as recovering old or traditional values, and would exclude practically all the fantasies that Jackson foregrounds. Of course there is insight to be gained by focus on one area: but in the end one learns as much about the critic's views as about the thing itself.

English fantasy has at least six modes, each containing different authors – secondary world, metaphysical, emotive, comic, subversive and children's fantasy. Any definition, to be adequate, should cover all these. Further, there are considerable differences between fantasies of different times and places. Nineteenth-century English fantasy is very different from twentieth-century, 1950s from 1960s; England's fantasy is radically different from Scotland's, and both from America's. Equally, in the children's literature we shall be looking at, the fantastic vision of one writer may be completely opposed to that of another writing in the same kind. Therefore, our definition is best where as said it is rule of thumb, where it strikes a spark: no more, or we will find no end to it, and no justice to all the writers. The most comprehensive recent book on the nature of fantasy by Kathryn Hume settles for a not dissimilar formula: '*Fantasy is any departure from consensus reality*.'[10]

As for *children's* fantasy, it is fantasy either written or published for a child readership up to eighteen, and which some children have read, whether voluntarily or not.[11] On the whole this also means that it will (as observed) have child characters, an exciting plot and a happy ending (though the last two are less essential for the teenager); and we might add absolute distinctions of good and bad. Naturally the fantasy will vary in character according to the age, sex or period of its addressees. Moreover insofar as childhood itself can in different times end now earlier, now later – today for instance one girl in six is said to reach puberty before age eight, and half are fertile by ten[12] - a book directed at a particular age group in one generation may be largely irrelevant to the next.[13]

For children, on the whole, read middle-class children. Children's fantasy is for most of its history a middle-class literature, written with a strong sense of family and educational values. There are till recently few 'working class' writers of English children's fantasy, and therefore relatively little sense of the often quite different values and problems of less financially secure members of society. Gestures are made at broken homes and lives by Kingsley in *The Water-Babies* (1863) and E. Nesbit in *Harding's Luck* (1909), but all is soon forgotten or cleared up;[14] only in the 1970s, with Helen Creswell in *The Winter of the Birds* (1973), Jill Paton Walsh in *A Chance Child* (1979), or Robert Westall in *The Watch House* (1979), do we begin to have books that look to a wider and less stable world; significantly, these are among the few English children's fantasies that are set in cities.

The peculiarly English character of these fantasies must await the end of this book, when we will have the materials with which to describe it. For the time the definition must be more external. By 'English' in 'English children's fantasy' is first meant books first published in England by either English or domiciled writers, and having a primarily English readership. This includes certain Scots writers living and writing in England, such as George MacDonald, J. M. Barrie, Andrew Lang and Kenneth Grahame: their fantasies are also often either set in England or have 'English' characters. There are also special cases such as W. W. Tarn and Eric Linklater, the first an Englishman writing about Skye, and the second a Scotsman whose children's fantasy is English in character and part of the English tradition. Naturally, there are influences from beyond England, such as Grimms' or Andersen's fairy tales, and these have become almost a part of the English children's fantasy tradition; and more recently American fantasy writers from Ursula Le Guin to R. L. Stine have taken a not inconsiderable slice of English children's reading. Nevertheless, in general English children's fantasy is less influenced by others than influential on them.

English children's fantasy has the distinction of having been the first on the international scene. Aside from the work of Hans Christian Andersen and of Heinrich Hoffman (of *Struwwelpeter*), neither the continent nor America produced anything of note until the last decades of the nineteenth century, by which time England had seen the children's fantasy of Thackeray, Edward Lear, Lewis Carroll, George MacDonald and others.[15] It was the strength of the genre in England which stimulated other countries to follow suit. Children's fantasy enjoyed a golden age in England from about 1850 till the First World War, and drew in some of the ablest writers of the time – Browning, Ruskin, Thackeray, Dickens, Wilde, Kipling. And this happened in the teeth of much early opposition to the fairy tale as frivolous and irresponsibly fanciful.

What made England and children's fantasy go so well together? There were probably two main factors. First, the views of childhood and the imagination were changing. In the eighteenth and early nineteenth century 'the child' was seen from a developmental point of view, as a creature of wayward tendencies to be carefully educated towards adulthood; and equally the free imagination was often frowned on as irresponsible and even socially dangerous. (Not that children did not pick up numbers of the latter's productions from chapbooks or their nursemaids.) But Blake's pictures of oppressed childhood innocence in his *Songs of Innocence* (1789), and Wordsworth's famous *Ode on the Intimations of Immortality* (1807), together with both poets' celebrations of the unconfined energies of the imagination, were symptoms of a changing view.

By these lights, the 'child state' was seen not as something to be educated away, but as a happy condition of natural innocence which the world too often crushes. The child becomes seen as a being in its own right rather than as part of a process. On this view adults should become more like children rather than the other way round; and children's literature should be what appeals to them, not what adults think proper for them. Children's fantasy moves between these two extremes of attitude in the nineteenth century, so that where the moral tale is dominant in 1800, imagination and the child are almost unchallenged by 1900. In Kenneth Grahame's *The Golden Age* (1895), the children abolish adults from their lives, and E. Nesbit's *The Book of Dragons* (1900) is a collection of purely fanciful and entertaining tales without any moral at all. From being a potential demon, the child has become a god.

The point of change, according to Kimberley Reynolds, is the 1860s, when the idea of the 'beautiful child' begins to take hold in the Victorian mind, and a specific genre of children's literature makes its first appearance.[16] At this time the pervasive Calvinist notion that children are fallen creatures of sin who have to be brought by teaching to salvation finally gives way, through the late popularisation of the more nostalgic theories of Rousseau, to an idea of the child as

> the pure, blameless link to the prelapsarian world. ... In this new version of childhood, what the child acquired through instruction and experience of the world was not a state of grace, but a loss of perfection – the consequence of contact with what Rousseau pejoratively termed 'civilization.'

Childhood thus becomes an object of nostalgia and veneration. And it also becomes a state divided by its purity from adulthood. The arrival of 'childhood' instantly provided a new market for publishers, for 'without an established concept of childhood, there can be no children's literature.' Reynolds goes on to argue that it is 'precisely *because* childhood is presumed to be innocent that so many writers have felt it safe to let their private fantasies find expression in writing for children.'[17]

But there is one further feature which gives children's fantasy its appeal to a wide Victorian public: and that, oddly enough, is the Industrial Revolution. In England the transformation from a rural to an industrial economy, from handcraft to factory, occurred far earlier and with far greater speed than in any other nation. Large numbers of cottage workers were abruptly made redundant by the new methods of factory production, and forced to congregate in towns to find work: soon the country itself became partly blighted by industry and the spread of urban slums. The country slowly ceased to be the place where most people lived and worked, and a sense of a lost good place lodged deep in the national psyche, to surface in the elegiac strain that pervades much late eighteenth- and nineteenth-century poetry. Such a feeling readily identified itself with the child, whose innocence is lost in adulthood. Children's fantasy thus met a strong emotional need in the general public, because it often portrayed another and often pastoral world in which the imagination could be free and evils might be overcome. Not a few Victorian novels have a parallel idiom, in which wrongs are defeated, justice is dispensed, and the hero and heroine retire to a country cottage. And this marriage of children's fantasy and pastoral in the adult mind endured over a century, until fantasy became more accepting of the mainly urban lives of modern children: even now there is still an impulse to associate children with innocent nature.

A word here about the 'precious old' English fairy tale – 'Jack and the Beanstalk,' 'Jack the Giant-Killer,' 'Childe Rowland,' 'Tom Thumb,' 'The Three Little Pigs' and others. Though these were made known to children in the eighteenth and nineteenth centuries by way of chapbooks and (later) in fairy tale collections, the strange fact is that the source and stimulus of English children's fantasy came more from foreign tales, particularly those of Perrault, Grimm and Andersen. The actual number of English traditional fairy tales was scant in comparison to any of these. And though translations of national collections of fairy tales from all over Europe came into England throughout the nineteenth century, it was not until 1890 that the first, relatively thin, collection of English tales appeared, edited by Joseph Jacobs. However, while the home fairy tale may have played a limited part in the development of English children's fantasy, it will be found to exhibit many characteristics in common with it – demonstrating a similar national temper in the working of fireside wonder-stories as in those penned from literary escritoires. These features include a strong practical streak and an emphasis on working things out; a domestic and often house-based action; concern with family relationships rather than with romantic ones; small interest in advancement to royal rank; and a recurrent penchant for putting miniature people beside giants.[18]

As said, over the last twenty years children's literature has become the focus for a large number of critical methodologies, all of them founded on a notion of literature, and a self-awareness in examining it, radically different from before. These have raised many questions, and challenged many assumptions. The very idea that there can be a *children's* literature, since the genre emerges from adults who can only construct their notions of childhood at a distance, has as we have seen been challenged by such writers as Jacqueline Rose and Karen Lesnik-Oberstein. There have been those such as Peter Hollindale and Peter Hunt who advocate a 'childist' criticism that tries to see the texts as children might; and 'reader response' and psychoanalytical critics such as Nicholas Tucker, Lois Kuznets and Margaret and Michael Rustin, who portray the ways in which texts can be transformative of children's psyches. John Stephens, Murray Knowles and Kirsten Malmkjær have analysed some of the linguistic means of ideological control in children's literature. Structuralists such as Maria Nikolajeva see children's fantasy as the continual reconstitution/recycling of a few narrative devices or fantasemes; while deconstructionist criticism on the other hand attempts to show the ways in which texts do not cohere. Feminist and gender-based criticism, such as Lissa Paul's or U. C. Knoepflmacher's, traces the impulse against male authority in children's literature. The approach of new historicism, as in the work of Mitzi Myers, changes our understanding of past literature by exposing the paternalistic and other assumptions of previous historical critics. Intertextual criticism, as by John Stephens or U. C. Knoepflmacher, supposes that the meaning of a text may be determined through its relations with others.[19]

Many of these approaches are de-centrist in aim. They want to get away from the idea of a cultural focus, and they question the old literary canon; they want to see history not as given past facts but as a multiplicity of biased present interpretations; they wish to remove the idea of the work, the 'text,' as the single centre of meaning, and substitute the multitude of its various readings or intertextual relations; they oppose a criticism that speaks of a work in terms of its unity, or its governing themes; they prefer the amplitude of the unconscious to the straight and narrow line of the conscious mind.[20] Philosophically this is often a choice of idealism over empiricism; politically it is Marxism over conservatism; sexually it is feminism over masculinism; and personally it would seem to be doubt over certainty, were it not that the practitioners of this new criticism are often no less certain than those of the old of the rightness of their views. Though this criticism would see itself as putting literary interpretation on a much more self-aware, theory-grounded and scientific footing, it occupies no more and no less of the truth than the approaches it dismisses.

The view here is that the conscious mind is as real as the unconscious one, that texts are singularities as much as they are shared, and closed systems as much as open ones. The procedure has been to start from individual texts, and then to see similarities with others belonging to the same cultural period, until whole groupings with similar concerns are built up, ultimately founded on a matrix of social history. At that point one sees how one period gives way to another, and has a process of psychic development across the entire genre. There is nothing new in this procedure, and by the lights of current criticism of children's literature it is outdated, for it gives authority to the text and not the critic, and it supposes that there may be an 'objective' world, a world 'out there,' in which both text and history exist. On present understanding this limits my approach no less than those of the recent theorists; but on the evidence there is also as much lingering - or growing - support for it.

The kinds of books I have therefore found most useful for my purposes have been the reference works and histories – Ruth Nadelman Lynn's annotated bibliographies, the *Oxford Companion*, the *Cambridge Guide*, the histories by F. J. H. Darton, Gillian Avery and Peter Hunt. While I find earlier critics of children's literature such as Marcus Crouch, John Rowe Townsend and Margery Fisher a great encouragement in their enthusiasm, they do not always see as far as I would like into the texts.

Previous accounts of the genre itself have also been very helpful. Ann Swinfen's *In Defence of Fantasy: A Study of the Genre in English and American Literature since 1945* (1984) was suggestive, although her approach is in terms of types of children's fantasy rather than its development. I also found Humphrey Carpenter's *Secret Gardens: The Golden Age of Children's Literature* (1985) very congenial. Sheila Egoff's survey of international children's fantasy, *Worlds Within: Children's Fantasy from the Middle Ages to Today* (1988) was a mine of information. The structuralist analysis in Maria Nikolajeva's *The Magic Code: The Use of Magical Patterns in Fantasy for Children* (1988), while a remarkable picture of the range and recurrent limits of the fantastic imagination, necessarily ignores change in the genre, even though the author at one point claims that recently it has become more complex in its deployment of fantasemes.[21] Patricia Smith's *The Fabulous Realm: A Literary-Historical Approach to British Fantasy, 1780–1990* (1993) is particularly useful on what she calls the 'diversionary' fantasy of the period 1900–1949. Other books of note which cover selected works of English children's fantasy are John Stephens's *Language and Ideology in Children's Fiction* (1992), U. C. Knoepflmacher's *Ventures into Childland* (1998) and Margaret and Michael Rustin's *Narratives of Love and Loss* (rev. ed., 2000). Though their interests differ from mine - Knoepflmacher is concerned with changing gender roles in children's fantasy from Ruskin to Christina Rossetti, Stephens with how authors control their readers ideologically, and the Rustins with empathetic reader-response and emotional change - their individual interpretations have often been illuminating.

My main obligations in writing this book are really to the writers themselves, whose books have given me pleasure I often missed when I was young.

2 VICTORIAN CHILDREN'S FANTASY

There is an extraordinary growth of children's literature in the nineteenth century, particularly in the area of fantasy. This was a time when English fantasy as a whole was enjoying a renaissance after over a century of comparative neglect.[1] The imaginative impulse had returned to favour after long being viewed with suspicion, and was expressing itself in a series of inventive, diverse and often chaotic-seeming works, from Carlyle's *Sartor Resartus* (1836), Tennyson's *Poems* of 1842, or Dickens's *Bleak House* (1853) to Browning's *Men and Women* (1855). In this energetic, even explosive atmosphere, expressing the expansive character of the age,[2] fantasy, the very home of the imagination and invention, flourished and produced some of its finest, and wildest, examples.

But in this period it was not known as 'fantasy,' but as 'fairy tale.' This is because its form often took something from the traditional fairy tale as found, say, in Grimm or Perrault; or it was thought to be the descendant of such tales, even though as a literary and invented narrative it was often radically different. Thus even Douglas Jerrold's adult satire *A Man Made of Money* (1848–9) begins with a magical transformation by a dwarf; and George MacDonald's *Phantastes* (1858) is launched by a fairy granting a wish. Thackeray's 'fireside pantomime' (1855) has a ruling fairy and a fairy-tale plot, and continually parodies fairy tale; Kingsley subtitled his submarine fantasy *The Water-Babies* (1863) 'a fairy-tale for a land-baby'; and even though they have scarcely any resemblance to the traditional fairy tale, this is how Lewis Carroll described the *Alice* books. There had been an earlier cult of the fairy tale started by adults in French aristocratic salons in the late seventeenth century out of préciosité and for amusement, and this was pursued in eighteenth-century England, but the Victorian fairy tale is generally much more inventive, and frequently directed at children.

The craze for 'fairy tale' – for it was to become a craze, like that for the medieval romance or the Elizabethan sonnet or, for that matter, the Victorian ghost story – really began with the first appearance of a children's Grimm, in Edgar Taylor's two-volume translation, *German Popular Stories*, of 1823–6. The huge popularity of these stories stimulated an increasing volume of translations of fairy tales throughout the nineteenth century, from the influential and often invented stories of Hans Andersen (1846) to the twelve *Fairy Book* collections of Andrew Lang (1889–1912) – Norse, Persian, French, Japanese, Russian, ancient Greek, Indian, Finnish and others; only the English traditional fairy tale itself remained strangely uncollected (see chapter 1, above), though many individual tales were in print. From being deplored in the eighteenth century as a menace to the rational calm of the English child's mind, both the traditional and the literary fairy tale gradually became accepted over the nineteenth century as a source of imaginative enrichment: the whole period from the 1830s is full of fairy operas, ballets, pantomimes and paintings.[3] One may surmise that the form of the traditional fairy tale, with its strict rules of magic and its clear rewards of merit and punishments of vice, appealed to that side of all anxious Victorians which welcomed a genre founded not just on the imagination but on moral certainties and an ordered and just universe. This, after all, is the idiom of much of their supposedly realistic fiction too.[4]

Two contrary impulses have often fairly been said to dominate in children's literature, particularly during the nineteenth century – the wish to instruct, and the wish to amuse.[5] (The former is unfortunately almost always viewed negatively.) Sometimes the instructive side was dominant, and the amusement side was reduced to being its sponsor; sometimes amusement was primary, and the instruction might become vestigial: the two were not often in balance or fused. It is between these two impulses – which may also be put as morality and imagination – that early children's fantasy negotiates.

Instruction, whether moral or pedagogic, is to the fore in the period from about 1750–1860, when the magic of a fairy tale may even be explained away to the reader as a device for the better inculcation of the lesson. Till 1800, indeed, few traditional fairy tales, apart from those circulated in chapbooks,[6] or the occasional *rara avis* such as Horace Walpole's privately-printed *Hieroglyphic Tales* (1785) survived the atmosphere of Evangelical and rationalist control. However the techniques if not the content of such tales were not infrequently taken over into more instructive stories;[7] and a genre developed in which animals or objects were made to speak of their lives and reflect morally on their involvement with humans, particularly children: examples are Dorothy Kilner's *The Perambulations of a Mouse* (1783) or Sarah Trimmer's *History of the Robins* (1786).[8] In her enduringly popular *The Governess: or, Little Female Academy* (1749), Sarah Fielding admitted two anaemic invented fairy tales under strict caveats, voiced by her Mrs Teachum to her infant charges: "'Giants, Magic, Fairies, and all Sorts of supernatural Assistances in a Story, are only introduced to amuse and divert.... Therefore, by no means let the notion of Giants or Magic dwell upon your Minds'".[9] This however comes not from any joyless dislike of entertainment for children, but from a concern that they should not lose the spiritual benefits of the story through the distraction from its contents. In 1803 Lucy Aikin, in the preface to her *Poetry for Children*, boasted that 'dragons and fairies, giants and witches have vanished from our nurseries before the wand of reason.' Mary Martha Sherwood, who rewrote Sarah Fielding's *The Governess* under her own name in 1820, banished all but one pious fable from her book, which nevertheless reached its sixth edition by 1840. As late as 1870 we find George Cruikshank, at the end of his marvellously illustrated *Fairy Library* of four well-known tales,[10] not only bidding his readers to dismiss the fairies and giants as mere pretence, but reasserting his right to alter what he saw as the 'immoralities' of the originals, to conform to a universal prescription of 'TOTAL ABSTINENCE from ALL INTOXICATING LIQUORS.'

However these restrictions on the use of fantasy lessen somewhat over the period, especially as the new status given to the imagination and the child by the Romantic poets begins to be more widely accepted.[11] We find Coleridge (1797), Lamb (1802), Elizabeth Rigby in *The Quarterly Review* (1844), and Dickens (1853), lamenting the dominance of the moralists, and calling for the return of the fairy tale for its own sake. 'The world is too much with us, early and late. Leave this precious old escape from it, alone,' writes Dickens;[12] though his own attempt at it, 'The Magic Fish-bone' (1868), was both implicitly didactic and feeble. In the preface to his translation of the Grimms' tales, Edgar Taylor complained that

> The popular tales of England have been too much neglected. They are nearly discarded from the libraries of childhood. Philosophy is made the companion of the nursery: we have lisping chemists and leading-string mathematicians: this is the age of reason, not of imagination; and the loveliest dreams of fairy innocence are considered as vain and frivolous.[13]

Such protests were to bear fruit, if in the form of invented rather than traditional English fairy tales. By 1837 we have the first partly 'made-up' fairy tale published to amuse children, Robert Southey's 'The Three Bears,'[14] which, at the same time as it is moral concerning beasts that are more civil than humans, is a charming and unforgettable portrait of ursine 'domestic life.' Nevertheless such tales are at first rather furtive, being hidden in larger works. Catherine Sinclair's 'Uncle David's Nonsensical Story of Giants and Fairies,' in her *Holiday House* (1839), is quite effectively instructive in its depiction of the fate of the idle boy No-book, delivered by the Fairy Do-nothing into the hands of Giant Snap-'em-up; but also comic in its picture of No-book hung up by his hair from a hook in the giant's larder, with his mouth stuffed with suet, gazing at the joyous frolics on a bank nearby of the Fairy Teach-all's virtuous little charges. Indeed there is a certain ambiguity in the pictures of the two fairies, the naughty one an alluring grande dame, and the other a watery plain Jane with a bundle of books: morally the point may be that it is only from the outside that sloth seems alluring and virtue insipid, but imaginatively the former wins hands down. One cannot forget that *Holiday House* was written in celebration of children's unconstrained natures.

But there is no uniform development away from the dominance of morality. It is a matter rather of more and less. John Ruskin's *The King of the Golden River* (1841; first published 1851) has a pervasive moral of selfishness punished, but is also a brilliant recreation of the Grimms, in terms of a magically-altering landscape and the fantastical but menacing figure of the South West Wind Esquire. Here landscape and teaching are integrated, for Ruskin the Romantic embeds his lesson of generosity in nature, which withdraws its generosity just as the brothers did theirs, and returns to giving only after Gluck has given his all to the needy. In Robert Browning's 'The Pied Piper of Hamelin' (1842) the moral of keeping one's promise is left rather banal in what has become a fantastic story of revenge. On the other hand, in the Rev. Francis Paget's *The Hope of the Katzekopfs: or, The Sorrows of Selfishness* (1844), the moral is literally underlined. Prince Eigenwillig (Self-willed), plagued by the dwarf Selbst (Self), and intermittently instructed by old man Discipline, must "'*Learn to live hardly; Deny yourself in things lawful: Love not comforts; Think of others first, and of yourself last*'":[15] but (however aptly) calling the prince's mother Ninnilinda is not in the cause of gravity, nor is the picture of the refractory Eigenwillig magically pulled by his fairy godmother in a string through a keyhole before being wound into a ball and kicked about. The imagination has here temporarily slipped control.

It should be said that for children at least the moral impact of several of these tales would be blunted by the fact that that they are not directed specifically at them. 'The Three Bears,' *The King of the Golden River* and 'The Pied Piper of Hamelin' do not have children at the centre of the action (Goldilocks was a later and sentimental import into 'The Three Bears'). And if we look more widely we find the same true of Mark Lemon's *The Enchanted Doll* (1849), W. M. Thackeray's *The Rose and the Ring* (1855) and much of Frances Browne's *Granny's Wonderful Chair* (1856). Young men and women, yes: but not children. It is not till the 1860s that children are more consistently made the actors in children's fantasy. Furthermore the morals that are levelled in many of these earlier tales are more applicable to adults than to children, having to do with nosy neighbours ('The Three Bears'), financial greed (Ruskin, Browning, Browne), envy at others' worldly success (Lemon), or acquiring the qualities necessary for good kingship (Thackeray). A third factor limiting moral effect is that a great many of these stories are set in other worlds – a land where bears are house owners, a country of giants and fairies, a mountain realm swept by a goblin wind, an imaginary medieval Hamelin, the kingdom of the Katzekopfs, Paflagonia, the land of King Winwealth (*Granny's Wonderful Chair*).

It is the few fantasies of this time that are set in our world – in which, it may be added, we find most of the child characters – that have the more instructive effect. In Margaret Gatty's *The Fairy Godmothers* (1851), we find more direct and sustained moral seriousness, handled with considerable wit and humanity. It should be said that the concern here is not with improving children, but with making them happy; indeed the story is written in celebration of the innocence of childhood, which the vain child spurns for spurious adulthood. The story describes how the fairies experiment with christening gifts, to see which will make a child most content: such benefactions as beauty, riches or being universally loved all lead to misery, and only one attribute succeeds, the mystery gift of the Fairy Ambrosia to her little protegée, for her gift is The Love of Employment. A rather strange moral is behind Mary and Elizabeth Kirby's *The Talking Bird, or, The Little Girl Who Knew What Was Going To Happen* (1856), which unites a lively and psychologically penetrating picture of a family of three children in this world with a warning of the dangers of knowing more than one should. In so vivid a human context it is the magic, in the form of a witch and a future-telling bird, that seems out of place. Even in the rather stern educational air of A.L.O.E.'s *Fairy Know-a-bit, or, A Nut Shell of Knowledge* (1866), there is fun in Philibert's recalcitrance over the rather prim little fairy's demands, and considerable wonder in the magic mirror through which he is taught the strange origins of everyday things. Clearly, if morality might not coexist easily with the fantastic imagination, it quite found itself in a human and domestic context where the observation and humour of the writer could come into play. This idiom was later to come into its own when it was more hospitable to the fantastic imagination.

But at this time the fantastic was beginning to go off on a course of its own. In Edward Lear's *A Book of Nonsense* (1846) we have a work almost devoid of instruction. Thackeray's *The Rose and the Ring* (1855) is only slightly more moral. The absurd possibilities of magic and of the traditional fairy tale are fully exploited by Thackeray, until the end of his pantomime, when the silly Prince Giglio is made to learn his lessons and how to look after himself properly, after which he is given preposterous magic armaments to enable him single-handed to defeat an entire army and regain his kingdom.

By the 1860s the shifting duality of morality and imagination was on the whole veering to the latter side. The ideas of the 'beautiful child,' and of childhood itself as a separate state, were beginning to take wider hold. Now the imagination, not morality, takes the dominant role. And the imagination that does so is a singularly wild one, operating by free invention. Where Thackeray's *The Rose and the Ring* parodied the traditional fairy tale, pantomime, and the romances of G. P. R. James, here there are no such controlling yardsticks. Kingsley may use Rabelais for the chaotic form of *The Water-Babies* (1863), but the images are his own. And though they may sometimes take their cues from Kingsley or from one another, Lewis Carroll's *Alice in Wonderland* (1865), Annie Keary's *Little Wanderlin, and Other Fairy Tales* (1865) and Jean Ingelow's *Mopsa the Fairy* (1869) are often without literary precedent, full of wild flights of creative novelty.[16] Here we find the imagination ranging freely in just the way that Sarah Fielding or Lucy Aikin feared. And this is no less extreme a condition than that of unrestrained moralising was before.

In part this new accent on the imagination is facilitated by being given ampler room to spread, in the gradually increasing length of the invented fairy tale to 1865. As Humphrey Carpenter has said, this partly mirrors an increasing confidence both in the writing of fantasy and in writing it for children.[17] In the 1830s it is in the form of the short story; in the 1840s it is usually the long story; in the 1850s, in the shape of *The Rose and the Ring* or *Granny's Wonderful Chair*, it is of novelette length; and in the 1860s, in Kingsley's *The Water-Babies*, it takes up a short novel. The habit of thinking of the fairy tale in terms of the brevity and control of the Grimms or Perrault, eventually gives way to a much more expansive and digressive mode. Instead of imposing discipline on the modern writer, the literary fairy tale now turns into an omnium gatherum, a bag for holding almost anything. And this formal change parallels that from the primacy of instructional control towards free entertainment.

The children's fantasies of the 1860s often depend on how much they can admit rather than on what they exclude. The worlds of *The Water-Babies*, the *Alice* books, Annie Keary's fairy tales and Jean Ingelow's *Mopsa* are crammed with creatures and objects. Kingsley's Tom has to open his heart to the wonder of an ever-expanding world, and George MacDonald's Mossy and Tangle in his 'The Golden Key' (1867)[18] have to travel to deeper and wider knowledge of the spirit until the final opening of their souls in death. This contrasts with many more exclusively moral fantasies, where parts of the self have rather to be denied – as when Catherine Sinclair's No-book has to reject the side of himself that responds to Fairy Do-nothing if he will have the benefits of Fairy Teach-all, or Juliana Horatia Ewing's Benjy in 'Benjy in Beastland' (1870)[19] has to have his propensity for ill-treating animals driven out of him. Where the more moral tale is concerned with ordering and settling the individual and society, these more intensely imaginative tales also reveal something of what is being omitted.

The structure of such tales can be loose, chaotic or dream-like, reflective both of a free mind and a multiple universe. The idea of a clear unity or directional plot is often in abeyance: Kingsley says that 'The idea of self-evolution in a story, beautiful as it is, is just one of those logical systems which is too narrow for the transcendental variety of life and fact,'[20] and Lewis Carroll composed *Alice in Wonderland* out of a mass of images and linguistic games he had first jotted down separately.[21] Everything is uneven, and the strangest things keep appearing. In *Alice* we move from a talking White Rabbit, down a well, through a pool of tears, and into a garden where we encounter a Mad Hatter's tea party, a game of croquet played with living things, and a trial of the Knave of Hearts. In *The Water-Babies* there are constant digressions to consider issues beyond the story, such as spirit-rapping, cram-systems of education, the fishing in Yorkshire or Hampshire, Abraham Lincoln, the 'hippocampus minor' controversy concerning man's simian ancestry, and many more. *Alice in Wonderland* has no particular direction, so that almost everything comes as a digression. *Mopsa the Fairy*, which takes its cue from *Alice*, is also a dream-sequence of strange images and events apparently unrelated to one another.

At the same time identity is unstable. Tom the chimney-sweep is changed to a water-baby and later becomes a fairy; and in parallel his larger body, his environment, which expresses his spirit, changes as he develops and moves, from narrow stream to river, estuary and ocean.[22] The world is full of metamorphosing creatures, going up and down the ladder of creation. In *Alice* everything has the plasticity of dream: Alice alters in size, the Cheshire Cat shrinks to a grin, the Countess's baby turns into a pig, the whole court at the end is transformed into a pack of cards. In Annie Keary's 'Mrs Calkill's Wonderful House' naughty children are turned to vegetables, bees, frogs, earwigs and snails, and in her 'Gladhome' to a variety of household objects. In MacDonald's 'The Golden Key' flying bird-fish change to creatures called aeranths; in Ingelow's *Mopsa* parrots become fairies; and in Mark Lemon's *Tinykin's Transformations* (1869) a boy is changed into a series of beasts by the Fairy Titania. And almost all these fantasies take place in worlds where everything – humans, animals, objects – talks to everything else: Kingsley's Tom converses with a fly or a lobster, Alice with a caterpillar or a pudding, Keary's children with a slate pencil, sugar tongs or a carrot.

That all these fantasies are implicitly written as dream narratives is suggested by several wider features they have in common. In previous fantasies we are in one world throughout, whether our own or another. For instance in *The Rose and the Ring* the narrative stays in Paflagonia, and nobody from our world travels to it, or from it to ours or another; and in Kirby's *The Talking Bird* we are in our world all the time, and the evil fairy and her bird appear within it. But the 1860s fantasies of Kingsley, Carroll, Keary, MacDonald and Ingelow all start with characters from our world who then enter the fantastic one, as Otto and Bertha cross into Mist-Land from their world in Keary's 'Gladhome,' or Jack in *Mopsa* crawls through a hedge and then finds himself shut in a world of fairies. These transitions often suggest that from waking to dreaming: and this is reinforced by the way that Kingsley's Tom is described as falling asleep and dreaming in the stream, Alice wakes up from dreaming at the end of her story, and Jack's long absence in Fairyland is quite unnoticed by his parents.

Significant adult fantasies of the time – William Morris's early prose romances (1856) and *The Death of Guenevere and Other Poems* (1858), and George

MacDonald's _Phantastes_ (1858) – are also in the form of dreams. Dreams were of great interest to the Victorians, either as testimonies to the spirit world or as revelations of the mind:[23] Dickens, for instance, had a knowledge of contemporary scientific dream theory, often wrote about dreams, and used them in his novels;[24] and _Great Expectations_ (1860–1) often has the hallucinatory character and narrative disconnections of dream. Dreams also condition several later children's fantasies, though never to the extent of disconnection of those in the 1860s: George MacDonald's _At the Back of the North Wind_ (1871) and the _Princess_ books (1872, 1883), Christina Rossetti's _Speaking Likenesses_ (1874), Mary Louisa Molesworth's _The Cuckoo Clock_ (1877) and _The Tapestry Room_ (1879), Lucy Lane Clifford's _Anyhow Stories_ (1882), Alice Corkran's _Down the Snow Stairs_ (1887).

Darker, more frightening things also appear in these 1860s fantasies – and in others of the Victorian period. One of the key texts here is the frequently-reprinted translation of Heinrich Hoffman's _Struwwelpeter_ (1848), where an idle boy's uncut hair and fingernails turn him into a monster, and where disobedient Little Suck-a-Thumb is at last visited by 'The great, long, red-legged scissor-man,' who cuts off his thumbs with giant scissors. The horror is compounded by the sheer disproportion of the punishment, something we also see in _The Water-Babies,_ where Tom is turned into a creature of prickles for stealing sweets; or in Christina Rossetti's story in _Speaking Likenesses_ (1874) where a child's discontent at her birthday party is re-run in hideous form, with the guests turned to loathsome grotesques; or in the hellish torments of naughty children in Alice Corkran's _Down the Snow Stairs_ (1887).[25] Grotesquerie abounds throughout the period, further examples being the huge Land Crab that pesters little Snow in Keary's 'Quiet Shoes,' or the man who pulls off his nose and replaces it upside-down in Edward Knatchbull-Hugessen's 'The Nose (1871),[26] or the mother who changes to a wooden-tailed monster in Lucy Lane Clifford's 'The New Mother' (1882).[27] The phantasmagoric Other-end-of-Nowhere in _The Water-Babies,_ the carnivorous Jabberwock in _Alice,_ or the children in Keary's 'Mrs Calkill's Wonderful House,' shut in repellent bodies and screaming to get out, all suggest a different side of the liberated imagination in 1860s children's fantasy – a side that stimulated the nightmare aspect of dreaming. Indeed, all these 1860s fantasies are pictures of punishment or education in a form of afterlife – purgatory in Kingsley and Keary, fairyland-purgatory in _Alice_ and _Mopsa_ – reflecting contemporary concern with the nature and existence of hell.[28]

So far as the moral or instructive sides of 1860s children's fantasies are concerned, they are variously affected by the new emphasis on the imagination and the lessening of control. _The Water-Babies,_ for instance, may be moral, but the morality is often unconventional. The Rev. Kingsley used his fairy tale as a repository for heterodox opinions which he could not readily display in the pulpit. In *The Water-Babies* he makes his central moral that 'your soul makes your body, just as a snail makes his shell.'[29] So he has Tom the water-baby's shape change according to his behaviour, and his body in the environment enlarge as he travels down to the ocean. Kingsley also believed in a law of spiritual (d)evolution throughout nature, whereby at death the soul goes on to inhabit the creature whose form expresses the moral condition it has reached in its past life: so that the whole process of life itself becomes a continuous purgatory. This for him made the whole of creation spiritually interconnected, and transformed Darwin's concept of natural selection (*Origin of Species*, 1859) into one of moral choice. Kingsley's idea was certainly eccentric, and was attacked by the contemporary scientist T.H.Huxley, but for us the interest here is that he felt he could make it central to a fairy tale for children as he could not in his adult fiction.[30] *The Water-Babies* is crammed with perfectly conventional morals about being considerate to others, learning one's lessons, and not being greedy or cruel, but its whole view of reality is so different from that of other moral fairy tales as to be a transformation of them.

In the *Alice* books, the complacencies on which morals and moral fairy tales are based are continually being undermined. "'Everything's got a moral, if only you can find it'", the Duchess tells Alice. But in the world of the *Alice* books the finding is a problem, for with few exceptions the adults, the repositories of morality, are mad, from the neurotic White Rabbit or the psychopathic Queen of Hearts, to the bullying Humpty or the nitwitted White Knight. None of them can manage anything properly, from a trial to a chess game. Many of them try to order Alice about, but she frequently answers them back, for their absurdity removes their authority. Alice is the first child in children's fantasy to learn no moral whatsoever, unless it is the 'morality' of changefulness itself.

This seems the more extraordinary when we recall the Rev. Dodgson's strong Christian belief;[31] indeed there have even been those who argue that he is mocking it here.[32] However there are ways in which existence in Wonderland, charming though it may appear to the reader, is a form of hell for the characters. Alice's very story there refuses progress, goes nowhere for sense to be made out of it: her time there is a series of visits to wildly different creatures, all of them in a state of eternal recurrence, in which it will always be time for the mad Hatter's tea party, the game of croquet or the trial of the Knave of Hearts. Change in both *Alice* books produces the reverse of human evolution, in that it goes from a baby backwards to a pig, a queen to a sheep or a kitten, and from whole societies to a pack of cards or a set of chess pieces; while correspondingly, animals and things are promoted, as flowers to people, or an egg to a philosopher. In this light Wonderland can be seen as a seductive hell of serial recurrence, stasis and self-dissolution.

In *Through the Looking-Glass* (1871) there is more sequence in the continual chess game, but we are not made strongly aware of this, since we again spend more time on lengthy visits to extraordinary characters. Our sense of direction is also undermined by the fact that to go forward in this looking-glass world often involves going back, or else running hard to stay in one place, and a Queen can scream with pain before she has pricked her finger. Running on the spot also comes from having traditional or folklore figures who behave according to set patterns, rather than the sheerly novel ones of Wonderland – as Tweedledum and Tweedledee, Humpty-Dumpty and Haigha and Hatta. Such an irrational context of dream reduces the scope for a moral plot, though plenty of morals may be freely offered.

Nevertheless a moral framework may be at least putatively present here, if we can consider the story, with its limited, even spiral, form of narrative progress through the chess game, as an image of purgatory. In which case *Through the Looking-Glass* becomes the *Purgatorio* to *Wonderland*'s *Inferno*: *The Divine Comedy* was a particularly popular poem at this time, and Carroll might have been particularly drawn to Dante by his similar (and doomed) love for a young girl –though he later professed never to have read the poem.[33] (Might this then make *The Hunting of the Snark* a form of mystic quest for the absolute, and *Sylvie and Bruno* a new Beatrice and Dante traversing the crystal spheres of the *Paradiso*?!)

From 1870 we find a change in the writing of children's fantasy. The dominant writers become for the time mostly women rather than men – Mrs J.H.Ewing, Mrs M. L. Molesworth, Christina Rossetti, Dinah Mulock, Mary De Morgan, Lucy Lane Clifford, Alice Corkran. Fantasy is written more often in the form of short stories, partly owing to the establishment of serials for children, particularly *Aunt Judy's Magazine* (1866–85) and *Good Words for the Young* (1868–77).[34] There is now a class of fantasy which is much more domestic, more moral, and less wildly inventive; which as often takes place amidst the day-to-day lives of the child characters, as it follows adventures in the outside world; and in which the environment is not infrequently houses and rooms. This fantasy becomes more internalised – in every sense, for there is more attention to children's minds and feelings. The change to some extent parallels that in the contemporary novel, which, with Thackeray and Dickens now replaced by George Eliot, Trollope and Meredith, is much more involved with psychological realism. But it also comes from a greater concentration on 'the child.' Where previously – in Paget, Thackeray, Kingsley or Carroll – the protagonist of children's fantasy was either an adult, or a child shown entering an adult world, now fantasy more often tries to enter the world of the child. For the time this change from an adult to a more child-centred perspective is quite crucial, and prepares the way, however moral the fantasy may still be, for the far more indulgent fantasy of the 1890s and beyond, when 'the child' became king. Yet for now it is still most often the solitary or selected child we meet, not the child among children: and the company of this child is adults, or fantasy figures who have an adult role.

With the move away from flights of invention towards a more sober realism, the earlier opposition of imagination and moral purpose in children's fantasy slips to one between imagination and truth. Now the question becomes: what scope is there, with a narrative based on everyday life, to accept fantasy as anything else but a dream or a symbol? It is less often, 'Does the imagination deprave the mind?' than 'Does it delude it?' And in these fantasies such a question is additionally provoked by the now often solitary and indoor child characters, and by the way they often have their fantastic adventures when they may be asleep. Nevertheless, we should recall that questions concerning the reality of the 'supernatural' were acute in England at this time, when Spiritualism had become very popular, and there was a great wish to prove the next world a reality, in the face of increasing religious doubt.[35]

The fantasy of George MacDonald, a Scottish novelist who lived and wrote in England, is full of the topic of 'truth' versus illusion. MacDonald confronts the issue by inverting the terms. For him fantasy is deeply real, while the common, 'solid' reality we live by is often seen as an illusion. As a Christian with a mystic faith in the imagination as God's seat in man, MacDonald believed that the strangest fantasy could be far more true than the 'real world' itself. In his *At the Back of the North Wind* (1871), the London cab-driver's son Diamond is visited at nights by the lady of the North Wind, with whom he travels the streets and the world, and goes to the strange country at her 'back.' Eventually he becomes ill and dies. No-one in London has believed in his magic experiences, and we are left to accept the truth of them if we will. Dreaming and daytime activity seem opposed. But MacDonald once wrote, 'When a man dreams his own dream, he is the sport of his dream; when Another gives it him, that Other is able to fulfil it.'[36] Meanwhile London itself, could we but understand it, is full of angels and mystic symbols; and points beyond its twisted and pain-filled streets to a truer and holier London, could we but build it.

Belief in the unseen is an issue also in MacDonald's 'Princess' books, *The Princess and the Goblin* (1872) and *The Princess and Curdie* (1883), where the young Princess Irene has a strange 'great great grandmother' living at the top of her house, and first she and then her friend the boy Curdie have to believe in her reality. In *The Princess and Curdie* the material world is seen as a delusion compared to the spiritual world which the imagination, good or bad, sees. The solid-seeming gold the citizens of the city of Gwyntystorm dig so obsessively for becomes a mere chimera, and ends in the destruction of the city itself. This novel shows people seeing the world not as 'it is' but as their inner natures make it, so that all perception is essentially spiritual. Curdie the miner and his father may see a strange lady they meet in their mine as beautiful, but the superstitious villagers nearby have perceived only an old crone they call Old Mother Weatherwop; and she herself says that to a thief she would seem "'the demon of the mine, all in green flames. ... I should be all the same, but his evil eyes would see me as I was not'".[37] And the whole object of the lady of *The Wise Woman* (1875) is to train two girls away from the evil vision that sees reality only as something to be grasped with their hands.

The issue of the truth of the magic is heightened by the magic being far less public than in earlier Victorian fantasies. There, for example, the Pied Piper of Hamelin piped both rats and children out of the town in full sight of its citizens, Prince Eigenwillig was transformed to a string before his mother's eyes, and both little Ellie and Professor Ptthmllnsprts saw Tom the water-baby. There, too, there was much more sense of a whole society in which the protagonist was immersed – Paflagonia, the marine world, Wonderland, Fairyland (*Mopsa*). But in later fantasy children are more alone, and the magic is either further off or hidden from others.

In one of the stories in Christina Rossetti's *Speaking Likenesses* (1874), spoilt Flora has left her discordant and quarrelsome birthday party, and is by herself. The afternoon is 'soporific' and she finds herself in a sinister room (her own mind?) where another ill-tempered birthday party is going on, and all the children are covered with hideous quills, fish-hooks, or sticky or slimy fluids, expressive of their unpleasant natures. The suggestion is that the vision was a projection of her upset conscience, rather than imposed by any supernatural or fairy authority from without. But the vision itself is far more violent than the trivial and scarce-realised naughtiness it is meant to condemn, and there is a sense of paranoia in the story, a feeling that one cannot be too careful, when the slightest lapse may generate a landslide of horror and punishment. There is a not dissimilar feeling in Rossetti's earlier poem *Goblin Market* (1862), where the girl Lizzie's thoughtless purchase of lovely fruits from the goblins puts her in a coma from which it takes her sister's desperate resistance of them to rescue her. This sense of nervous strain seems to come from Rossetti herself, who was throughout her life afraid of the power of her own stifled emotional and physical nature. The magic world of fairy tale becomes expressive of the repressed unconscious.

The separation of fantasy from the world, and the isolation of the protagonist, can produce that hopeful looking beyond death so frequently seen in 1870s literature. That 'Death is the theme that most inspired George Macdonald,'[38] is sufficiently evident in his *At the Back of the North Wind*. Prince Dolor in Dinah Mulock's *The Little Lame Prince and his Travelling Cloak* (1874) is so distanced from the world by his exile to a lonely desert by his subjects, that he can never quite rejoin it when asked. He spends his (successful) reign as king thinking of his dead mother, and looking longingly on the Beautiful Mountain to which she has gone. Here again, Dolor's experience of the supernatural is confined to him – his fairy godmother came to the tower and gave him a magic carpet with which he secretly travelled and learnt about the world. The story is also a picture of how the inner world is no longer in harmony with the outer one. It is in complete contrast to Dinah Mulock's much more domestic *The Adventures of a Brownie* (1872), about the mischievous pranks of a brownie who is met by a family of children staying on a farm.

Another increasingly otherworldly writer of the time is Mary Louisa Molesworth. At first in her work she seems to scorn fantasy as a delusion. In her domestic fairy tale 'The Reel Fairies' (1875), solitary Louisa is mocked for making imaginary companions out of the reels in her mother's workbox. When the reels actually come alive and try to force her to be their queen, she learns the error of her ways and joins the 'real' world. So too in 'Con and the Little People' (1875), the fancy-struck Irish boy Con is taken by the fairies, and only just escapes. Con is a Peter Pan figure, but he leaves his Never Land and grows up in the real world. The (limited) irony of these stories is that it takes fancy to write them.[39]

In *The Cuckoo Clock* (1877), *The Tapestry Room* (1879) and *Christmas Tree Land* (1884), however, Molesworth gives fancy increasing pride of place. *The Cuckoo Clock* still has one foot very much in reality, with rebellious Griselda and the rather patronising wooden cuckoo in the house of the well-meaning but too-old aunts Grizzel and Tabitha. But then Griselda is given three trips by the Cuckoo, to the Country of Nodding Mandarins, Butterfly Land and the Other Side of the Moon. Of course these are meant to entertain Griselda, but it is clear from the beauty and intensity with which they are described, that they are a source of wonder for the narrator too.

The Tapestry Room goes further, with English boy Hugh and French girl Jeanne taken through a strange tapestry in Jeanne's house to a magic land. In this story the 'realistic' context is far weaker than in *The Cuckoo Clock*, where the two maiden aunts are well characterised. Here Jeanne and Hugh are left on their own in the house. The narrative is also less focused, and there are two long inset stories, one a version of 'Beauty and the Beast,' the other a tale of the house a century ago. We have the sense of being cut off from reality, with a magic land within a house, and stories within a story. The fairy tale, with its theme of double selves (beast and man), and the duality of the house in the present and the past – even the two children themselves, who never leave the house and have little individual character – suggest that here identity is multiple and shifting.

With *Christmas Tree Land*, we are out in a strange forested country, where two children are taken to stay with their coldly rational cousin Lady Venelda. In the forest Rollo and Maria meet a magic fairy godmother figure, who lives in a cottage with two children, Waldo and Silva; and they all go on several magical excursions. There is an implicit sense of the wood being the unconscious behind the civil country house; also that the children met in the forest are the deeper selves of Rollo and Maria; and even that the magic 'godmother' could in part be the other side of the rational Lady Venelda. Here again the sense is of going deeper into an interior, even though this time we are outside buildings for most of the time.

Yet Mrs Molesworth swings back to her 'anti-fantastical' side again in *Four Winds Farm* (1887), written while she was writing her 'realistic' children's books, such as *Daddy Darwin's Dovecote* and *Jackanapes*. The farmer's child Gratian is a lazy dreamer – the view of fancy here – who is bullied into better ways by the four winds. He then helps lame rich boy Fergus with his lessons, and as a reward, is given help to go to a good school, and thus makes himself useful to society with his talents. Clearly this utilitarian fiction is at an opposite pole to the fantastic, and shows how divided between the two writers could be at this time.

Juliana Horatia Ewing, daughter of Margaret Gatty, is often paired with Mrs Molesworth, but is far more consistently a 'realist,' writing her few short fairy tales to teach, as did her mother, good behaviour in this world. In her tales the fantastic itself is made a source of punishment. Sam in 'The Land of Lost Toys' (1869) is told a story of a land where naughty children have to mend the toys they have broken. Spoilt Amelia in 'Amelia and the Dwarfs' (1870) is haled underground (into her conscience) to wash the clothes she has dirtied, live on the food she has rejected, mend the dresses she has torn and the ornaments she has smashed, and pick up all the threads of conversation she has broken, until she reforms. 'Benjy in Beastland' (1870) gives similar training to a child who is cruel to animals.[40] Apart from these, Ewing tried in her *Old Fashioned Fairy Tales* (1882) to adapt traditional fairy tales to infant moral benefit, but, lacking the vivid nursery milieu that inspired the others, these stories are rather bloodless and allegorical.[41] There is really no scope for dreaming and the imagination in Ewing's work: everyone is busy becoming or being made better. Nevertheless her stories give us some of the most alive child characters in nineteenth-century fantasy: the naughty Amelia before she meets the dwarfs is a wonderful portrait of a spoilt child.

Nearer to the dreaming side is Mary De Morgan, in her story-collections *On a Pincushion* (1877), *The Necklace of Princess Fiorimonde* (1880) and *The Windfairies* (1900).[42] Many of these tales show a disdain for materialism and a Pre-Raphaelite love of decoration and beauty: Mary De Morgan's brother William was part of the Craft Movement and a maker of beautiful tiles, and was a friend of Morris and D. G. Rossetti, whom Mary also often met. Nevertheless her tales do operate as oblique reflections of the problems of our own world. Indeed one of their recurrent themes is the evil of cutting oneself off from reality. A woman falls in love with her own reflection and is punished by elves; a gnome feeds on the lives of young women to evade his own death; a queen is obsessed with the beauty of her hair; a village is blighted when its people let a wizard live there for a bribe; a succession of people try to cheat one another for services they cannot pay for; a princess gains all knowledge and finds she cannot live.[43] More narrowly, we are back with that perennial target of Victorian fantasy, greed and selfishness. The answer of course is self-giving and sacrifice, which involves exposure to the world and pain. In other stories we have a queen who can only keep her husband's love for her and her child by killing herself, a woman who lets herself be changed to a magic harp to lift the curse from a village, and a prince who has to endure seven terrible years of servitude to an evil magician to save the life of his princess.[44] Yet this sacrificial impulse carries a drive towards death and the quitting of this world, too. There is throughout the stories a hatred of materialism and a longing for a happier world that readily translates into a longing to leave this one. This is a theme we saw in George MacDonald, where it had a Christian basis: and it reappears in later writers, notably Laurence Housman.

How far these tales have genuine symbolic force is debatable. The human behaviour in them may be parallel to ours, but the circumstances and locations in which it is shown may be too far from our experience for the connection to be made. It is hard without more encouragement to translate an escapist gnome, an omniscient princess, or a queen devoted to her own hair into the terms of our own reality. However, the Andersenian 'The Toy Princess' seems more nearly to reflect Victorian society, in its portrayal of a prim and unfeeling people who exchange their lively and refractory princess for an artificial one who behaves just as she should. And in 'The Necklace of Princess Fiorimonde' we have a picture of such coldness at an individual level, in a woman who collects adoring lovers and turns them into beads – a true *femme fatale* (a figure often seen in the literature of the time). Yet even as these tales make to cross the gap between their world and ours, they are held back by our feeling that the authoress is half in love with the very creations she condemns – with the beauty of the beaded necklace, the intricacy of the toy princess, or the wonders of the queen's hair; and indeed with the very construction of fairy tales themselves as beautiful artefacts.

Such 'beautiful' fantasy, seen also in Mrs Molesworth's stories, becomes more common in the late 1880s and 1890s via Pre-Raphaelitism and the Aesthetic Movement. But one children's fantasy writer remains, who analyses more subtly than any so far both the strengths and the dangers of fantasy – Lucy Lane Clifford, authoress of the enigmatically-named *Anyhow Stories, Moral and Otherwise* (1882).

Lucy Clifford was a friend of Henry James, and shows in her stories something of the same psychological penetration and sense of the complexity of experience that we see in James's novels. A cobbler's boy, who wastes his life in fancies, still passes on his delight to other children ('The Cobbler's Children'). A heartless girl who comes into the world from outside, and asks people why they work and suffer as they do, is still asking questions that deserve thought from those too busy to give it ('From Outside the World'). More simply moralistic fairy tales would have labelled the boy a dreamer, and the girl a prig. In one of Clifford's poems in *Anyhow Stories*, 'The Paper Ship,' the doll inhabitants of an artificial world ask, '"What shall we do to be real?"'. In another, 'The Imitation Fish,' a toy fish, treated as real by its long-ago child owner and 'released' into the sea, is found on the shore years later by his mother, as her child, now dead, never can be. None of these stories is created as a world to be enjoyed for its own sake: they are all sharply engaged in a quest for truth. The contrast with other fantasies we have seen is marked.

In Clifford's celebrated 'The New Mother,' two children listen to the falsehoods of a travelling girl rather than the truths of their mother, whom they so disobey that eventually she leaves them; whereupon a new and terrible mother comes, with glass eyes and a huge wooden tail with which she smashes in the house door. This story, even more traumatic to children than the mutant infants of Rossetti's *Speaking Likenesses*, seems, like that story, a grossly repressive treatment of childish naughtiness. But the underlying metaphysical truth is that here the fantasy the children have pursued – their longing to see a little dancing man and woman supposedly inside a tramping girl's box – is linked to evil. The travelling girl is a form of the devil, and has a still more sinister companion: and her box, like evil itself, actually has nothing in it. The children have given themselves away for nothing, and henceforth they can be seen as suffering the idiot disproportions of hell, by which their mother forsakes them, a horror comes in her stead, and they end in the houseless wilderness their minds have become. For the once ordered and love-filled cottage was an image of the civilised self, which, when wrecked as the cottage is by the children on the girl's orders, turns the inner world to a chaos and the outer to a monster. The children then go to the wilderness outside because a wilderness is what they have become.

But it is part of Clifford's complexity that the story can be read not just as judgement on these children, but also at a psychological level, as a portrayal of all children's deepest fears about the world, and a prime subject of their nightmares. What if Mummy took away all the security we learn to trust in? What if she threatened to leave? What if she left? And what, still more, if the naughty things we did made her go? And then, supposing the Mummy we know loves us and is warm and loving turned into a monster mummy who wants to do us harm? In destroying spiritual harmony the children can be seen as liberating the terrible unconscious, which in a sense here represents the child's secret terror of the other mother, the monster who punishes rather than loves. That the story can thus sustain two opposed views of children – metaphysical judgement and psychological comprehension, imaged by the two mothers themselves – is a measure of its power.

In this world fantasy itself is evil: it is the nasty little girl with her box of tricks, it is the fantastic lies she tells the children, and it is the grotesque false mother who is sent to them. Had the children held to love and normality, they would never have entered the inverted world that engulfs them. A similar view of fantasy is also present in Clifford's other well-known story 'Wooden Tony' (1892):[45] but here it also has a more redemptive side.

Whereas in 'The New Mother' the children failed their mother, in 'Wooden Tony' parents fail their child. Set in Switzerland, the story describes a carpenter's dreamy autistic son, whose father, regarding him as useless, one day gives him into the uncertain employ of a passing stranger (another devil in disguise), who eventually turns him into a wooden figure in a cuckoo clock. Here parental 'realism' is stupidity: Tony's father does not understand his son's condition, seeing it simply as a failure to bring in money. His gross materialism contrasts with Tony's dreams. Tony 'knows' a beautiful song from the mountains, which the stranger to whom he is given prizes; and Tony's beliefs about the world not only enliven reality by inverting it, but can even come true, if in a terrible manner. Seeing how people appear to grow smaller as they move away from him, Tony thinks that if he goes far off he will get small too: and indeed this comes to pass, when he is turned into a wooden mannikin by the clock-maker traveller and put in the clock. Tony made the virtual real, but the traveller makes the real Tony virtual. And just as the mother had two forms in 'The New Mother,' here the father 'is' in a sense both the Swiss carpenter and the wood-carving traveller: the first belittles Tony and calls him 'Wooden Tony,' while the second makes him small and wooden indeed. In this story the fantastic visions given to Tony by his autism may make him ignorant of reality, but it also makes him capable of visionary truth.[46] And here it is the child who is shut out, and not the mother: and with him a vein of fantasy and spiritual perception that might have transformed reality.

The preoccupation with the pulls of fantasy and reality is continued, less coherently, in the work of Andrew Lang and other writers of the 1890s, with the accent now increasingly falling on the value of dreaming and fantasy. At first Lang's fantasy tends towards realism. *The Gold of Fairnilee* (1888) tells of a boy stolen into fairyland by its glamour, who one day comes by magic to see that the enchantment is a fraud, with all the fairies sad, old or wounded, their feasts coarse pulses, and the land itself a desert waste. Rescued back into this world by his friend Jeanie, the disillusioned Lord Randal thereafter settles to the good management of his estate. A similar but more lighthearted story of disenchantment is found in Lang's earlier tale *The Princess Nobody* (1884). But we find quite the opposite in his *Prince Prigio* (1889) and *Prince Ricardo of Pantouflia* (1893), for both are set in magic realms, where the marvellous and the faery reign supreme. Indeed one of the central issues of *Prince Prigio* is belief in fairies and magic, at first foolishly scorned by the over-educated Prigio. And it is Lang who produces twelve *Fairy Book* collections for children from 1889 onwards: his interest in fairy tales was very much that of the cultural anthropologist, but it was also that of a man who admired our primitive forebears with their 'unblunted edge of belief, [and] ... fresh appetite for marvels.'[47]

With *Prince Prigio* and *Prince Ricardo*, we enter a charmed-circle world of fun and magic. Both are indebted to Thackeray's *The Rose and the Ring*, which Lang inverts in *Prince Prigio* , by having Prigio over- rather than under-educated. But Lang has no satiric, moral, or parodic points to make about the reality outside his texts, which are much more relaxed and desultory than Thackeray's, and lacking in the compressed, witty dialogue of *The Rose and the Ring*. Lang's characters are all suburbanites in ermine, whereas those of Thackeray are royals whose robes let through vulgarity. What Lang does well are his huge and beautiful monsters, the Firedrake (a volcano) and the Remora (a snake-like glacier), and their battle; and in *Prince Ricardo* the picture of the giant Earthquaker which, about to destroy a city, is 'slain' with a huge mass of intellectual stupidity. (Here, however, he draws to a considerable extent on Kinglsey's book of geology for children, *Madam How and Lady Why* (1869)). But no longer is it suggested that the monsters are from within the self. Fantasy is on the way to embracing the illusion entirely.

This fantastical enjoyment of high life and exotic imagery is also seen in the tales of Oscar Wilde in the sumptuously-produced *The Happy Prince* (1888) and *A House of Pomegranates* (1891). These stories owe a considerable debt to Hans Christian Andersen, particularly in *The Happy Prince*, where they are more directed at children than the rather more philosophical *A House of Pomegranates*.[48] But where Andersen's recurrent theme is vanity, Wilde's is the more Victorian one of charity. 'The Happy Prince' describes a jewelled statue which steadily gives away all its gems to help the poor; in 'The Selfish Giant' a jealously-protected garden is thrown open to children by its changed owner; the bird in 'The Nightingale and the Rose' gives its life to help a poor student win his lady-love. So too the innocent in 'The Devoted Friend' goes on helping the parasitic miller until it kills him; the Star Child regains his beauty and his kingship when he learns humility and charity; and in 'The Young King' the hero removes his royal trappings when he learns of the sufferings of the poor in making them. Contrastively, 'The Birthday of the Infanta' describes a lack of charity, in the thoughtless Infanta, who cares only for people when they amuse her, and has no time for their sufferings. Wilde's stories often end in Christian transfiguration of those who have leant charity – the Happy Prince, the Selfish Giant, the Young King.

But this theme goes only so far. In 'The Happy Prince' Wilde is interested in the jewelled statue's sacrifice, not in its result in helping the poor: he traces its self-stripping and the gradual dying of its swallow-helper day by day, and stage by stage, almost as a ceremonial, an ornate ritual in reverse. The creation of beauty is often the object in Wilde's stories of self-sacrifice, whether a red rose, a blooming garden or a new king. Even 'The Remarkable Rocket' describes an object whose purpose is to be beautiful while burning out: the story is modelled on Andersen's 'The Darning Needle,' whose poor central figure Wilde has altered. When the king in 'The Young King' learns of the pains of labouring men and strips himself of his clothes, the point is the spiritual beauty of the act itself, for no help is either intended or offered to the poor themselves.

Indeed if we look at Wilde's contemporary work *The Soul of Man Under Socialism* (1891), we find him saying that a socialist society should be created only so that the artist and the individualist may be released from their chains: he has no time for charity, which he sees as 'interfering' in other people's lives. To Wilde the vast mass of the public are conformists, and his sympathy for the poor is qualified by their 'barbarism.' 'The true artist is a man who believes absolutely in himself.'[49] This, one should observe, is a defence of the dandy, of the Remarkable Rocket and the chilly little Infanta.

Nor even is Wilde's moral – that natural is better than artificial beauty – borne out by his stories. The manufactured rocket, vain though it is, is right about its magnificence. The red rose that the nightingale makes with her blood fails to win the girl, because it does not go with her dress, and in any case '"the Chamberlain's nephew has sent me some real jewels, and everybody knows that jewels cost far more than flowers" (76). Of course we know that in fact the rose 'cost' the nightingale its life, but that is not the only point here: the jewels are not more but less artificial than the flower, which has been unnaturally created out of season. Arguably the student is out of touch with changing reality, for he has turned a feminine whim into an absolute: it is appropriate that he returns to his philosophy tomes at the end. At the centre of the story is not the rose but the beauty of the bird's vision of love and of its gradual death through giving. Again, in 'The Birthday of the Infanta,' we seem bound by the story to prefer the little dwarf from the forests to the bejewelled courtly setting of the little Infanta. But the fascinating and lengthy descriptions of the court again show where the sympathies of the story lie.

Wilde described his stories as 'an attempt to mirror modern life in a form remote from reality,' but such remoteness, as with Mary De Morgan's 'aesthetic' tales, can forfeit their relevance to life.[50] This begs the question why Wilde chose such a remote form in the first place. The obvious attraction was that the fairy tale could be made the home not only of magic but of the exotic and the beautiful. But Wilde was also attracted by the formality of the fairy tale – its set patterns, mythic base, age-old characters, rules of three and happy endings. Wilde's style is itself formalised, influenced as much by the Bible as by the Aesthetic Movement, and his narratives progress through measured, usually threefold, steps to their end. What in the fairy tale is normally a triple movement to worldly gain is in Wilde's tales often a three-stage process of self-stripping or sacrifice leading to death. Three times the swallow returns to the stone Prince; three stages of decline bring the rocket to its end; three temptations must be overcome by the Fisherman; three areas of human misery are visited by the Young King to transform his spirit; three acts of kindness bring the Star Child back to his true self. But the luxurious and ceremonial manner compromises the spareness of the form, and we are less prepared to accept the tales' renunciation of the world's glories than to see Wilde striving to capture new experiences of beauty in the life of the spirit:

> And the child smiled on the Giant, and said to him,
> 'You let me play once in your garden, to-day you shall come to me to my garden, which is Paradise.'
> And when the children ran in that afternoon, they found the Giant lying dead under the tree, all covered with white blossoms. (32)

The 1890s were a period when children's fantasy became largely playful and escapist: questions of illusion versus truth, or of dreaming versus reality, largely disappeared, because they had been settled on the side of illusion and play, and 'the fashion for sentimentality towards children and childhood was at its height.'[51] The fairy tale collections of Laurence Housman – *A Farm in Fairyland* (1894), *The House of Joy* (1895) and *The Field of Clover* (1898) – owe much to Wilde's stories for their Aesthetic charm, but Housman's are pure fancy, carrying with them no larger meaning. Prince Noodle in 'The Bound Princess,' in *A Farm in Fairyland*, has to go to immense lengths to rescue an enchanted princess, including acquiring a super-fast plough, water from a Thirsty Well of clutching hands and mouths, a burning rose from the cloud of a giant's dream, and the magic breath of the Camphor Worm. In all of these he shows he is not so much of a noodle after all, but nothing is made of this. The tests are quite unrelated to one another, being simply a series of bizarre inventions. In 'The Rooted Lover' (1894) a ploughboy can only gain the princess by being turned into a poppy in her garden, in the hope that she will touch him with her lips: this is doubtless potentially egalitarian, but the point is the crossing of a gulf, not the levelling of society. The rocking-horse that wants to fly home in 'Rocking-Horse Land' (1894) might have had a theme of exile, but simply provides a little temporary tension to a story which otherwise might go nowhere. Housman made no claims for his stories, except that they should convey delight: 'The true end and object of a fairy-tale is the expression of the joy of living. . . . Its value consists in its optimism.'[52]

In the 1890s we also find the fairy tale increasingly used for light-hearted parody. In F. Anstey's version of Perrault's 'Les Fées,' 'The Good Little Girl' (1893),[53] young Priscilla's fondness for telling others how to behave is rewarded by a fairy, who says that henceforth every time she utters an improving remark a jewel will fall from her lips. This certainly makes Priscilla's hearers as receptive to her little lessons as she could wish: only, her popularity abruptly ceases when the jewels are found to be fakes. Anstey here mocks both the absurdities of fairy tale and the many moralising books for children: but his story also continues the topic of fantasy versus reality. Priscilla could be said to meet the fairy because she has a fairy-tale picture of herself: and the gems prove as false as her fancied virtue. A more successfully child-oriented version of the theme is 'The Story of a Sugar Prince' (1892),[54] where a prince made out of coloured sugar is placed in the centre of a table at a children's party, and entertains romantic notions about a little girl opposite him, until she eats him. Another and more straightforward fairy-tale parody, 'The Reluctant Dragon' (1898) by Kenneth Grahame, describes a dragon who is too lazy to take on St. George, but in the end agrees to a pretend fight for the sake of appearances.

Meanwhile, in another landscape altogether, an expatriate English writer was writing fantasy with a contrastively stark sense of reality. Rudyard Kipling's *Jungle Books* (1894, 1895) tell of the Indian boy Mowgli who, brought up in the jungle by the beasts, has to fight for his position and eventually becomes the animals' master. In his Indian jungle, Kipling created one of the first secondary worlds with its own laws in children's fantasy; and he also married the pastoral impulse of *The Water-Babies*, the *Alice* books and Richard Jefferies' *Wood Magic* (1881) to the savage facts of wild animal life. The books were instantly hugely popular, for they united fantasy with the adventure story of faraway lands; though secretly they were also an allegory of the way Europeans should try to relate to the culture and variety of the Indian peoples. The idea of humanity joining with the animals is later extended by Kipling to linking with one's own history, in *Puck of Pook's Hill* (1906) and *Rewards and Fairies* (1910). In one way it is an urge to find roots, to break down modern man's loneliness and alienation, which is seen later in other writers such as E. M. Forster and D. H. Lawrence. Even Kipling's *Just So Stories* (1902), with their search for the origins of the leopard's spots, the elephant's trunk or the crab's shell, are part of this impulse.

The English Nineties are full of fantasies for children, for this was a time when both childhood and fantasy were becoming more widely desirable to adults. Fantasy writers now often get on their knees for children: there is a return to the wilder fantasy of the 1850s and 1860s, but now simply to revel in the absurd. Often, though, there is an element of clumsy, if benign, patronage; adults are amusing themselves as much as their imagined audience. The results, which are frequently imitations of the *Alice* books, are on the whole overstrained exhibitions of adult whimsy. Maggie Brown's *Wanted – A King, or How Merle Set the Nursery Rhymes to Rights* (1890), presents a child who enters the land of nursery rhymes to overthrow the wicked giant Grunter Grim, who has made the rhymes end unhappily, and to set up a good king Baby Bunting to rule them. Without Jack and Jill falling down the hill or Miss Muffet being frightened away by the spider any longer, one wonders just what is left of the rhymes themselves after this moral witchhunt. Jonathan Cott works it too hard when he calls the story 'an amazingly "modern" ... reflection ... of the Victorian era's post-Darwinian ontological anxiety.'[55] The book is however quite well told, with a novel idea, and a unity and drive to the plot.

In these whimsical books there is little attempt to understand children, or to do more than address the adult idea of childhood. Typical are the nevertheless popular *Wallypug* books of G.E.Farrow, also written in the *Alice* tradition, starting with *The Wallypug of Why* (1895), which describes an upside-down realm of feeble jokes and 'funny' characters, where the king is for long treated as a servant rather than a ruler. Also popular were the wild books of Judge Edward Abbot Parry – *Katawampus. Its Treatment and Cure* (1895) and *Butterscotia: or, A Cheap Trip to Fairy Land* (1896). Children's ill-temper is called Katawampus, and is caused by a bug, which can only be removed by handing one's children over to a strange old man called Krab in his magic cave (no comment). Here bad behaviour is like an illness, to be sympathised with, and to be removed like tonsils, only under the most entertaining conditions. This shows starkly the change in attitude to children since the early nineteenth century. *Butterscotia* is as its name suggests, a fairy treat, a visit to a magic land of fun and adventure. This aspect of being a treat is to become more and more the nature of children's fantasy.

In all these books, we may note, something is being 'put right,' particularly in those of Brown and Farrow, where kingship is being restored to an unruly kingdom. In that limited sense they reveal themselves as anti-fantastic, for they are removing the chaotic inversions of the world on which their own fantasy depends. (This idea of restoring order to kingdoms from outside can also be seen as an imperialist one.) Here Evelyn Sharp's collection *Wymps and Other Fairy Tales* (1897) and *All the Way to Fairyland* (1898), are a contrast, delighting in turning things upside-down. Sharp is fond of anti-fairies, whom she calls 'wymps,' who play practical jokes on people and cause chaos; and she delights in inversions. In the 1898 stories a princess takes on the role of a prince and seeks her fortune ('The Story of Honey and Sunny'); another princess finds an ugly poet beautiful ('The Princess and the Poet'); 'The Wonderful Toymaker' has the idea that true silence is full of sound. Evelyn Sharp's later involvement with the Women's Suffrage Movement is quietly anticipated in the feminism of some of these tales: but she was a radical thinker throughout her life.[56] The witty character of her stories often anticipates those of another contemporary female rebel, E. Nesbit.

3 THE LONG IDYLL: 1900–1950

The more indulgent attitude to the child and childhood that appears in the fantasy of the 1890s continues, with local modifications, until after the Second World War. If we put Kenneth Grahame's *The Wind in the Willows* (1908) beside Beverley Nichols' *The Tree That Sat Down* (1945), we find the same English pastoral note; if we compare E.Nesbit's *Five Children and It* (1902) with Mary Norton's *Bonfires and Broomsticks* (1947), we will see a similar idea of fantasy as a collection of treats. Where previously children's fantasy could be viewed as a serious threat to the imagination, as an essential release to the Victorian spirit, as a symbolic source of moral truth or as a way to religious or mystical understanding of the world, from now for another 50 years it is to be seen mainly as a form of entertainment, with only licensed credibility and little or no relation to the wider concerns of life. With few exceptions, fantasy becomes less a place for learning or growing than a sort of prolonged secondary world where the imagination can feel at home – a safe world where youth never ages, where magic and wonder are ever-present, and where dangers and difficulties simply heighten the pleasure as they are overcome. This world is not infrequently equated with England itself, as a sea-girt land of nature and wonder – a linkage which is part of the larger merging of patriotism with pastoral in this period. This has much to say of the consolatory function that children's fantasy and fairy books served throughout a time of growing urbanisation and decreasing social assurance. And indeed war, Depression and collectivism eventually begin to make themselves felt even within the precincts of fantasy.

The new attitude to the child and fantasy is epitomised in Hilaire Belloc's *Cautionary Tales for Children* (1907). Written in the idiom of *Struwwelpeter*, but more unambiguous, these are comic exposures of the moral fairy tale, just as Anstey's 'The Good Little Girl' was of the moralist; the increased literariness is typically Edwardian. 'Jim' portrays a naughty boy who leaves his nurse's side at the zoo and is eaten – gradually – by a lion: when the lion is called off by his keeper, '"Ponto!" he cried, with angry Frown. "Let go, Sir! Down, Sir! Put it down!"', all that is left is Jim's head. Jim's parents coolly mark the moral: his mother comments, '"Well – it gives me no surprise. / He would not do as he was told!"' Then young Henry King – no evident satire on the seventeenth-century poet of that name – eats bits of string until he dies, moralising his story as he goes. When one George is given a balloon which bursts and kills his entire family, we are informed that 'little Boys/Should not be given dangerous Toys.' The model child is Charles Augustus Fortescue, whose infant worth showed itself in his fastidiousness, his devotion to Latin and Maths, and his passion for mutton scraps at table: in later life he rises, marries well, becomes rich and builds a huge house,

> Where he resides in Affluence still
> To show what Everybody might
> Become by
> SIMPLY DOING RIGHT.

Or in other words, doing right can be translated into doing right by oneself. This is the age when, in literature at any rate, the naughty child is preferred because it has vitality.

Naughtiness is behind several of the animal fantasies (1902–1918) of Beatrix Potter, which portray disobedient and disruptive kittens, rabbits or squirrels. Tom Kitten ruins his clothes, and causes a riot upstairs while his mother has guests to tea; Peter Rabbit steals Mr McGregor's vegetables, even though forbidden; Squirrel Nutkin is extremely rude to the owl, whom his sisters try to placate. But the models of behaviour – Peter's or Nutkin's siblings – are as water beside wine: 'Flopsy, Mopsy, and Cottontail, who were good little bunnies, went down the lane to gather blackberries. But Peter, who was very naughty, ran straight away to Mr McGregor's garden...' We find the same preference in the contemporary stories of E. Nesbit, where it is the high spirits and wild imaginations of the children that cause all the delight – though they are never quite disobedient or rude to their elders. The idea of restraining the self is relatively in abeyance. Only magic may do the restraining from outside, as with the daily wishes that end every sunset in *Five Children and It*.

This too is the age of the animal story – of Kipling's *Just So Stories* (1902), *The Wind in the Willows* (1908), Walter de la Mare's *The Three Mulla-Mulgars* (1910), *The Story of Doctor Dolittle* (1920), the *Pooh* books (1926, 1928), John Masefield's *The Midnight Folk* (1927), T.H. White's *The Sword in the Stone* (1938) and C.S. Lewis's *The Lion, the Witch and the Wardrobe* (1950). In these stories the animal is treated as though rational and capable of speech: the impulse is partly pastoral, looking back to a time when all the now divided orders of being could be imagined together; it is also at times sentimental and overly anthropomorphic. By the early 1950s it is on its way out, as the Talking Beasts of Lewis's Narnia become fugitive companions, liable to lose their speech or die out. In Richard Adams's *Watership Down* (1972) or William Horwood's *Duncton* books 1980–93), animal and human societies live quite separate lives.

Beatrix Potter's books are so good not least because she is able to play with her own anthropomorphism: she lets the civil rest lightly on the rude. Peter

Rabbit may have clothes and be told not to go into Mr McGregor's garden, but he is also simply an impulsive little rabbit who might have become a stew: the sense of both realities makes the fiction a game. Frogs sit on lily pads and frogs eat minnows, so in *The Tale of Mr Jeremy Fisher* (1906) we have the hero sitting on a lily pad in his raincoat with a fishing rod and hamper. In *The Tale of Mrs Tittlemouse* (1910) there is a sort of interplay between animals-as-humans and the plain animal. Mrs Tittlemouse lives in a hole which she likes to keep very tidy, but a spider, a cluster of bees and a toad are making use of it, as they might in real life; the spider is sent off with a 'scolding,' and Mr Jackson the toad is enlisted to remove the bees' nest. The story ends with a tea party for Mrs Tittlemouse's friends, from which Mr Jackson's rather greedy and dirty presence is excluded by her making the door smaller, though he is later handed acorn-cupfulls of honey through the window. Here the unwanted guests of human life mix with those of the animal world. In *The Tale of Pigling Bland* (1913), we have dressed-up pigs setting off on their own to walk to 'market' – which (here perhaps only for adults) shimmers in and out of its more sinister meaning.

Clothes, which distinguish man from animal, are an issue in many of Beatrix Potter's stories: Peter Rabbit and Tom Kitten lose theirs, Pigling Bland has to keep his, and walk on two legs in the human world, or he may be treated as a mere pig. The fox in *The Tale of Jemima Puddleduck* (1908) is taken for a benign 'gentleman' by the witless duck because he wears clothes and reads the newspaper; but the child reader is given superior knowledge. The frog in *The Tale of Mr Jeremy Fisher* (1906) escapes being devoured by the trout because the fish dislikes the mackintosh he is wearing. In the ends of many of the tales, however, conversation gives way to uncivilised action, or clothes are shed in kittenish riot, mad rabbit flight, or the sudden throwing off of a disguise. Animals are a delight to us, and we may turn that delight into human dress if we will; but we are never allowed to forget that animals are a delight to one another also, and for quite different reasons.

Many of the stories involve going out into the world and taking risks. Jemima Puddleduck wants to find a place to lay her forbidden eggs; Jeremy Fisher is sitting exposed in the middle of a pond; Peter Rabbit goes twice into Mr McGregor's garden; Pigling Bland sets out to market; the Flopsy Bunnies imprudently fall asleep in Mr McGregor's rubbish heap; Squirrel Nutkin pushes his luck with the Owl until he pays for it with his tail; Timmie Willie the country mouse visits his cousin Johnny in town, and Johnny visits the country. All this is not unlike a child making its first ignorant forays into a world of boiling pans, electric sockets, fragile ornaments and muddy ponds.

After the risk and the escape, there is domestic retreat. Peter Rabbit and Tom Kitten are sent to bed, Jemima Puddleduck goes back to the farm to lay her eggs, Pigling Bland just escapes back across the county boundary, the town and country mice return happily to their own territories, Jeremy Fisher resolves not to go fishing again, Mrs Tittlemouse shuts out Mr Jackson from further invasion of her house, the Flopsy Bunnies run home. The world is a place of casual menace or alienation: only by living soberly and with good sense can one be sure of escaping it – but then, who would not tease it a little?[1] And the idyllic aspect of these stories is always that death and pain are escaped, the happy country life is preserved, and recklessness does not have its usual price.

The only inescapable enemy of idyll is time. At the end of Kenneth Grahame's *The Golden Age* (1895) Edward has gone away to school and will never be the same again; at the end of his *Dream Days* (1898) Harold, Charlotte and the narrator have followed him. But time as change is rarely felt in this period's children's fantasy – with the exception of *Peter Pan* (1904). The Never Land is a delightful idyll, but with one exception the children must grow up. Peter is in a sense insubstantial and a half-man, which is why he stays an elusive fairy and a boy. *Peter Pan* was such a decades-long success because it appealed to what was then a universal sentiment about childhood, as well as giving children the pleasures of magic adventures, and adults reassurance in their loss.[2]

When we turn to the magic books of E. Nesbit, however, we find that though time is one of her most frequent themes, its effects of loss, growth or mortality are spurned altogether. Nesbit writes about children of the same ages from first to last. Several of her fantasies involve time-defeating journeys to the past (*The Story of the Amulet* (1906), *The House of Arden* (1908) and *Harding's Luck* (1909)), in which the past may be used to better the present, or a wrong in the present may find its resolution in history. Her children do not often look backwards to their own past experiences, or make comparisons that would enable them to learn. In *Five Children and It* (1902), where four of them meet a 'sand-fairy' and are granted one wish per day, they never learn to ask for something that will not cause them difficulties, and try as they may, they never really profit from their mistakes. As for Nesbit herself, it could be argued that her very writing of children's stories was a defiance of time more than for most other writers, for she claimed that she could recall exactly what she did, felt and thought as a child, so that when she wrote she had a child's vision with an adult's perception.[3] Nesbit's own unconventional and ever-active life in part expressed a desire to stay young. Her adult novels, written in middle age – *The Red House* (1902), *The Incomplete Amorist* (1906), *Daphne in Fitzroy Street* (1909), *Dormant* (1912), *The Incredible Honeymoon* (1916) and *The Lark* (1922) – are mostly about the passions of youth.

Nesbit's magic books up to 1906 are written as a series of children's treats –if treats with qualifications. In *Five Children and It* the children can use their daily wish to acquire gold, beauty, wings, giant size or adventures, and all these things and some of the pleasures they bring are granted:

> The wings were very big, and more beautiful than you can possibly imagine – for they were soft and smooth, and every feather lay neatly in its place. And the feathers were of the most lovely mixed changing colours, like the rainbow, or iridescent glass, or the beautiful scum that sometimes floats on water that is not at all nice to drink. (95)

It is typical of Nesbit to add that last realistic touch: but she gives the impression through her three similies that the experience is something being described now, rather than a literary construct. So too in *The Phoenix and the Carpet* (1904) both the bird and the carpet can grant wishes, and *The Story of the Amulet* is a series of visits to the remote past in search of the missing half of the magic amulet.

These treats are made more real-seeming by their qualifications and by the often ludicrous 'scrapes' the children get themselves into with them. The gold they are given turns out to be in spade guineas, which are no longer legal tender, and cause problems in the local village. Wishing one's baby brother would 'grow up,' brings considerable difficulty in stopping the resultant young man from going up to London to his club. Asking a magic carpet to bring back from its native land '"the most beautiful and delightful productions of it you can"', brings one hundred and ninety-nine very hungry white Persian cats to the nursery. Travelling through time to Atlantis might suggest all the pleasures of exotic tourism, but it also means having to escape the tidal wave that finally engulfs the city. But, as in Beatrix Potter's tales, all these difficulties add spice to the stories' enjoyment, especially when everything turns out happily – or at least, safely.

Nesbit has a special art in 'pressurising pleasure,' for she often uses logic and mathematics to control the magic, particularly in her many short fairy tales.[4] In 'The Island of the Nine Whirlpools,' not very bright Prince Nigel has to do sums to release a princess from a whirlpool- and dragon-guarded island, after learning that the whirlpools fall quiet and the dragon sleeps for five minutes each per day, and that each day the whirlpools are quiet five minutes earlier and the dragon three minutes later. In 'Melisande: or, Long and Short Division,' Prince Florizel has to rescue a princess cursed with rapid-growing hair: cutting the hair off the princess does not work, for it simply grows twice as fast, and when he tries rather cutting the princess off her hair, it is then *she* who grows enormous: so he has to find a logical answer.[5] Nesbit is fond too of hidden double meanings and puns that solve fairy-tale problems.[6]

Each of her magic books is like a compendium of games. There is a series of short, separate adventures loosely linked together, each wildly different, and exposing different aspects of the magic and the children alike: here a visit to a

French tower with treasure in it, there a trip to the South Sea Islands, to a Fire Insurance Office or the theatre. And everywhere the most odd things are thrown together – a tropic island and an Edwardian cook, a nursery and a cow, or a well-regulated insurance office adoring its god the Phoenix. In all Nesbit's comic fantasy we find this delight in mixing opposites, and somehow making a new unity out of them. The traditional fairy of the Tinker Bell variety would certainly not have recognised Nesbit's sand-fairy or Psammead, which emerges as 'something brown and furry and fat' from the children's diggings in a gravel-pit:

> Its eyes were on long horns like a snail's eyes, and it could move them in and out like telescopes; it had ears like a bat's ears, and its tubby body was shaped like a spider's and covered with thick soft fur; its legs and arms were furry too, and it had hands and feet like a monkey's. (27)

This creature, with its bad-tempered and contemptuous manner, somehow comes across as a single organism, and as one of the dominant personalities in the book. And this is true of all Nesbit's magic books, where she thrusts the most diverse things together, and yet manages to give a sense of unity.[7] There is much in her imagination that is like Lewis Carroll's. And her interest in maths recalls not only Carroll, but the several fantasy writers of the nineteenth century who were mathematicians or scientists or closely related to one – Kingsley, Carroll, George MacDonald, Mrs Molesworth, Mary De Morgan, Lucy Lane Clifford, E. A. Abbott.

This idyllic picture, however, has to be qualified with Nesbit's later magic books for children, *The Enchanted Castle* (1907), *The House of Arden, Harding's Luck* and *The Magic City* (1910). The magic in *The Enchanted Castle* is both more frightening and more mystical. Here E.Nesbit is exploring a more religious side of her nature, the side that could believe the supernatural potentially real and not necessarily amenable to human wishes. There are statues of dinosaurs in the castle grounds that come to life, and a group of dummies (the 'Ugly-Wuglies') which, dressed up by the children as an audience for a play they are acting, suddenly move and speak; and there are statues of the Greek gods and goddesses who meet when the moon is full. The Ugly-Wuglies do not destroy the idyll of the wonderful garden, to which the awakened gods give a divine basis, but they are an element that is not part of the scheme of things – a random irruption of the sinister. Nesbit had a frightened addiction to the macabre, which appears elsewhere in her numerous ghost and horror stories, and which spilled over here.

In *The Enchanted Castle* we are more concerned with the inner world of the spirit, than with the outer world of objects and doings. This is symbolised by the story being in the house and its hidden gardens: all Nesbit's subsequent books are set in and around houses also. A strange girl met by the children, who have happened on the castle, tells them that she is a princess, and they believe her, until they realise that she lives partly in a fantasy world of her own. Yet the notion of her as a princess never quite goes away, and the boundaries of fiction and reality overlap. What was solid and real in the earlier books, is less certain here. A statue may come alive, a dummy may turn into a half-person, a girl into a princess: nothing is what it seems. We are partly in a world of the imagination, partly in one of magic, and who is to say which it is? Where in the earlier books the imagination came real, here the real becomes the imagination. And where the earlier books took place mainly in the day, these later ones often have night-time settings. It is as though Nesbit had passed from a materialist to an idealist attitude towards magic.

In the 'Arden' books, *The House of Arden* and *Harding's Luck*, nothing is what it seems in another sense, for the true heir to the Arden seat is not middle-class Cousin Edred, as is thought, but little lame Dickie Harding, a wandering tramp's companion. The harsh realities of Dickie's life are vividly portrayed by the Fabian side of E.Nesbit's temperament, but in the end no upset to the status quo is caused, for Dickie finds an estate and a knighthood prepared for him in the seventeenth century, into which he disappears, so managing matters that the castle and its treasure will after all go to Edred three hundred years in the future. But this happy arrangement, where everyone belongs somewhere in time, and poverty turns out to be hidden nobility, is undercut by the earlier picture of Dickie's wretched life as a social outsider in Edwardian England.

Whatever we say about Nesbit's skill in deploying temporal laws in these books, she has used time as a sort of extensible bag in which to find a place for those who do not fit the present: and all her 'metaphysical' views about time and space being '"only forms of thought"'[8] are conditioned by an inability to face and struggle with problems in the here and now. The 'Arden' books may still be centrally concerned with providing 'treats' for the characters, and, through time-travel to the comparatively pastoral seventeenth century, for the reader; but the books lack the sense of enjoyment central to idyll. Everyone is concerned with arranging other people's lives – Dickie with Beale or the children, the old nurse who explains what to do, the continual plots in the Jacobean world, the magic 'mouldiwarps' who organise the time-transfers. And everyone always has a future object in view, so that there is little scope for enjoyment of the now elusive present moment.

The Magic City, less idyllic still, enlarges space rather than time. 'Deserted' by his much older sister Helen, who has married and left him with her new husband's daughter Lucy, young Philip consoles himself by building a model city out of domestic objects in the library of the house. By magic he then suddenly finds the city big enough for him to enter it, and there finds another library with another toy city with living people in it, which again becomes large enough for him to enter...[9] Meanwhile Lucy has followed him, and then becomes lost. Philip has to find her, and then both have to work together to deliver the city from seven perils. There is a constant atmosphere of fear and tension, even when most of the terrible-seeming tasks and creatures the children face turn out to be enlarged versions of items they used in building the first toy city. Play here is no idyll. It has rightly been said by Lois Kuznets that the toy adventures in the story are symbolic means by which Philip is brought to move beyond his earlier sense of betrayal by his sister to acceptance both of his new relation to her and of his new family.[10] Fantasy here serves as a means of finding one's place through displacement.

These later books have 'themes' in a way that the earlier ones do not. *The Enchanted Castle* is about the imagination, the 'Arden' books are about time, and *The Magic City* is about making. Philip and Lucy can enter their town because they made it, and everybody who contributed to making the household objects inside it is an honorary citizen. If it is made well, it comes to life in another dimension. Obvious thoughts concerning well-made literary fictions and *their* reality, not least that of Nesbit's own stories, are invited. And these books differ from the earlier comic ones in another way also: they are much more concerned with helping others than with only amusing the self. In *The Enchanted Castle* the children rescue the little girl from her lonely imaginings about herself as a princess, before they proceed to discover the real magic about the castle. The 'Arden' books show Edred's and Elfrida's vain efforts on their own behalf to find the Arden treasure and take up the Arden inheritance: they have to be given the help and generosity of an unexpected other to succeed. The idea of doing something for others goes a stage further in *The Magic City*, for by rescuing Lucy through accomplishing the seven tasks, Philip and she become deliverers of the entire city from the tyranny of the renegade nurse, while at the same time they deliver the 'city' of themselves from the tyranny of their anger.

After Nesbit, children's fantasy was never quite the same again. She showed just how much fun could be made of bringing magic into the ordinary domestic lives of children: and she introduced to children's fantasy the idea of the group of different children, rather than the frequently solitary child of earlier books. Her books demonstrated that fantasy could be wildly inventive and yet follow its own peculiar laws. She was also the first children's fantasy writer to explore time-travel, and the source of much of its later development

And Nesbit is, perhaps most distinctively of all, one of the first children's fantasy writers to use the idea of a single thread of directed narrative over a novel length. Previously most longer children's fantasy had been episodic or desultory in form and drive, from *Alice in Wonderland* to Nesbit's own *Five Children and It*. (Even MacDonald's *The Princess and the Goblin* is as much about the princess as it is about the goblin(s).) It is likely that some of this comes from Nesbit's having written for older children, who might be expected to manage reading a whole book at a time; and here we might note that a good deal of nineteenth-century fantasy is aimed at younger children, often because they are supposed more formative, or more innocently receptive to fantasy. The same progress from episodic to 'joined-up' narrative is seen in Nesbit's 'real life' children's books, which start with the anecdotal *The Treasure Seekers* (1899) and *The Wouldbegoods* (1901), but move to a single continuing narrative with *The Railway Children* (1906). Actually Nesbit's writing from the 1890s to the war follows a pattern, in that she first writes for the very young (for example *Pussy Tales* and *Doggy Tales* in 1895), and then for progressively older children. This was not in parallel with the growth of her own children, born in the early 1890s: when she was writing her children's fantasies, they were in their twenties. What the changes show is the way that childhood itself was being enlarged by the nostalgic adults of the time; nor should we ignore the effect of the Education Acts of 1870 and 1902 in extending the school leaving age and thereby lengthening childhood.

In 1906, when Nesbit's *The Story of the Amulet* was published, there appeared Kipling's *Puck of Pook Hill*, which also portrays visits to the past. But in Kipling's book it is England's past that is the subject, and numerous figures from that past visit two Sussex children, rather than the other way round. Under the aegis of Puck, last of England's fairies, and England's spirit itself, Dan and Una hear the stories of a Roman, a Saxon, a Norman, a medieval craftsman, a usurer and others, and even the tale of how the old fairies left England at the time of the Reformation. Kipling's book is not a wistful look to the past, but rather a panegyric to the present, into the making of which all these characters and their actions have gone. It shows the children just how much more rich and various their country is than they could have imagined, and it gives them a historical sense, by which they can see themselves as parts of a long-growing tree of history. In a way it denies time, by suggesting that these contributions from the past go on, and that the total present being of England is the stream of time that has made it.

Just as idyllic and celebratory of England is *Puck*'s sequel, *Rewards and Fairies* (1910), which deals with episodes from England's eighteenth- and nineteenth-century history as well as with further earlier ones, almost all within the little world of Sussex. Many of the episodes in *Rewards and Fairies* are more intellectual and esoteric than those in *Puck*, where we have strong and exciting narratives, and the perspective is more national than local. Neither book keeps to chronological order, but puts Romans after Normans, or Queen Elizabeth before the early Iron Age. But then, this shuffling of times can be seen as Kipling's way of making them all one. One other feature of the books stands out, and that is Puck's ensuring that the children entirely forget every episode. This might seem to make their instruction useless, did we not reflect that just as England's forgotten past continues a submerged action on the present, so Dan's and Una's minds are unconsciously shaped by the stories they hear.

The idea of community in time is furthered by that of one in place. Not a story passes without tying characters and events to particular places: the 'insider' detail on Sussex in *Rewards and Fairies* is marked, and a close parallel is drawn between the children in their play 'kingdom' and Gloriana, Queen of England, in her more serious one (*Rewards*, 27–42). And everything is very sensuously felt,[11] from the cold weather of Hadrian's Wall to the way a horse's tail 'brushe[s] the glassy water' of a pool in which it stands drinking (*Puck*, 29–30). There are no solitary people in the stories, they are all deep in a network of relationships: much of every story is conversation; and the children often interrupt to ask questions, reminding us that each story does not exist on its own, but is being related, in both senses of the word, to others. Continuity, the flow of one thing into another, is the key, in contrast to Nesbit's technique of opposition and reversal of expectation. In a similar way, in Kipling's *Just So Stories*, all the animals change, and many are parts of their background; while the abrupt and absurd alterations the fantasy gives them – proposing, for instance, that the Elephant got its long trunk from a tug-of-war with a hungry crocodile, or that the leopard had its spots painted on it by an Ethiopian[12] – point to the much more gradual evolutions of reality, where creatures change in a continuous environment rather than from chance and singular events.[13]

Perhaps the purest idyll, because the most pastoral, among Edwardian children's fantasies, is Kenneth Grahame's *The Wind in the Willows* (1908). Strictly the book might not appear to be for children at all, since the characters are so clearly ex-public school chums, of the sort Grahame clubbed with on his escapes from his job as Secretary of the Bank of England. Its paradise is found among the weekend retreats of the Thames Valley, in then relatively unfrequented parts of the river: it imagines a world remote from mankind, where woodland animals, clothed, civil, and usually rational, live a life of pleasure in close contact with the earth and water, as citified man cannot. It celebrates life freed from modern routine, as the Mole, possessed with delight at a bright and beckoning spring day, throws aside his household work and comes out of his dark burrow into the gleaming air. The subsequent days of 'messing about in boats' with his friend the Water Rat is one of the happiest things in literature: and it is given a mystic basis, when the two creatures meet Pan, spirit of the woods, at the Wild Wood's heart.

One of the main touchstones of emotion in the book is the idea of home. From the Mole's dark tunnels, of which he is ashamed until the Badger tells him it is just what he himself likes, to the Rat's bankside house with its watery views and sounds; from the Badger's snug but rambling home underground in the woods, stumbled on just in time by the snowbound Rat and Mole, to the brick-built Hall of Mr Toad, with its large rooms and rolling lawns: all these are homes where each animal can be not only safe and comfortable, but fully at home with itself. The Mole feels his long-forsaken house call to him from beneath the winter ground:

> Home! That was what they meant, those caressing appeals, those soft touches wafted through the air, those invisible little hands pulling and tugging, all one way!... Shabby indeed, and small and poorly furnished, and yet his, the home he had made for himself, the home he had been so happy to get back to after his day's work. And the home had been happy with him, too, evidently, and was missing him....(81)

The pathetic fallacy almost justifies itself. Even the manic Toad loves his home, and puts his eventual return to it in loud and repeated triumphal tones, "'The Toad came home!'" (244–5). And beyond the individual animals and their homes there is the larger home of the River Bank itself. This home is not without its threats, in the shape of hostile weather or invasive weasels; nor without its nearby mysteries, in the shape of Pan: but it is the wider locality that all share and have chosen to live in.

This responsiveness to the idea of home is very much an Edwardian phenomenon. We see it in novelists and poets from Forster to Rupert Brooke; and it is strongly present in the children's fantasy of E. Nesbit, in *Peter Pan*, and in Kipling's *Puck of Pook's Hill* and *Rewards and Fairies*, where it relates to England itself. And this concept of home often has a divine or mystic sanction, the *genus loci*, from its wild woodland god Pan, an Edwardian favourite, to the English Puck.

But to some animal spirits home is not enough. It is not just the Mole throwing aside his whitewash brush for a long holiday, which still alows home its eventual place: but it is those more restless spirits, the Rat and particularly the Toad, who feel the draw of wider horizons.[14] Mole is drawn out at the call of 'Spring...with its spirit of divine discontent and longing' (p.1); but the Rat, who continually wonders, "'*Why* can't fellows be allowed to do what they like *when* they like and *as* they like...?'" (20), is more dangerously and irresponsibly truant, a ready victim for the Circean nutbrown traveller's clichéd tales of far and romantic places (ch.IX).

But of course the extreme is Toad, driven by one wild craze after another in his lust for "'a horizon that's always changing'" (24): he is the one who actually leaves the Wild Wood because of it; while the Rat is steadied by having to help him. Toad is personally vain and ambitious beyond his station, behaving like a human, with his brick-built house, his boats, caravans and cars; he is the only animal who uses money. In consequence he alone comes into disastrous contact with humans. Living out of all reason, he is unreasonably punished with twenty years' imprisonment; having lost touch with reality, he is placed in an anachronistic jail staffed by medieval soldiery. And because he is absent from home, Toad Hall is taken over by the weasels, and only the help of his patient friends restores it to him. There can be no final certainty, despite Toad's repentant declarations, that he will not turn to yet another craze before long: both he and the Rat are described in terms of being drugged, but Toad is an addict.

Yet judgement alone will not do. Toad may go too far, the Rat nearly lose his mind through romantic bewilderment, and the Mole, least of the sinners, may blame himself for irresponsibility: yet the whole book demonstrates that their variously wild urges are at root as natural as their more domestic pleasures. And of course none of them in this fantasy is able to translate these sparkles in the blood into that alternative natural current: love, sex and children. All of the animals are hearty bachelors and there is not a female in sight (though the Otter has produced a baby from somewhere). After all, having women around makes the idea of 'home' quite a different thing. But ambition, wild joy, longing (authenticated in Pan) and even occasional irresponsibility are justified by the book, if the madness to which they can lead is not. Reject them, and one rejects much of the passion at the heart of life, for the even tenor and the seasonal round, and nothing new *happens*. It is the Toad's actions that suddenly give the book a direction and a plot.

What Grahame portrays here are really two impulses of idyll, both based on longing, or *Sehnsucht*, in a decade when the pace, routine, and crowdedness of life were considerably increasing. There is a side that desires simply to rest, to be, to contemplate: it is even a languid and a lazy side, Grahame's Reluctant Dragon drawling, "'I always let the other fellows – the earnest fellows – do all the fighting, and no doubt that's why I have the pleasure of being here now'".[15] On the other hand there is the equal emphasis we find in idyll and pastoral on ambition and action (*Lycidas, Adonais, In Memoriam*, for example). Some idyllic children's fantasies are actually full of continual activity and doing – Kingsley's *The Water-Babies*, Carroll's *Alice* books, Jean Ingelow's *Mopsa the Fairy*, E.Nesbit's magic books: what is desirable is the variety, the busyness, the changing sights of the world and the acquisition of more and more wonderful experience, à la Tennyson's Ulysses. Others stay more still, and invite a good deal of contemplation – George MacDonald's, Mrs Molesworth's or Laurence Housman's fantasies. *The*

THE LONG IDYLL: 1900–1950

Wind in the Willows can at best make only a temporary truce beteween the two impulses: the position of rest reached at the end is in part an illusion.[16]

But then, the animal characters themselves are partly an illusion. For of course this is an artificial world, not a fully natural one. Moles and rats do not wear clothes and go for picnics in boats, and toads are usually found in more intimate contact with roads than that of driving cars over them. Nor do badgers and others rally to the help of the outcast, or the reproof of the foolish, but are more likely to eat them if they do anything at all. Here of course Beatrix Potter's animal stories are a contrast, for they deliberately play their own artificialities against the facts of animal life. But Grahame's story is to be taken simply as pathetic fallacy and as wish fulfilment. He has grafted human attributes on to animals to create an ideal natural world, one in which the virtues of 'good fellows' find themselves at home, and weekending Edwardian man may feel that his values are mirrored in the natural order.

Central to these values and to the idyll is friendship, and the balance that comes from it. The friendship between Mole and Rat is at the heart of the book; the Mole balances the Rat's wilder emotions, while the Rat stirs up the torpid Mole. Sharing and playing are seen as great joys here. But also caring: Ratty saves Mole in the snow, and Mole later helps to bring his friend back from the madness of his wild longing. And of course Mole, Rat and Badger help Toad out of many of his difficulties: whether in turn the obsessive Toad will ever be able to think of anyone else besides himself is another matter. At the centre of the Wild Wood, its spirit, Pan, is called 'the Friend and Helper': and it is on a mission to find one of the Otter's lost children that Mole and Rat meet Pan.

In two other children's fantasies before 1914, Walter de la Mare's *The Three Mulla-Mulgars* (1910) and W. H. Hudson's *A Little Boy Lost* (1910), we find that the idyll is on the side checked in *The Wind in the Willows*, that of wandering and adventure in far places. The protagonists of *The Three Mulla-Mulgars* are three monkey creatures with human attributes, who journey over a strange African jungle land in winter, to a mysterious land called Tishnar where they will find their long-lost father. Largely drawn from Purchas's *Pilgrimage*, the story is in the form of a journey through life to the land beyond death: but its exotic setting makes it rather more of a wonderful journey through a fantastic world to a mystic paradise. For the characters their trek is both arduous and dangerous, and it is the reader who draws pleasure and romance from it: the 'idyll' for the monkey heroes is always in prospect. The story is filled with romantic desire, or *Sehnsucht*, which becomes an increasing part of (adult) fantasy into the 1920s and 1930s.

In Hudson's *A Little Boy Lost* we are also in a strange and remote continent, this time South America, transformed through the author's vision and the child character's magic-making mind. Little seven year-old Martin leaves his family home on the pampas and wanders far over the country to the sea, where a ship finds and takes him. On the way he meets a sinister old shepherd, mirage-people, savages, black sky-people, wild horses, a lady with a leopard, underground dwarf people, mist people, and the Old Man of the Sea. These beings have their strangeness through the child's vision: for instance, we would call the black sky-people vultures. Martin makes 'people' of every creature he meets, in order to relate to them. But Martin's journey is also a mystic one through a truly magic land: natural mysticism comes readily to Hudson, particularly in his South American romance *Green Mansions* (1904). So too was the journey in *The Three Mulla-Mulgars* mystical, but more in relation to a goal, a world beyond this one.

Where Grahame in *The Wind in the Willows* animates the familiar, these books make the unfamiliar (Africa, South America) more strange. Where Grahame tells us of home, these give us a sense of the world as alien, and show us how we do not comfortably belong. As to belonging, the protagonists are never allowed to stay in one place; and they leave home altogether at the outset, whereas Grahame's characters return to it. Both these books are dealing with fantasy in Tolkien's sense of desiring dragons – what is remote from oneself, and therefore exciting. They are in short making 'other worlds,' or in Tolkien's terms, 'secondary' worlds of the imagination: 'Fantasy, the making or glimpsing of Otherworlds, was the heart of the desire of Faërie.'[17] De la Mare's and Hudson's stories are among the first fantasies to create secondary worlds based simply on a desire to make an alternative reality. Lewis Carroll, for instance, is not creating a world in Wonderland, rather a loose federation of strange characters and views in a variously pastoral setting. The making of alternative realities is in some degree an expression of the new relativism in scientific thought.[18]

Virtually no children's fantasies of distinction were published in the period 1911–1919, with the possible exception of W. W. Tarn's story about Skye, *The Treasure of the Isle of Mist*, written in 1913–14 and first published in 1919. This describes two Anglo-Scottish children searching for lost Spanish treasure near their home on Skye. It is a book about belonging, and like *Puck of Pook's Hill* or *The Wind in the Willows*, it has a *genus loci*, here in the shape of the local fairies. One of the children, the more sensitive Fiona, is brought to learn through the help of the fairies that the search itself is better than its object (143), for it shows her more fully the nature of her home. The material treasure is not found, for it is guarded from men by the fairies: but Fiona, who rescues her foolish brother from Fairyland, is given by the fairies a far greater treasure, "'the spirit of the island ... the freedom of the island, and of all living things in it'"; for the King of the Fairies tells her:

THE LONG IDYLL: 1900–1950

'All that is there has passed into your blood. ... You can walk now through the crowded city and never know it, for the wind from the heather will be about you where you go; you can stand in the tumult of men and never hear them, for round you will be the silence of your own sea. That is the treasure of the Isle of Mist. . . .' (148–149)

Here the feverish plot of the fantasy, the desperate struggle with a villain also seeking the Spanish treasure, is rejected for the more contemplative side of 'being' and enjoying what is, rather than trying to get more out of the world: Badger versus Toad. The story is shot through with the marine beauty of the island, and its mysteries, and it is full of that current of desire or *Sehnsucht* for seen and unseen alike, that is frequently present in the fantasy of this time. Here that desire is fired not by far-off places, but by the wonders of one's home, which by grace and her own generosity of heart Fiona is able to take with her when she is far away.

After 1918 and the war, we no longer find the same kind of weight being put on childhood innocence as a value from which adults can benefit. Children's fantasy becomes marginalised and less distinctive. What takes its place is popular entertainment in the form of comics, 'rewards' books, adventure stories and endless series; now children's books are to amuse the 'kiddies,' more than to reflect an area of human experience.[19] The spread of literacy among children, and the affordability of books to a wider public, created a mass market, and mass tastes were increasingly its determinants. Children's fantasy lost much of its cultural *raison d'être*, and became intermittent and sometimes flat or strained. Mixed with gleams of better things, this was to be the situation for the next thirty years.

Children's fantasy of the 1920s and 1930s was frequently written in series. There had been sequel books before, such as *Through the Looking-Glass, The Princess and Curdie, Prince Ricardo, The Second Jungle Book* or *Harding's Luck*, but now they were more the norm, and often ran to more than two: thus the *Doctor Dolittle, Martin Pippin, Flower Fairy* (Cicely Barker), *Rupert, Pooh, Little Grey Rabbit, Hoojibahs, Professor Branestawm, Mary Poppins, Mumfie, Worzel Gummidge* and *Sam Pig* books, not to mention the wider children's literature context of Elinor Brent-Dyer's endless Chalet School stories, *Billy Bunter, William, Jungle John*, and Arthur Ransome's and Enid Blyton's books. Writers tended to stay in a niche, or else be confined to one: they did not often surprise, like E. Nesbit with *Five Children and It* or Kenneth Grahame with *The Wind in the Willows*. This is because they gained a mass readership which liked the 'formula' and the 'attitude' of their books, and therefore to earn a living it was best to continue in the same vein. But this meant a degree of conservatism and intellectual comfort: there was to be nothing a readership was not prepared for or receptive to. Books became variations on a theme, and the reader entered a created world where the mind could be at home. In a sense all these books are 'secondary' or alternative world fantasies, even when they are set in this world. Hugh Lofting felt he had done with Doctor Dolittle after the first book; and then was asked for more, and then more.

In the 1910s and 1920s there was a continued vogue for fairies and fairy books, furthered not least by the enduring popularity of *Peter Pan*.[20] These fairies can be seen as sharing the place of the image of innocent human childhood: many of them are winged children. It was a time for enchanted pastoral images and Never Never lands, whose power was demonstrated by the comfort they could afford even the shell-torn army in Flanders.[21] This was the heyday of fairy artists and illustrators such as Edmund Dulac, Arthur Rackham and William Heath Robinson; and, in the 1920s, of new figures such as Margaret Tarrant, Cicely Barker and the Australian Ida Rentoul Outhwaite (whose fairy book *The Enchanted Forest* (1921) had a huge following).[22] Many of these, particularly the latter three, reflect a gracile, feminine, and desire-filled vision of fairyland, which became closely linked with the beauties of the imagination, and is reflected in such adult fantasy writers as Lord Dunsany, Kenneth Morris, Stella Benson, E. R. Eddison, Margaret Irwin, Hope Mirrlees and Gerald Bullett. There are mingled currents in these of mysticism, nostalgia, feminism and, after the war, social disengagement. So far as children's fantasy is concerned, the main 1920s examples of this strain are Eleanor Farjeon's *Martin Pippin in the Apple Orchard* (1921), and, more complexly, the stories of Walter de la Mare and John Masefield.

Martin Pippin in the Apple Orchard was not at first seen as a children's book, but gradually became regarded as one.[23] Redolent with that peculiar strain of yearning for enchantment in the 1920s spirit (which so influenced C.S.Lewis that he later made it the romantic basis of his theology and fiction), *Martin Pippin* relates such desire specifically to the experience of romantic love. Six magic love stories are told by Martin Pippin to the six damsels who hold the keys to the well-house in which the fair Gillian is held captive. Each of them is finely told, with mocking wit, a good sense of character, a feel for traditional fairy tale, and a love of the English countryside – all of which makes them much like Shakespeare's *As You Like It* (then one of his most popular plays). And like many other 1920s fantasies, they are set in a Morrisian medieval imaginary world, infused with magic and peopled by blacksmiths, shepherds, sailors, gardeners, kings, lords and princesses. Much of their magic lies in the way that, through love's working, one person may turn into another, and what was 'real' become enchanted. In 'The King's Barn,' the young blacksmith for whom the king drudges turns out to be the woman who appears magically at midnight every week on the nearby hilltop. The shepherd boy in 'Young Gerard' is both 'lord of the earth' and a hidden king, whose love, unknown to him, undoes an evil spell. 'The Mill of Dreams' has love's reality pass into lovers' dreams, so that we can no longer tell whether they met or imagined meeting.

A central idea is that only by living and working simply and without pride, may one gain love and enchantment. This is what Martin Pippin himself does in telling these stories on behalf of another: for he finds when he has released Gillian that she loves him. Similarly 'Proud Rosalind and the Hart-Royal' has a princess who must learn humility disguised as the low-born and inept Rusty Knight, who is the only figure apparently prepared to defend her honour. Putting aside the self is to go with the grain of reality, which, these stories benignly assure us, is love. There is no socialist impulse here, simply a desire to obliterate distinctions. The brother in 'Open Wilkins' who gives up all his wishes to save his siblings is the one whom the lady loves. Turning away from the world, to win one's own soul through a monastic life, is rejected in 'The King's Barn,' when the king finds that his supposed apprenticeship to a blacksmith has been a service to love. Even the stories themselves break down the walls of their 'selves,' for they are continuously interrupted by the listening damsels' questions and Martin's badinage with them. This dissolving of the self into the current of love is a very Romantic impulse, replete with 'nameless longings'; and it is of course finally no more moral than it is escapist and *voulu*.[24]

Walter de la Mare's children's stories, collected in *Broomsticks* (1925) and *The Lord Fish* (1933), are part of the same broad current of feeling expressed in his friend Farjeon's book, but they have a greater sense of death and the sinister, and are closer to the real world. Like Farjeon, de la Mare writes to a vision of his own, and only occasionally with children in mind: and this is true for many writers and readers in the 1920s, who annexed a fairy vision normally assigned to childhood as their own. Where the Edwardians tried to recapture or even preserve childhood, these 1920s adults took childhood over. (What happened to actual children in the process may well be asked: A. A. Milne's son Christopher is a case in point.)

Many of de la Mare's stories are set in houses and/or involve people in conditions of stasis, whether through captivity or inertia: and they thus often naturally suggest the mind. As with Henry James's supernatural stories, to which de la Mare was indebted,[25] they repeatedly deal with situations where the supposed supernatural event may in fact be a delusion in the human witness: so that it both 'happens' and is imagined, and one cannot tell how much of which is the case. In some ways the plots of the stories are at variance with this, for the object is always to escape from the deceptive and solipsistic enclosure, symbolic of the desire to touch unquestionable truth and reality. The girl in 'The Lovely Myfawny' is kept prisoner by her father, till her lover wins her; in 'Miss Jemima' a girl is tyrannised by the housekeeper of her uncle's house; the retired robber in 'The Thief' lives shut in his house with his paranoia. The three sweeps of 'The Three Sleeping Boys' are bullied and finally unsouled by their tyrannical master, until their release from enchantment; the centuries-old grandmother in 'Alice's Grandmother' tries to persuade Alice to live for ever in her frozen old house. In 'Broomsticks' a cat continually breaks out of its home to fly with a witch; and in 'The Dutch Cheese' Griselda's brother John shuts her indoors to keep her away from the fairies. Many of these stories deal with the antagonism of the old towards the young: in a real sense they are not about childhood but about getting away from it into a free life. De la Mare's poetry on childhood is full of the sense of death.

The theme of possession and entrapment continues variously in *The Lord Fish*, with tales of captive girls, a self-centred admiral, a greedy giant, a selfish witness of a fairy, and an intelligent monkey reduced to a public spectacle. All de la Mare's adult supernatural tales and ghost stories are on similar themes – 'Seaton's Aunt' (1923), 'The Green Room' (1925), 'All Hallows' (1926), 'Crewe' (1930), 'A Revenant' (1936).[26] Most of his children's stories may end happily, for they are after all fairy tales, but the repeated enclosures, darknesses and tyrannies from which their protagonists escape remain as real as the escapes from them – escapes which are not so obtainable in the ghost stories. De la Mare's work is full of compassion at life's confinements, and the releases at the ends of his stories are often like flights to a better world outside this one, for which he also hoped:[27] so that they are a strange mixture of fear, regret and desire.

Like de la Mare, John Masefield was a poet, but of a more open and exuberant nature, with a less reserved sense of delight in the world. His children's fantasies, *The Midnight Folk* (1927) and *The Box of Delights* (1935) are stories of voyages to South America and the past, in search of lost treasure. Masefield always had a love of adventure, and his novels *Sard Harker* (1924) and *Odtaa* (1926), which anticipate the Kay Harker stories for children, are exotic tales involving strange journeys. Where de la Mare often starts from a very ordinary human situation which then becomes something more, Masefield mixes reality and the fantastic straight away, so that young Kay has his ordinary life so interwoven with magic that we cannot tell which is real.

Masefield writes fantasy with something of the dislocated and abrupt manner of dreams. There are no chapter divisions in *The Midnight Folk*, and Kay switches between daily lessons with his governess, and travel by miniature sailing boat to South America, or life as a bat. The story is a mélange of romanticised literary figures – highwaymen, pirates, witches, mermaids, talking animals and birds. Love of romance and excitement possesses it, and also a love of nature and all creation; but at the same time it is a picture of a young boy's shooting mind, whether awake or in dreams, based on Masefield's own childhood. And what do all boys want, by this prescription? Why, treasure of course, and the excitement of finding out where it is – even if as in *The Midnight Folk* it has to be given back in the end. Where de la Mare writes with an adult's perspective on life, Masefield in *The Midnight Folk* sticks close to the perceptions of a child. There are no 'themes' in this book, evil and death are not real, and ugliness and misery are not in evidence. This is an idyll for a boy.[28]

It is rather different in Masefield's later *The Box of Delights*. Here Kay is older, a teenager, and the evil is more truly malign, and threatens a whole society. Quite what the villains want is never clear, for they first want Kay's strange magic box, then they want to use it to obtain the Elixir of Life from a long-dead magician, and finally they become keen to stop a cathedral Christmas service. It may be that there is an implicit analysis of evil here, as a sort of swelling power-lust with no particular direction: and certainly the wicked seem to have that marked 1930s disease, megalomania. The more 'epic' character of the book is seen in Kay's having to save a whole world; and in the evil being a collective conspiracy who use aeroplanes and a submarine, who are helped by a black-clad company of 'Wolves,' and who seem to be able to call up help from devils.

The Box of Delights itself enables Kay to grow small or travel to the past, but it also reveals to him the far larger box of delights that is life in its infinite variety. Such delights Kay experienced less thinkingly in *The Midnight Folk*: in a sense the Box gives him back the vision he has partly lost in growing older, providing what Tolkien was three years later to call 'Recovery', the 're-gaining . . . of a clear view.'[29] Recovery is its true function in taking one to the past, and in that sense the Box is the book itself as a time-travelling fantasy. However the Box is also a box with knobs and controls, an artefact made by a wizard, or early scientist, called Arnold of Todi, for his own purposes, and therefore by this book's lights dangerous: the evil people in the story habitually use machines. The book reflects the strong current of pastoralism in 1930s thought which was hostile to technology, a view illustrated variously in Aldous Huxley's *Brave New World* (1932) and the adult fantasies of C. S. Lewis, Tolkien and T.H.White. White and Lewis, incidentally, are highly indebted to Masefield's Kay stories.

The happy ending of *The Box of Delights* is less idyllic and 'earned' than that of *The Midnight Folk*. The threat offered by the evil figures goes far beyond the covers of the book into contemporary politics, and cannot be so readily wished away. Masefield's story tries to contain it with the religious sanction: God and the church are bigger than Abner Brown (the villain); the triumphant Christmas service in the cathedral at the end is meant to shout evil down. But the cathedral is at first in the darkness of a power cut, and the service when it takes place is a charmed circle in the midst of a larger and more implacable dark.

THE LONG IDYLL: 1900–1950

Alongside the strain of enchantment and desire in children's fantasy of the time runs another current, that of animal and toy fantasy. This continues the pre-war interest in the subject shown in the *Jungle Books*, *The Wind in the Willows* and *The Three Mulla-Mulgars*, but with the difference that where previously animals were shown living away from human society, now they are portrayed with a much closer relationship to man. This is increasingly an age of pathetic fallacy, which leads on the one hand to Disney and on the other to genocidal dictators who talk with their Alsatians. Animal stories are particularly prominent in the 1920s. They are seen in the books by Hugh Lofting about the 'animal rights' hero Doctor Dolittle (1922 onwards), in Margery Bianco's pioneering animal and toy fantasy *The Velveteen Rabbit* (1922), in Kenneth Walker and Geoffrey Boumphrey's *The Log of the Ark* (1923), Mary Tourtel's *Rupert* books (1924 onwards), A. A. Milne's *Pooh* books (1926, 1928), Masefield's *The Midnight Folk*, and Alison Uttley's *Little Grey Rabbit* stories (1929 onwards). These often reflect a desire to escape from human society and its concerns into kinship with a supposedly less vicious animal world: a desire mocked by David Garnett in *Lady into Fox* (1922) and *A Man in the Zoo* (1922), where a man struggles to relate to his wife after she has suddenly turned into a vixen, and where a jilted man in a rage offers himself as an exhibit of *homo sapiens* for a zoo. However, most of the stories do much better than the slightness of their impulse might suggest.

The *Doctor Dolittle* books are an unusual mixture of science and fantasy. The *savant* veterinary Doctor Dolittle learns the different speeches of animals, birds and fish, and thus becomes a genuine citizen of the world. He organises and educates the creatures until they acquire something of the civility of man without his vices; while at the same time he learns immensely from them. In a way the books are about communication: they set up a sort of animal League of Nations. Lofting began his books partly out of shame at the brutalities he saw done to horses on the Western Front: his doctor becomes the sole human friend of animals, first and foremost because he heals them of their sicknesses. Only two modest humans are admitted into the Dolittle world as helpers and friends: otherwise the Doctor's house and garden remain shut off from his kind.

The *Doctor Dolittle* books are quite happy to be fantastical, introducing us to strange creatures such as the Pifflosaurus or the Pushmipullyu, mixing seventeenth-century sailing ships with post offices, or travelling to the moon on a moth, but their interests are also practical and empirical. Sometimes they read like accounts by Swift's Gulliver or Defoe's Crusoe. And of course today there is considerable scientific interest in understanding the intelligence and speech of animals. 'Dolittle' is an ironic misnomer: the Doctor is continually planning and doing, and his concern is to solve practical problems, make life more efficient and happy, and pass on his knowledge; he never rests to enjoy his successes, nor does he philosophise, nor does he make his relations with the animals any more than that of helper and friend. This is *work* as idyll.

It might be said that the *Doctor Dolittle* books do not invite deeper levels of reading: it is after all their point to be scientific and to speak plainly and with clear meaning. Nevertheless there are frequent hints that Dolittle is a God-figure, making a happy garden of animals who relate once more to man as they did in Eden, tending to all living creation, and trying to write a book about it (which has to be passed on to Stubbins, his apprentice). The originally final book of the series, *Doctor Dolittle's Return* (1933) has continual semi-apocalyptic overtones, with the Doctor returning from the moon as a giant. Nevertheless this is a god who ministers more to animals than to man, a scientist God determined to bring joy to all neglected creatures; and a God, too, who is not all-knowing but continually trying to find out. In one sense the books reflect a strand of contemporary belief in the power of science to answer the ills of the world, and a no less potent readiness to believe in some Messiah prepared to bring it about.

They also express a contemporary belief in the spiritual worth of animals and nature beside most of mankind, which comes out in such adult fantasies as Violet Murray's *The Rule of the Beasts* (1925) or John Lambourne's *The Kingdom That Was* (1931), both of which teach man by animal example how to live a better life. So too in Ronald Fraser's *Flower Phantoms* (1926) a girl on the edge of a proper marriage to a worldly man prefers the loves of the plants in a Kew glasshouse; in Kenneth Walker and Geoffrey Boumphrey's *The Log of the Ark* (1923), the whole object of the humans is to save the animal race; and the 1920 novels of D. H. Lawrence are often concerned with the animal side of human nature.[30] It was in the 1920s that an interest in keeping pets really expanded in England.

An idea behind the Doctor Dolittle books is that the idyll has to be made. Where talking animals are a 'given' in *The Water-Babies* or *The Wind in the Willows*, here communication between animals and man is possible only through hard work and study. This notion of idyll as earned is also seen in several minor fantasies of the period. Kindness, perception and courage win Fiona the gift of the island paradise in *The Treasure of the Isle of Mist*. In Edith L. Elias's *Periwinkle's Island* (1919) the children have to learn to be better-behaved before they are allowed on to the wonderful island, and then they have to rid it of its 'one dark spot,' the evil Creepingo. In *The Marvellous Land of Snergs* by E. A. Wyke Smith (1927), the children enlarge their paradise by journeying to the interior and taking on the evil Mother Meldrum. Sometimes the message is that happiness comes from learning to accept oneself, as in Esther Boumphrey's *The Hoojibahs* (1929), where the absurd Hoojibahs spend the story trying to be humans because they are ashamed of their own ways – which, when they come at last to value them, are the true source of their happiness. And in A. E. Coppard's *Pink Furniture* (1930), the deluded Toby Tottel spends the whole story looking all over a fantastical world for pink furniture, only to find that it was at home all the time in his love for the girl next door. This idea of the mind making the idyll will be found central in the *Pooh* books, where Christopher Robin's mind is the source of the action;[31] and it is also seen in Masefield's *The Midnight Folk*, where it is in Kay's imagination that the creatures come alive. All this is in contrast to Edwardian children's fantasy, where there might be a Butterscotia or a Psammead around for the discontented child, and where the earthly paradise of the River Bank lay only a few stations west of Richmond. It seems to mark a sense that the happy place is no longer so easily to be found. Humphrey Carpenter has said, 'It must have been harder to dream up River Banks and Never Never Lands after the experience of the Somme.'[32]

One aspect of the change is that whereas before 1914 children's fantasy often had a fairy or other supernatural manager, in the 1920s this is much less common, and characters have to find happiness for themselves. And this in turn may be because children themselves are often absent from 1920s fantasy. Christopher Robin is only occasionally present in the *Pooh* books, and in any case has a parental role towards the other characters; the *Doctor Dolittle* books are often child-free; *Martin Pippin in the Apple Orchard* is about young adults; Walter de la Mare's stories only intermittently have child characters; only Kay in *The Midnight Folk* stands out as an exception. Also, as we have seen, the sense of a child readership is much less marked in 1920s fantasy too, because adults were more interested in enchanting themselves than children. At any rate children return in the 1930s, and with them the idea of the fantastic ring master who looks after matters, in such forms as Mary Poppins, Worzel Gummidge, Mr Leakey and Merlin.

A few 1920s fantasies have political overtones. The *Doctor Dolittle* stories of animal internationalism are obvious analogues for human behaviour. Less intentionally, *The Hoojibahs* could be an allegory of the poor trying to ape their supposed betters. *The Marvellous Land of Snergs* suggests the kind of cooperation among peoples enshrined in the recent League of Nations (1925). And Walker and Boumphrey's *The Log of the Ark* portrays a happy community of animals which is brought to savage dissension by an evil creature called the Scub. This kind of (potential) engagement with the adult world is comparatively rare in English children's fantasy.

Nevertheless the primary impulse of post-Great War children's fantasy is inward-looking and retreatist. In *The Treasure of the Isle of Mist* the treasure is the island itself, which enables Fiona to remain a happy island self when she is far from it in cities. Then there are Periwinkle's Island, Doctor Dolittle's garden,

Martin Pippin's apple orchard, the enclosure of the Ark in *The Log of the Ark*, the houses in Walter de la Mare's stories, Hundred Acre Wood, the Hoojibahs' cut-off village, and the posthumous paradise of *The Marvellous Land of Snergs*. This does not always make these places escapes, however. Several of them have the idea of a poisoned Eden: Periwinkle's Island is stained by the machinations of the evil Creepingo, the Scub poisons the animals, the children's paradise in *The Snergs* is menaced by the witch, and Kay's home in *The Midnight Folk* is threatened by the governess and Abner Brown. These fantasies exhibit an unease with escape which underlay the 1920s: the wider world with all its problems was not to be ignored: however much the door might be shut against it, it still found a way in.

The *Pooh* books of A. A. Milne, *Winnie-the-Pooh* (1926) and *The House at Pooh Corner* (1928), however, are quite untroubled by such wider matters, being about a highly marginal society. Indeed it is just possible that the *Pooh* books were a reaction against the *Doctor Dolittle* stories' portrayals of animals who live by good sense and make their own civilisations. Nearly all the creatures in the *Pooh* books are inept – Pooh himself, the Bear of Very Little Brain, the credulous Piglet, the dimwitted Owl, the cretinously sullen Eeyore, the skittish Tigger, the blunderingly vain Rabbit. Indeed, the creatures could be seen as potential cases for psychiatric treatment in any other context: Pooh for memory loss and neural failure, Eeyore for manic depression, Tigger for hyperactivity, Owl for dyslexia and Piglet for paranoia. It can fairly be said that where the *Doctor Dolittle* books show the animals making more sense of the world, the creatures of the *Pooh* books make progressively less. When Pooh calls on Piglet and gets no reply, he goes home, to find Piglet there waiting for him: at which,

> 'Hallo, Piglet,' he said. 'I thought you were out.'
>
> 'No,' said Piglet, 'it's you who were out, Pooh.'
>
> 'So it was,' said Pooh. 'I knew one of us was.'
>
> He looked up at his clock, which had stopped at five minutes to eleven some weeks ago.
>
> 'Nearly eleven o'clock,' said Pooh happily. 'You're just in time for a little smackerel of something.' (*The House at Pooh Corner*, 2–3)

In the world of the *Pooh* books, Milne has made an idyllic society which should fall apart but does not. The creatures cannot make connections, as when Pooh and Piglet fail to see that the Woozle footprints they are following are their own, or Eeyore thinks that his new house is actually his old one moved by the wind. Not one plan they make comes to fruition. Pooh's attempt to get honey with a balloon ends in disaster, Eeyore's birthday presents are eaten or burst, Rabbit's plan to kidnap Baby Roo goes wildly wrong, the Expotition to the North Pole ends with Eeyore falling into the stream. The books are like Eeyore's 'house' at Pooh Corner, a mass of odd sticks. Even the creatures themselves are ramshackle, being a cross of animal and toy, a teddy bear obsessed by honey, a morose old donkey who has been loved to death, or a stuffed kangaroo with a child in her pouch; and sometimes they are inverted clichés, like the witless Owl. This diverse and disconnected assemblage, incapable of making sense of their world or of surviving in it – quite opposite to the Dolittle animals – is nevertheless held together by love, by the dreaming mind of childhood which confers eccentric life on its toys, and above all by a humorous author writing a comedy, which precisely depends on upsets, inversions and disconnections.

More than any other book in English literature, the *Pooh* books celebrate play. That is Milne's childhood idyll and the last word of the books; and it runs through all the poetry of *When We Were Very Young* (1924). Milne has managed to make a world of play somehow immune from time and circumstance, and one which through his understanding of childhood illogic he has made enduringly appealing to both adults and children. This is the world we lose at five, to work and routine, those enemies to the free mind: but while necessarily there is a sense of loss, the adult who recreated this world tells us that we could do so too.

Before we turn to the 1930s, however, we should note the contrastive picture of young people presented by Richard Hughes in his adult novel *A High Wind in Jamaica* (1929), for this effectively is an exposure of the happy view of childhood fostered in the 1920s and 1930s. Set at first in nineteenth-century Jamaica, this tells of seven children captured reluctantly by pirates – that source of fascination for many 1920s to 1940s minds, with their apparently raffishly romatic life outside convention and law – on their way to school in England, and eventually released. Their time with the pirates is portrayed as a slowly waning idyll, in which they delight in the ship and their situation, and the pirates have a certain avuncular pleasure in relating to them. But this idyll is founded on ignoring a mounting series of horrors, from the accidental death of one of the children and the whoredom of another, to the murder by young Emily of a captured Dutch captain. When the children are finally handed over in relief by the pirates to a passing Dutch steamer, their view of their past life, encouraged by their fellow-passengers, shifts to one of loathing: as a result the pirates are caught by a gunboat and, thanks to the children's false evidence, a number of them are hanged. The story looks back to the darker views of childhood in Henry James's *The Turn of the Screw* (1898) and forward to William Golding's *Lord of the Flies* (1954). But Hughes's picture of the unfathomable savagery of children passed by the benign children's fantasy writers of his time. Indeed such a vision has proved almost impossible for children's literature ever wholly to assimilate, which is why it still has an essential vein of triviality. In Hughes's story reality dismisses the idyll, whereas in children's fantasy the idyll usually dismisses reality. Much more typical of children's literature are the romantic views of pirate life in *The Midnight Folk*, Mervyn Peake's *Captain Slaughterboard Drops Anchor* (1939) or Eric Linklater's *The Pirates in the Deep Green Sea* (1949).

In the 1930s many children's fantasies are not so much continuous romantic stories as jerky sequences of 'treats,' excitements in the midst of a dull or regulated life. In part they continue the method of E. Nesbit's Psammead and Phoenix stories, though with less skill and fluency. A. E. Coppard's *Pink Furniture* (1930) is a series of absurd adventures had by Toby Tottel, who is himself absurd for having left home to look for pink furniture in the first place. John Buchan's *The Magic Walking Stick* (1932) is a story of a boy magically able to travel anywhere and have a range of exciting adventures. Norman Hunter's *The Incredible Adventures of Professor Branestawm* (1933), the first book of a series, is a witty and highly inventive picture of a scientist who constructs Heath Robinson-like machines out of household junk and has wonderful adventures and mishaps. P. L. Travers' *Mary Poppins* (1934) and its sequels portrays the nursemaid to a family of children who is also a fairy of amazing power. Mary Poppins transforms the domestic lives of the children, talking to the dog next door, shutting a cruel former governess in a birdcage, or taking afternoon tea a few inches from the ceiling. The title of Masefield's *The Box of Delights* speaks for itself, though in effect it is not quite so delightful as it promises. Barbara Euphan Todd's *Worzel Gummidge* (1935) and its continuations describe a scarecrow who comes to life for two children holidaying on a farm. Kathleen Tozer's *Mumfie* stories begin with *The Wanderings of Mumfie* (1936), which portrays a journey by toys to see who will qualify to be given to human children in a Christmas stocking. J. B. S. Haldane's wonderfully inventive *My Friend Mr Leakey* (1937) is a series of stories involving the travels and parties of a super-magician who, like God, can turn anything into anything else. J. R. R. Tolkien's Bilbo in *The Hobbit* (1937) is given the (to him initially unwelcome) treat of a series of adventures in quest of treasure. T. H. White's *The Sword in the Stone* (1938) is a collection of treats for the Wart (King Arthur, as yet unknown). The wizard-tutor Merlin gives him several transformations into a number of animals, so that he can see life from their varied points of view. And in Hilda Lewis's *The Ship That Flew* (1939) a magic flying longship allows a variety of trips to the past.

In many of these the human is an onlooker, as at a conjuring show. Mary Poppins continually fascinates or badgers the children, Worzel Gummidge forever turns life and himself upside-down, Mr Leakey entertains his guest, Mumfie amuses his owner, Merlin delights the Wart. There is not the interaction between humans and magic that we see in Kingsley, MacDonald, Molesworth or Nesbit. Even Masefield's Kay is a more shadowy figure in *The Box of Delights*. Tolkien's *The Hobbit* is one exception, for Bilbo's character emerges strongly as he struggles on his fantastic journey. This one-sidedness happens even though the magic is often set in a 'real life' context where one might expect some inter-action: Mary Poppins lives as nursemaid to a suburban English family, Worzel Gummidge and Mumfie live in contemporary rural and urban settings among ordinary people. The idea here is that daily life should be shown as open to visits by magic, and that children should be cheered up with the thought that Christ-mas and birthdays might not happen only once a year. If one happens to be a scarecrow like Worzel Gummidge, there might even be birthdays for each part of one's body (*Worzel Gummidge*, 122–3). The 1930s idea that fantasy exists as a counter to boredom is relatively new. Of earlier fantasies with this motive only Mrs Molesworth's *The Cuckoo Clock* and E. Nesbit's *The Story of the Amulet* come to mind: and these are special cases, for Griselda is staying with her elderly aunts, and Nesbit's children have been left for months by their parents in the care of their old nurse in her dull London house. All this suggests that the 1930s were a particularly boring and confining time for middle-class English children – which might just be true – or that parents were so out of touch with 'kiddies' that they considered amusements not as things they shared but as gifts they conferred.

Most 1930s fantasies are set in 'this' world: but towards the end of the decade there is a change, as the threat of war grows. In 1937 and 1938 we have, in Tolk-ien's *The Hobbit* and T. H. White's *The Sword in the Stone*, two fantasies which entirely forsake their time to create the imaginary alternative worlds of Middle-earth and Gramarye. Both writers see fantasy as having an escapist, or consola-tory, aim, and Tolkien in 1938 delivers a famous lecture 'On Fairy-Stories' to say so. In 1939 appear two books that leave their time to travel to the past – Hilda Lewis's *The Ship That Flew* and Alison Uttley's *A Traveller in Time*. In the 1940s fantasy often exists in imaginary worlds, in the work of Elizabeth Goudge, D. Watkins Pitchford, W. Croft Dickinson, Eric Linklater, Rumer Godden and Beverley Nichols. The same process is seen in adult fantasy from 1935, in the work of C. S. Lewis, Herbert Read, Ruthven Todd and Mervyn Peake.

With the exception of *The Box of Delights* and *The Hobbit*, most 1930s fantasies do not have an overall thread, but are simply a list of episodes until the magic stops. They are situation fantasies in which a fairy nursemaid, a magic walking stick or a magician scientist are presented, and then run through their tricks. This means that the stories are rather 'stop and start,' and, in the absence of en-gagement by the child characters as any more than spectators, they lack depth, complexity and humanity. Indeed their interest is often directed at the fantastic alone rather than at human children interacting with it. A clenched, manic cheeriness pervades them all.

They are also highly extravagant in the use of fantasy. Even with Nesbit's tales of hairy princesses or lovers turned to hedgehogs one was prepared to suspend disbelief, because they were made parts of witty little systems: but here the fantasy is much more of a loose cannon. We are presented with a scarecrow which lives unremarked in human society (*Worzel Gummidge*), a pillar box that talks broad Scots (*Here Comes Mumfie*, ch.2), or a little wooden horse on wheels whom everybody talks to as though it were perfectly normal (Ursula Moray Williams, *Adventures of the Little Wooden Horse*, 1938). Wilder flights pervade the Professor Branestawm, Mary Poppins and Mr Leakey books, whereby Branestawm invents a life-giving elixir that animates the contents of his waste-paper basket,[33] Mary Poppins has a dance with the Sun, or the guests at a fancy-dress party have themselves turned into a comet, a lobster, William Shakespeare and 'a regular icosahedron' (*Mr Leakey*, 86) Even Masefield's *The Box of Delights* shows this, with Arnold of Todi, the Trojan Wars and King Arthur alternating with tea and crumpets.

There is often a sense of strained ingenuity or of mad laughter here, as though something has to be drowned or shut out. It is all wild fancy rather than organic imagination. The books are very busy and noisy, with continual action and abrupt and jerky style: there are few moments of rest and contemplation.

> The hamper packed itself again, and Clementina, who was all right by now, tied herself round it. Pompey's brazier was filled up with charcoal, and the carpet spread out. 'I think we might go on round the world,' said Mr Leakey. 'Of course it is night to the east of us, but magic carpets travel much better by night, like radio messages. Where would you like to go in America?' (*Mr Leakey*, 64–5)

(This is worth comparing with the less frenetic liveliness of E. Nesbit's *The Phoenix and the Carpet*, for example pp. 48–50.) Nor is there much thinking or planning: one simply gets on with things, makes mistakes and somehow comes out all right in the end. In England it is called 'muddling through.'

The magic in 1930s fantasy appears the more peculiar because it emerges not from something obviously strange, such as Wonderland or a Psammead, but from the everyday and unremarkable. Objects from a walking stick to a model ship, toys from a kapok-filled elephant to a wooden horse, people from a nursemaid to a kennel boy or an unexceptional hobbit – these are the decade's stuff of enchantment. The home to which the perfectly ordinary-looking Mr Leakey invites the narrator after he has saved him from a car accident is 'in a block of flats ... [with] a quite ordinary door, and the little hall of the flat was quite ordinary too, but when I got inside it was one of the oddest rooms I have ever seen' (*Mr Leakey*, 10–11). This whole idea of fantasy being assimilated within the ordinary is not wholly unlike the nature of 1930s experience: perfectly ordinary routine life went on while containing one of the most fantastic mutations of reality ever perpetrated; perfectly ordinary bigotry, racism, envy and fear were accepted attitudes, until a turn of the mirror showed their astonishing product. Shock and reversal are personified in the abrupt characters of Branestawm, Poppins, Gummidge and Leakey, and embodied in the violent changes in plots and directions in their stories: it is almost as though children's fantasy felt intimations of the earthquake to come.

One of the figures in vogue in 1930s fantasy is that of the scarecrow.[34] We find one in Walter de la Mare's 'Hodmadod' (*The Lord Fish*, 1933), where a scarecrow is made to seem alive by the presence in it of a fairy: and thereafter we have *Worzel Gummidge* (1936) and its sequels, Mumfie's ever-present friend Scarecrow, and even the scarecrow called Joe for whom Eleanor Farjeon's Sam Pig deputises while he is on holiday in Blackpool.[35] These scarecrows speak 'vulgar' and are dressed in rags, yet they come in from the wild outside and ape human behaviour: they are symbols of that fascinated horror with which the bourgeoisie imagined the proletariat muddying their lives. (E. Nesbit might have been anticipating them in her 'Ugly Wuglies.') The scarecrows are also like T. S. Eliot's Hollow Men (1925), 'headpieces filled with straw': they are sham people come alive, perhaps unconscious images of the 1930s psyche itself, a psyche elsewhere depicted in the people of Huxley's *Brave New World*, Greene's *Brighton Rock* and Orwell's *Coming Up for Air*.

Children's fantasy goes down a class in the 1930s, despite a sharpening of class divisions at the time. Several fantasies have 'lower class' fantasy figures who enter and influence the lives of middle-class families – perhaps reflective of there being closer proximity between bourgeois families and their now often single live-in help. Mary Poppins the nursemaid speaks with slight vulgarity – '"Strike me pink"', '"Spit-spot into bed"', '"a fair treat"' – and has her friends among the poor and the unemployed – a pavement artist, a gypsy, a balloon-seller. Her downright collisions with a pompous ex-governess or with Mrs Banks, the children's feckless mother, are full of the sense of class, and she has the curious pruderies of the 'servant classes,' such as getting undressed inside her nightgown. As for Worzel Gummidge, rural life at its lowest, he must be one of the rudest and crudest heroes in children's fantasy. It is the children who have to visit him, for he offers no relation to or feeling for them. He is a constant insult to the local grande dame Mrs Bloomsbury-Barton. Gradually in *Worzel Gummidge* more scarecrows appear, until they form a semi-animate society to question the human one. Close to nature they may be, and that has its charm, as in Gummidge making himself a home for birds or brushing his 'hair' with a hedgehog, but both nature and they are seen as coarse and intractable. And in the way that Gummidge and his friends are heaps of diverse cast-offs, always on the verge of collapsing or being destroyed, they suggest the final vulgarity of death, in which all classes will be levelled. In subsequent books, when Gummidge begins to enter the human world and sets up as a citizen – first as a gardener and later as a holidaymaker or a circus performer – he becomes less convincing.

Then there is Mumfie, the toy elephant[36] who befriends the proletarian Scarecrow, and who himself can say, '"Oh dearie me"', '"I ain't never had a Christmas tree, nor a stocking what had anything in it, nor nuffing"', '"'Elp"', '"Lawks!"', '"Well, fancy"' or '"Pardon"'. What we find with all these creatures is that they tend to have their own societies: Mary Poppins has her friends, Worzel Gummidge his fellow-scarecrows, and Mumfie his own life with Scarecrow: indeed for much of *The Wanderings of Mumfie* and *Here Comes Mumfie* we are away from children altogether. Much the same is true of Eleanor Farjeon's *Sam Pig* stories of the 1940s.

A levelling urge is also partly behind the finding of King Arthur in the guise of the Wart in T. H. White's *The Sword in the Stone*. But while Arthur is the most unpretentious and natural of kings, the later and more adult books of the story become the celebration of a civilised and on the whole noble society. Tolkien's gobbling, fearful and slightly vulgar hobbit Bilbo is dragged by dwarves into high adventures among figures of magic and myth, which his presence and their own revealed evils make far less ideal. And in Ursula Moray Williams's *Adventures of the Little Wooden Horse*, modelled on *Collodi's Pinocchio*, the hero not only meets common people, but has to do their work. He drudges on a farm, pulls a barge, works down a mine, labours for a blacksmith and performs in a circus, before he manages to swim back across the sea to his beloved master, Uncle Peder the carpenter.

Two 1930s books are in revealing contrast to this trend. In John Buchan's *The Magic Walking-Stick* (1932) and Hilda Lewis's *The Ship That Flew* (1939), the middle-class children have magic objects that give them powers of travel, which enables them to do noble deeds that would otherwise have been beyond them, and to visit the exotic past. Translate these magic objects as 'silver spoons' or 'privilege of birth,' and one has something of a parallel to the powers of avoiding painful reality that were open to the better-off in the period. In this decade class separation and race prejudice in harsh form existed side by side with a growing fearful admiration of the proletariat, seen as realised in the shape of Communist Russia, and faintly attractive to a bourgeoisie no longer certain of itself or its values.

T. H. White's *The Sword in the Stone*, with its picture of the ignored child the Wart become King of England, is in one way a picture of this uncertain spirit given imagined purpose. *The Sword in the Stone* is ostensibly an idyll of boyhood, in which the education of a child is made a series of wonderful treats and adventures. But it is also an idyll with a hidden direction, for, unknown to the Wart (and to the reader), it is preparing him to be King Arthur. The Wart, who does not know he is Arthur, is by seeming chance given Merlin as his tutor.

His education involves not only the 'usual' medieval subjects, but also being turned into a variety of creatures, a fish, a merlin, a snake, an owl, and a badger.[37] Through them he learns much about power, aggression, rule and sovereignty, without being aware of it. All the time he is both living a boy's idyll and growing the qualities with which he will leave boyhood. When that secret growth is complete, he one day finds a sword in a stone in a quiet London churchyard, and pulls it out, to give it to his foster-brother Kay. But he has now pulled out his adulthood, and kingship with it. There is much in the book that in retrospect seems prophetic of the war, and a call for readiness. But it was also a consolation for its time, in offering purpose where none was seen. It was a consolation which the war itself was soon to give to England in reality, in the certainty of being on the side of right against evil.

Tolkien's *The Hobbit*, an idyll of exciting adventures in a strange land, with a non-human hero, turns children's fantasy into the new channel of making fascinating secondary worlds quite removed from ours, which Walter de la Mare began, but without followers, in 1910 in *The Three Mulla-Mulgars*. Tolkien seems indebted to *The Three Mulla-Mulgars* for its basic premises of a strange land, a non-human hero and an object to be gained by an eventful journey through unknown territory: constant thrills and continuous suspense result. And like de la Mare's book, itself drawn from Purchas's *Pilgrimage*, Tolkien's also offers the pleasures of considerable invention. The account of Bilbo the hobbit's 'chance' finding of the Ring in the deep mountain-tunnels of the goblins; his riddle-dispute with the sinister Gollum; the encounter with the hideous nests of giant spiders in Mirkwood; the escape from elves in floating wine-barrels; the strange lake-town of Esgaroth; or the Mountain with the dragon coiled inside on its pile of treasure – these are all striking and often novel. Tolkien also puts us very close to events, with the dwarves hanging in bags of web from a high branch, Bilbo's struggling to stay upright on a barrel in the river, or the dragon rolling over fatuously to display both its gem-encrusted belly and its one weak spot to its admiring visitor. And in contrast to the later *The Lord of the Rings*, Tolkien is here both terse and specific in descriptions: 'A whirring noise was heard. A red light touched the points of standing rocks. The dragon came' (229). Tolkien himself seems so to have liked *The Hobbit* that he rewrote it in *The Lord of the Rings*, whose episodes and their sequence are often similar: indeed it is fair to see *The Lord of the Rings*, even allowing for its more epic intentions, as an overblown version of *The Hobbit*.[38]

A further distinction of *The Hobbit* is that, unlike not only *The Lord of the Rings* but most children's fantasy of the 1930s, it always goes for the realistic rather than the simple and one-sided. In the elves and dwarves, Tolkien show how people are a mixture of good and bad impulses. He puts us close to Bilbo's struggles, at once humorous and brave, to do the right thing, whether in saving the dwarves from the spiders, going to visit the dragon, or stealing the Arkenstone. (And on all occasions he is not simply heroic: he is also protected by his invisibility.) Bilbo also plays a dual role as hero and burglar: his great deeds involve thieving. His son Frodo is to be more plainly a heroic figure on his journey in *The Lord of the Rings*. Nor does Tolkien give us a simple story of treasure gained. His friends the dwarves claim it for their own and war against the rightful claimants, leaving Bilbo with divided loyalties. Though the treasure is eventually returned to its owner, it is shown to be often destructive in its influence: we are made to feel that the gold itself is nothing beside the treasures of nature, which return to the land desolated by the dragon after its death.

With Alison Uttley's *A Traveller in Time* (1939), the story of a girl who meets her Elizabethan forebears through the shared medium of their ancestral home, we look back to a supposed idyll in which houses and their surroundings, man and nature, were felt to be at one. Implicitly the book rejects the modern division of town from country, and indeed the housing explosion of the 1930s. Thackers, the Derbyshire house, is partly a working farm (based on the one in which Uttley was brought up), and we do not forget the cattle that supply the table nor the manure that renews the fields; also much of the life of the novel takes place in the kitchen, among housekeepers and servants. Though the kitchen is devoted to the comfort of the great people of the house, deference to rank in no way conflicts with equality. This 'harmony of opposites,' and the meeting of different times too, is only possible in an old rural family home, the book says, aligning itself with such seventeenth-century country house georgics as Ben Jonson's 'To Penhurst,' Thomas Carew's 'To Saxham' or Robert Herrick's 'To Sir Lewis Pemberton.'

Yet those poems were panegyrics to then existing houses: this is an elegy about a house that is gone. As fantasy this is no longer idyll or treat. The whole story rings with loss, made more poignant by the temporary meeting of the two times. The 'psychic' girl Penelope's powers of seeing the past of the house gradually fade, her lover in that time is lost to her, the Babington family that became dear to her is under threat, and Mary Queen of Scots whom they sought to rescue is even more harshly confined than before. In a sense these people are lost from the beginning, for Penelope knows what later happened to Anthony Babington and to Mary, and can do nothing to alter history. Such too was to be Merlin's fate in the later books of T. H. White's Arthuriad, *The Witch in the Wood* (1940) and *The Ill-Made Knight* (1941): as poignantly as in Alison Uttley's book, we watch the characters' acts of free choice creating, stitch by stitch the tapestry of their fate. Like White's *The Sword in the Stone*, too, *A Traveller in Time* has special resonance in the context of a world slipping into war.

Like White's also, Uttley's book depends heavily on past sources – which is in keeping with its theme. *A Traveller in Time* rewrites E. Nesbit's *The House of Arden*, with its account of the fortunes of the Arden family in Elizabethan and early Jacobean England. But Nesbit's book, more experimental, has greater concern with the external mechanics of plot and the paradoxes of time-travel than Uttley's much more psychological novel, which is a picture of the developing spirit and romantic feelings of the girl Penelope. With Alison Uttley's book children's fantasy in a sense grows up, for here we enter on a much deeper analysis of character than has been seen before – and one which is to return in 1950s children's fantasy.

During the Second World War more children's fantasy appeared than in the First, which had hardly any – and this even with paper restrictions. Children and the possible future had a far greater place in the national mind than in the First World War, which had been fought largely without purpose, and had involved more the death of the Edwardian past than the creation of a new order. Alison Uttley's *Sam Pig* series began in 1940, and was continued in 1941, 1943 and 1945; three *Mumfie* books (ending with *Mumfie Marches On* (1942)), and *Mary Poppins Opens the Door* (1944) appeared. The distinctive books, however, are Elizabeth Goudge's *Smoky-House* (1940), 'B. B''s (Denis Watkins-Pitchford's) *The Little Grey Men* (1942), William Croft Dickinson's *Borrobil* (1944), Eric Linklater's *The Wind on the Moon* (1944) and Mary Norton's *The Magic Bedknob* (1945; New York, 1943).

Smoky-House is a story of a quasi-mystical West Country village after the Napoleonic Wars, where smuggling ('free trading') is seen as a noble calling, here assisted by the Good People (fairies), a mule, two dogs and three children. With this help, the local smugglers (most of the worthies of the village) are saved from the gallows, a government spy is unmasked and made repentant, and the contraband saved. The story has a theme of 'comprehension': it is the animals and the fairies who know the truth, but at first the fairies are not seen and the animals are not understood. When the children do realise the truth, they have to persuade the adults. Meanwhile, a wandering fiddler who has been given hospitality in the village is secretly a government spy, and this is understood only in the end by the humans, the dogs having seen it first. But the humans are then capable of a comprehension beyond the animal, for they see that the fiddler, who could play so well must have some good in him; and by trying to understand him rather than condemn him, they bring him to this better self. The idea of the book is a community of all creation, imaged in the idea of 'free trade' or commerce. This idyllic community is established by the end of the book, and is given something of a Christian setting. "'Help,'" says one of the good People, "'extends through the whole universe, immortal, untiring help. Don't worry'" (176). The book has considerable charm, but this cosy optimism mars it. Anyone who could write in 1939–40, 'In this world when you can't last out any more you don't generally have to' (152), must have been well away from events.

Although most 1940s children's fantasies continue to be largely escapist in character, there are certain changes towards realism. One is that magic becomes less public or identifiable, more likely to be mistaken for something else, than in the more reckless and preposterous fantasy of the 1930s. This is partly owing to a less patronising attitude to children, and also to a broad increase in the seriousness of children's fantasy, which from about 1920 to 1937 had been largely comic and whimsical in character. Another development is the acknowledgement of sex. In *Smoky-House* it is clear that the teenage Jessamine's feelings about the young Squire are sexual from her first dance with him, even if it is put in romantic cliché: 'Speechless yet exhilarated she looked up at him. ... He was lean and hard with so much riding, yet graceful and supple in movement by reason of much laughter and lightness of his heart' (31). This was the year of the film *Gone With the Wind*; Hollywood had certainly left its mark. (However, when later Jessamine marries the Squire, her four babies are described not as being born but as being brought to her by an angel.) There had already been sexuality in Hilda Lewis's *The Ship That Flew* (1939) in young Humphrey's attachment to Matilda, a girl from Norman times; and in Alison Uttley's *A Traveller in Time* Penelope is in love with Anthony Babington. From now on there will be much more openness in child-portrayals. There will be those who bar it, such as C. S. Lewis, but the trace is there in his very expulsion from Narnia of the now adolescent and lipsticked Susan.

Much more of a bachelor idyll is a book published in 1942 by the naturalist, illustrator and Rugby schoolmaster Denis Watkins Pitchford (writing as 'B. B') – *The Little Grey Men, A Story for the Young in Heart*. The first children's fantasy to win the recently-established Carnegie Medal, this is the story of the last gnomes of England, three brothers living by a Northamptonshire stream, who decide to set out to look for for their fourth brother, Cloudberry, who a year earlier left home in search of the source of the stream. Encountering numbers of dangers, such as a mill-race, a stoat, a gamekeeper and a pike, the three are eventually forced by winter to return empty-handed, only to find Cloudberry back at home, having arrived from a summer trip north with the local geese.[39] Indebted though the book is to *The Wind in the Willows*, it has both a zest for life and an acceptance of nature's harsh ways that give it conviction – apart, perhaps, from the gnomes' (instigated) killing of the destructive gamekeeper. The gnomes themselves may not be individually characterised, but every natural scene they pass is vividly described: indeed the journey often seems conducted for the sake of the natural world it uncovers.

Yet one of the most memorable descriptions is not natural at all; it occurs when the gnomes, starving castaways on an island, find a child's model liner beached, and having worked out how to wind its clockwork motor through the funnel, sail away in it. (T. H. White must have been indebted to this for the miniature sailing-ships he has his Lilliputians build for themselves to sail the Malplaquet lake in his *Mistress Masham's Repose* (1946).[40]) Indeed, one of the particular pleasures of *The Little Grey Men* is its miniaturism. The model boat is a real steamship to the tiny gnomes, and the Drayton-like pictures of them milking a single teat of a cow's vast udder into a snail shell, or hiding beside the eggs in a bird's nest to escape a stoat, or sailing over a lake in a coracle made of frogskins, are striking. Miniaturism is a relatively common in children's fantasy of the 1940s and early 1950s, with White's *Mistress Masham's Repose*, Rumer Godden's doll and mice stories starting with *The Dolls' House* (1946),[41] and Mary Norton's *The Borrowers* (1952) and its sequels. It perhaps reflects the new power of realism in children's literature, which forces fantasy to be fugitive and undetectable.

Rather less successful is W. Croft Dickinson's *Borrobil* (1944), a story of how two children enter a magic circle of trees on Beltane Eve, and find themselves in land of dragons, knights, wizards and Vikings. The ways of Dickinson's world are very complicated, and the children are continually happening on a mythic action that must be explained to them. The effect is of rather a rush, and characterisation and believable action suffer. However, while it is true that Dickinson is highly dependent on Tolkien's *The Hobbit*, he is one of the first to give us modern children going into the secondary world, for which Alan Garner may later have been indebted to him; and his sources are distinctive, being more in folk-narrative and history than in epic and saga like Tolkien's. Centering the story on one narrative rather than a breathless sequence of them might have made this a better book.

Breathlessness of another kind is to be found in Eric Linklater's *The Wind on the Moon* (1944). Linklater said that this came from the fact that the story emerged from desperate attempts to keep his daughters amused,[42] but there is also an edge of violence about the story which may have come from his own impatient nature. There is at first something of Belloc, something of a female William in his truculent girls Dinah and Dorinda, who eat themselves into spheres and have to be rolled down the village street, and who defy every adult injunction presented to them; eventually they turn themselves into kangaroos to take revenge on the village, and are captured and placed in a zoo. But then the story becomes more desultory, with a frankly silly plot concerning an ostrich whose eggs are always being stolen, followed by an equally stuck-on allegorical plot where the girls' father is imprisoned in the land of Bombardy (or Germany) by a tyrant called Hulagu Boot, and has to be helped with the aid of a puma and two tunnelling sappers left over from the Crimean War who chance on the dungeons. Here we have returned to some of the forced absurdity of 1930s fantasy.

The Wind on the Moon won the second Carnegie Medal for children's books: but a much better and almost forgotten book by Linklater is his *The Pirates in the Deep Green Sea* (1949). Though indebted to Masefield, this is a magnificent tale of undersea adventure, full of rich characters, from the idle octopus Cully, or the herring shoal who swim and speak as one, to the hearty Davy Jones, or the oily pirate Inky Poops. Here Linklater continues to present people who are long 'dead' and in Davy Jones's Locker, but he does so from the first, and with care and preparation, so that we accept it. The idea of the story is faintly crazy, for the lines of latitude and longitude are portrayed as ropes holding the world together, knotted where they intersect. The pirates are seen as the enemy because they want to replace the old knots with new ones. This does not seem particularly evil, unless the knots are allegorised as traditional values or politics, which are being replaced with less reliable others: it is perhaps relevant that the pirates are finally unmasked in a church, and that the whole aim of the story is to preserve a world order (compare Masefield's *The Box of Delights*). Certainly the story is a celebration of 'age-old' things: the beauties of the sea, the glories of a sailor's life, and the worth of high courage and adventure in strange lands. It is also a celebration, as was the first book, of Englishness and of English eccentricity: hardly a Scot speaks, and it could as well have taken place on Lundy as on the Hebridean island of 'Popinsay.' Between them Linklater's two books cover the worlds of land and sea, and in particular the different kinds of creature to be found there: if the first book had a zoo, here Davy Jones is enthroned in a marine aquarium on wood from the gangplank of the Ark.

Perhaps the most talented writer to appear in the war years was Mary Norton, whose *The Magic Bedknob* (New York, 1943; London, 1945) is a *tour de force* of wit and lively characterisation. Three children help a prim spinster of their village, Miss Price, when she is injured while training to be a witch. They promise not to reveal the truth about her if she grants them some magic, and she makes them able to travel wherever they like by twisting one of the brass knobs on their bed. E.Nesbit-like disasters occur, since the bed must accompany the children: they are arrested in a London street outside their mother's house, and captured by cannibals on the Pacific island of Ueepe.

As interesting in the stories as the magic situations are people's characters. Miss Price with her secrets, whether it is sorcery or reading a naughty book; young Paul with his naïve directness; or the London policeman trying to explain his quaint off-duty hobbies to his Jaggers-like inspector: all these are as gripping in their way as the magic itself. Little sparks of humour are continually being struck, such as Miss Price saying that witches cannot make money, and "'That's

things to the creatures of the surrounding wood, but the evil Sam and his father run a rival Emporium which cheats its customers. This is a story of old British commercial values, supposedly founded on 'decency,' being overtaken by a new business rapacity – rather along the lines of Willy Loman's continual lament in Arthur Miller's contemporary *Death of a Salesman* (1947). Shopkeeper Sam, hating Judy, tries in vain by fraud to destroy her and her mother's business, moving from trying to strangle their custom, to hiring a witch and poisoning Mrs Judy's goods, and finally to attempts at murder. In the end there are lightly-touched biblical and apocalyptic hints, when Judy forgives Sam, and is transported to a beautiful country where she meets a prince and marries him. At the same time her mother sets up a new shop in this happy land: the seemingly trivial occupation of shop-keeping becomes in the end a symbol of the free commerce of souls. The little island idyll may be swept away here, but it will find a permanent resting place in a happy land elsewhere. All this happens within a book which is tirelessly comic, from Mrs Badger's disastrous body-odour, to the escaped circus bear Bruno trying to impress once too often with his minimal Russian, or the witch's beloved poison toads with their wicked rhymes. Nichols has the ability to make evil at once funny and repulsive, and good at once laughable and joyous.

Two further books about the Judys, *The Stream That Stood Still* (1948) and *The Mountain of Magic* (1950) are much less assured, not least because the first was complete in itself. Both portray new attacks by Sam, this time on the happy lives of Judy's children Jack and Jill – the first involving Jack's transformation into a fish in a stream, and the second being an attack on the children when they go on an adventure to a mountain. In both the evil are reactivated to make new plots, in an attempt to recreate the success of the first. However *The Stream that Stood Still* has merit in its descriptions of underwater life. And all of the books were quarried by other fantasy writers, which says something about their originality. Eric Linklater was almost certainly indebted to *The Stream That Stood Still* for the method of underwater breathing in *The Pirates in the Deep Green Sea*. C. S. Lewis in the Narnia books probably took the characters Mr and Mrs Beaver and the seemingly beautiful witch who seduces and enchants Jack in *The Stream That Stood Still* into his *The Lion, the Witch and the Wardrobe* (1950) and *The Silver Chair* (1953).[44] He may also have remembered Sam's use of the stupid bear to further his evil purposes against the Judys in *The Tree That Sat Down*, when he described the duping of the donkey Puzzle by the Ape Shift in *The Last Battle*. And the eagles and the volcanic mountain of *The Mountain of Magic* are remarkably close to the climactic events of J. R. R. Tolkien's *The Return of the King* (1955).

In a class all of their own – and eventually in an invented country all of their own – are the railway engine books of the Rev. W. Awdry. *The Three Railway Engines* (1945) and *Thomas the Tank Engine* (1946) began a list of twenty-six little picture books, published yearly after 1949 and ending in 1972. At first the engine heroes worked the railways of England, but in the late 1950s Awdry was to develop for them a land of their own called Sodor, situated between the Isle of Man and Morecambe. Here for the first time in children's fantasy we find a celebration of the world of machines,[45] if they are machines so personalised as to become voluntary, and thereby often portrayed as overenthusiastic or vain. Thomas the Tank Engine with his stumpy cockiness, irrepressible for all the lessons he learns, is the best known: but in every story the message is precisely one that machines never have to learn – one of self-control. Against this lesson are played the glowing personalities and colours of the engines themselves, and their shifting vanities. In these books it is man, in the shape of the Fat Controller, who is the creature of discipline, time-keeping, good work, loyalty and service, and the machines that defy him. (Yet the Controller is in one way uncontrolled: he is fat.) In some small sense the books are symbolic of human work itself, and the management-employee relationship. Of course none of this will matter to many children, who, like Awdry himself, love trains and the variety of them – a variety which Awdry had enjoyed in a childhood spent in houses next to busy railway lines, and with a devotee father. But there is in the stories, however benignly written, that lurking sense of machines developing lives of their own which underlies the modern experience of them. And below that is the sense that machines express our own alienation from ourselves, from what we can do and control directly with our own hands and bodies.

Such alienation is expressed in another form in the modern obsession with animals. Throughout the period from 1900 to 1950 animals have been a source of delight in children's fantasy, and an essential part of the idyllic vision. But by the 1940s we have reached a point where the animal, and other forms of existence generally, are valued as much or even more than the human. At first, Kipling's animals could not have succeeded without Mowgli to help them; and Grahame's were humans in animal skins. But the *Doctor Dolittle* books recognised the separate rights of animals, and based themselves on the supposition that they may have complex and intelligent societies of their own which our man-centred view of things prevent us from seeing. Margery Bianco's *The Velveteen Rabbit* (1922) is new in that it has the toy rabbit tell its own story. More and more the world was seen from an animal, toy, doll or even alien (hobbit or Little Grey Man) point of view. Toys, however laughable, are at the centre of the *Pooh* books: and Christopher Robin who in 'real life' is the child author of all their games, is put on the margins. Kay in *The Midnight Folk* owes his finding of the treasure to the wider creation beyond man, and to his being turned into animals. The toy elephant Mumfie is the central figure in his stories, and the children in the *Mary Poppins* and *Worzel Gummidge* books are reduced to ciphers beside an exotic nursemaid/angel and an obstreperous scarecrow. T. H. White's Arthur learns, like Masefield's Kay (to whose story White owed much), by seeing the world from different animals' perspectives. In Elizabeth Goudge's *Smoky-House* the animals complain that the humans are too stupid to heed the warning they are trying to give them; and a group of intelligent animal managers is found helping Maria in Goudge's *The Little White Horse*. In the pacifist Beverley Nichols' *The Tree That Sat Down* the animals are horrified at humans' propensity for fighting among themselves, and the Owl even argues that the world would be better off without them (160). Here a vision that was present in 1920s fantasy for adults enters the world of children.

And yet, within a few years, it was all gone as if it had never been. 1950s children's fantasy always has humans at the centre, even if once it is Borrower humans; indeed apart from the Talking Animals of Narnia, animals hardly appear. One reason seems not too hard to guess. The sceptical current that was fuelled by the First World War and its gradual slide into the Second had been swept away by what seemed a total victory over human evil, promising a new world of hope. And that hope was to be realised in the minds and spirits of the new generation. There were, of course, still those who had other views of this new generation, as shown by Golding's *Lord of the Flies* (1954): but they speak from within a different culture.

1946 saw the appearance in America of a book that was eventually to transform parent-child relations: Benjamin Spock's *Baby and Child Care*, not published in England till 1955. Since the Great War there had been often a 'Behaviourist' approach to child-rearing, whereby the child's individual mental makeup was seen as alterable by external conditioning, and social and parental needs came first. In other words, a child with a socially awkward character could be changed to conform to society, rather than society have to make room for the exception. But Spock insisted that the child was primary, and that love of children for what they were, rather than for what could be made of them, would produce social integration. It was a transformative moment, that was eventually to see the whole shift away from the notion of duty and self-improvement towards one of self-gratification, and from the emphasis on the wishes of the parent to those of the child. These changes were to have immense influence on the nature of children's literature. Even though 1920s and 1930s fantasy seems aimed at pleasing rather than controlling young children, the whole idea on which much of it is founded, namely that of children as passive and largely ignored receptors of entertainment provided by adults, is part of the manipulative approach.

Our last fantasy here, also published in Spock-less England in 1946, seems in many ways an intuition of Spock's ideas: Rumer Godden's *The Dolls' House*. Godden herself, who spent much of her life in India, found the English repressed and conformist.[46] Her 'family' of dolls are a highly individual group, comprising a wooden Victorian Dutch doll who is the daughter, Tottie; a battered father doll, Mr Plantagenet; a celluloid mother doll, Birdie, who is not quite right in the head; a soft plush boy doll called Apple; and a dog, Darner, made out of pipe cleaner with a darning-needle backbone. The dolls know that it was their child-owners Emily and Charlotte who made them into a family. Yet, made out of different materials, originating from different places and with different histories, these dolls feel as strong a love for one another as might be hoped for in any biologically-bound human family; and indeed Birdie gives her life to save Apple. Further, they relate to one another as equals: because they love one another as they are, they value each other's views and feelings, and nobody dictates behaviour. Indeed the personal limitations of the 'parent' dolls mean that Tottie often has to make the decisions. It is the vain doll Marchpane introduced into their dolls' house who tells them that they are inadequate and vulgar, and has them banished to the attic and kitchen as servants. Previously the doll family needed no servants, for they looked after themselves.

Through the power of their wishing, the dolls believe they are able to influence the actions of their owners Charlotte and Emily. In a sense they challenge the passive child-like relation in which they are themselves treated. Nevertheless, the story is to be unhappy with this need for manipulative will. From the dolls' point of view the children are in a sense *their* dolls: though they know that often their wishing does not save them from harm. Tottie tells her family to "'Wish that Emily and Charlotte can put our house in order and make it good again. Go on, all of you. Wish. Wish. Wish'" (39): and this duly happens, each separate item wished for – curtains, chairs, bed, couch, carpets – appearing as desired. Yet the cold Marchpane is also able to wish in opposition to the Plantagenets' desires, for she wishes herself out of her original attic and eventually into pride of place in the dolls' house. And, just as Marchpane dominates the others, so Emily the older girl sister overrules Charlotte.[47] There is thus literally a battle of wills in the story. But in the end will is proved futile, for Marchpane overreaches herself in persuading Emily to put little Apple too near a candle flame, and Emily grows somehow repelled by her: she is taken away and put in a museum, where her frozen conceit is permanently satisfied. Nor are the Plantagenets entirely better off, for Marchpane's will has brought about Birdie's sacrifice of herself to save Apple from the flame. However Birdie's instinctive, selfless act has put another value in place of will – love.

In the same way that she resists dictated behaviour, Godden here refuses to simplify or to organise her own fiction. Though the Plantagenets are free, there is no facile ending: good times come and go, like the bad, and everything passes, "'Everything, from trees to dolls'", says Tottie. When she comforts Mr

Plantagenet, she does so 'in her kind wooden voice'; when he asks how they can be happy without Birdie she tells him, '"Birdie would be very happy. She couldn't help it"' (112). Rumer Godden is more easily sentimental in her later, but still charming, doll stories of 1955–60, where everything turns out unambiguously happily.[48]

In this story the dolls, who have no relation to one another, nevertheless make up a real family, for it is based on love and on feelings for one another as individuals, rather than on the blind obedience and power politics of families united only by blood. Marchpane is the cold egoist who does well in such loveless families. But their time is now passing: the family as a loving and more equal group will prevail, as humans learn to behave like Godden's dolls.

In some of the fantasies of the late 1940s we begin to see something that has been absent from children's fantasy since E. Nesbit. That is attention to the child. There has been much attention to animals, toys, nursemaids, professors, wizards and little grey men, sometimes perhaps as substitutes for children themselves. But actual human young have not been the focus: more often than not we have simply seen through them as windows, or followed them doing things; as individuals few of them stand out, not even Masefield's Kay or Milne's Christopher Robin (who in his little world is more the intelligent governing 'adult'). But in Mary Norton's *The Magic Bedknob* or T. H. White's *Mistress Masham's Repose*, we begin to find more memorable children, whose characters stay with us, because the authors are interested in them as well as in the worlds they inhabit.

In the 1950s this is to go further. The attention will often be as much on the child characters' psychology as on their actions. Indeed there be rather *less* action of the crowded sort we saw in much 1920s and 1930s fantasy, and far less multiplication of characters. Children's fantasy will become more contemplative, and will stay much more in one place (fewer journeys); while locality will become more important. In short, stories will be closely joined to the immediate world in which children live. Children's fantasy will partly absorb the idiom of children's 'realistic' fiction, and this new genre of more 'realistic' fantasy will attract almost all of the major writers for children from 1950–2000.

4 INTO A NEW WORLD: 1950–1970

The war resulted not only in the defeat of Hitler but in the defeat of the old Britain. Within a decade much of the Empire had gone, together with our international military standing; and similar weakening of authority began to appear at home. The 1945 election brought in a radical Labour government committed to giving all, rich or poor, the right to free health, free education, state housing and secure employment in nationalised industry. Society began to be influenced not just from the top down, but from the bottom up. There was to be much counter-action by the rich and privileged, and the continuance of the British vice of class snobbery: but whereas the Britain of 1939 would have been broadly understandable to the Britain of 1909, by 1969 it had become quite alien.

The great agent of change was the new emphasis on education, which was seen not only as the birthright of every man and as the route to progress, but as the antidote to the ignorance and narrowmindedness that had produced the war. The international Children's Charter of 1942, signed by educationalists from 19 leading nations, had stated as its first principle, 'We believe that the personality of the child is sacred, and that the needs of the child must be the foundation of any good educational system.' The British Education Act of 1944 directed attention to youth, no longer as the inheritors of old cultural values or as a subject for nostalgia or idyll, but as the seedcorn of a new future. And as we have seen, in 1946 in America appeared Benjamin Spock's *Baby and Child Care*, which was to revolutionise the early nurture of children according to their individual needs, and not (as with the old 'Behaviourist' methods) society's supposed requirements. Though many of these changes were slow to take effect, the war had changed minds irreversibly. Indeed what we shall be seeing as we move through the decades to 2000, will be the slow dissemination of these shifts of heart.

Out of this, among other things, arose a wholly new sense of the importance of children's literature, as part of the training of the mind and spirit (the 1950s still saw it as 'training'). If in the 1950s this resulted in some censorship – with, for instance, the frequent exclusion of Enid Blyton's books from libraries on grounds of their linguistic simplicity and ethnic myopia – it nevertheless led to a greater sense of children's literature as a literary genre with an important function. Numerous children's sections were opened in public libraries, and educative children's literature was promoted.[1] A tradition of good writing in children's literature was established, particularly through the reviews of *Junior Bookshelf* (1936 on), through the annual Carnegie Medal for the best children's book (begun in 1936) and via the high standards of the Puffin book series, the leading imprint of children's books in England (begun 1941). With such a developing market, the number of children's books published grew considerably, and what has been called the second golden age of children's writing began.

If all this might suppose an emphasis on realism in children's literature, the best books published in the 1940s and 1950s were in fact mostly to be fantasies. Several of them still have something of the old past-oriented and pastoral-idyllic impulse that had lain behind children's fantasy for so long. One explanation for this is that all the authors were brought up long before the war, and several of them – Lewis, Tolkien, Lucy Boston and Mary Norton (b.1903) – had Edwardian childhoods, and were of an age at which one has usually lost the contact one needs with contemporary children to attempt writing 'realistic' fiction for them. This is not the least reason for the plethora of historical fiction in the 1950s and 1960s – though the educational purpose is also present. From the mid-1950s we find increasingly that writers for children are 40 or less: Alan Garner's first book (1960) appeared when he was 26. This is the most concrete expression of the way authors were closing the gap between themselves and their audience.

However the fantasies written in the 1950s are quite different from before in several respects. Most of them emphasise spiritual growth and development, something we have seen little of in children's fantasy since the Victorians.[2] A recurrent idea linked with this is freedom, escape from confinement: very appropriate to a decade bursting free from the restraints of postwar austerity and self-denial. A sense of the possibilities of the future began to rival the continued cultural allegiance to the past.

At the same time these impulses for growth and freedom are still set within or against a moral frame. Development enables one to become better integrated with the world, and 'fit in.' Freedom is rather from tyrannical or unnatural constraint than from the obligations of society. The solitary child is much less valued than before (as say in Milne, de la Mare, or Masefield): now the emphasis is on children relating to others and growing towards being part of the collective. Just as people all 'did their bit' in the war, so in peace. Many schools had murals depicting all the professions of society cooperating within one frame to a great goal.

That goal was widely seen as being achieved by science, which had helped win the war and was now transforming the standard of living in peace. The popularity of science has perhaps never been so great as it was in the 1950s, even while its more lethal discoveries were producing the paranoia of the Cold War. At the same time the empiricist and practical attitudes which had served Britons in war were pervasive for a long time after it. This had considerable impact on the nature even of children's fantasy, where we will see defensiveness in the use of the supernatural, empiricism, practicality and, in the *Borrowers* stories, the ethic of 'make do and mend.'

What we also see in children's fantasy is an interest in children's natures. If we look back before 1945 there is scarcely a memorable child in fantasy till we reach Edith Nesbit. The prime interest then was in the fantasy itself, as a treat for children, who were often onlookers in their own stories. But now, within a few years, we are to have Lewis's Pevensie children, Mary Norton's Arietty, William Mayne's children in *A Grass Rope* or Tom and Hatty in Philippa Pearce's *Tom's Midnight Garden*. As previously observed the effect is that children's fantasy often takes on some of the qualities of children's realistic fiction.

Some of the issues that became prominent in 1950s fantasy arose from the different currents that went into its making. One of the challenges was to combine the realistic portrayal of children with their fantastic experience. How can one fit the two together, when the one may challenge the existence of the other, and when both compete for importance? Then there is the issue of writing fantasy in an empiricist decade. Third, there is the problem of reconciling the new impulse for personal freedom and growth with the requirements of society.

C. S. Lewis's *The Chronicles of Narnia* (1950–56), the most celebrated of children's fantasies to emerge from the 1950s, would seem to set themselves against almost every one of these new values. Indeed Lewis himself positively gloried in the fact, portraying himself in the inaugural lecture of his Cambridge English professorship in 1955 as a 'dinosaur' and an 'Old Western Man'.[3] His fantasies have little or nothing to do with this world, being set in a Christian fairyland which is reached by the 'cut off' device of walking through the back of a wardrobe. They have even less to do with it than his earlier fantasies, which were set variously in the soul, the solar system, heaven and hell, and which all had some reference, educative or condemnatory, to the human condition. But Narnia is a relatively closed system. Children from this world are drawn into it, and do things for it, but there is scarcely a glance back at life in our world. It is not even allegory, though many have tried to read it so. The action of Aslan in dying to save Edmund may accord with the universal principle operative also in Christ's Passion on earth, but it is a unique event tailored to the particular landscape of the spirit that is Narnia. The children in Narnia may behave morally, but if readers learn from this, it is by indirection.

So far as science and empiricism are concerned, Lewis has little time for the humanist and materialist outlook on which they are based. The Narnia books repeatedly expose what is seen as the crass smugness of secular realism. In *The Lion, the Witch and the Wardrobe* (1950), Edmund refuses to believe Lucy's account of how she got into Narnia, and even when he has realised the truth he still tries to persuade the other children that she is making it up: he has a long and painful journey ahead of him. Other materialists in the books are Eustace in *The Voyage of the 'Dawn Treader'* (1952), the greedy Uncle Andrew of *The Magician's Nephew* (1955), and the cynical Dwarfs of *The Last Battle* (1956) who prefer their dingy picture of the world to the highly coloured reality about them. In *The Silver Chair* (1953), Prince Rilian of Narnia is held underground by an evil snake-enchantress who tries to persuade him that Narnia is a dream of his. She keeps Rilian bound for most of the time in a silver chair, lest in his rage he harm himself and others: the chair is a fantastic version of a straitjacket, and she is a Freudian psychotherapist of the sort that says that the perceived world is a projection of wants and fears. For Lewis believes in the solid reality of the world all right, without being a materialist: for him its solidity is not its own, but heaven's. In his *The Great Divorce* he depicts heaven as far heavier than our own world.

In the same way Lewis is not interested in children's 'characters' for themselves. Certainly the four Pevensie children are differentiated, but according to spiritual, not secular realities. Lucy is gentle, kind, forgiving, perceptive; Peter is bold and decisive; Edmund is suspicious, jealous, false and greedy; Susan is cautious and worldly: and all this in relation to a story where they must decide for Aslan or the Witch, heaven or hell. Of course there are charming moments and 'realistic'-seeming situations, as with the Faun or the Beavers, but they have their reality from Aslan, not from themselves. The idea of living by and for the self belongs here to the Witch. This does not mean that Lewis did not rejoice in people's personalities and idiosyncrasies: a glance at his literary criticism would show that he did. But he was not concerned with personality for its own sake: only for God's sake, as the expression of His creative variety. This of course could lead to a certain harshness: Susan is eventually excluded from Narnia for becoming a self-regarding teenager.

As for the 1950s theme of growth, that is certainly prominent in the Narnia books, but it has nothing to do with growth of the merely personal self. Every one of the books has a theme of freedom or expansion, but one that relates to approaching Aslan or his nature, not towards the betterment of a human state or society; Narnian society, yes, but that is seen as much more immediately in God's hand. As the wardrobe opens into the new world of Narnia, where God walks once more within his creation, so Narnia itself ends by opening on the wider world of heaven.

There is however a structural pattern of growth and expansion in each of the books. In *The Lion, the Witch and the Wardrobe* all Narnia is brought gradually to life, and from solitary figures to a whole diverse population, as the freezing power of the Witch (perhaps symbolic of the war[1]) is overcome, and long winter turns to spring. *Prince Caspian* (1951) describes a later and again enclosed Narnia, oppressed by a usurper king, which is revived by Aslan, the children in their larger Narnian selves, and the young rightful king Caspian. *The Voyage of the 'Dawn Treader'* is the story of a long sea journey out from Narnia to discover Aslan's far country. Whereas the previous books portrayed Aslan in his nearness, this explores his distance: it is a picture of a journey from the known world to the wholly 'other.' On its way the ship passes seven islands, each of which is an image of the cut-off self and of evil or delusion, while the 'Dawn Treader' itself, moving ever onward, is an image of the growing spirit. And so with the other books. The children in *The Silver Chair* free Prince Rilian from his underground enchantment, and open up the rich worlds beneath the earth. By escaping from his slave life in the land of Calormen, the boy Shasta in *The Horse and His Boy* (1954) discovers his much fuller identity as the long-lost son of the king of neighbouring Archenland. *The Magician's Nephew* shows the creation of Narnia itself out of darkness by Aslan. *The Last Battle* chronicles Narnia's decline and death, but as a prelude to its ever-growing life into a better country after death.

Meanwhile relationship and meeting ('real life is meeting,' Lewis wrote[5]) are also central ideas. The whole series is a kind of growing love-affair with Narnia, which goes on even beyond death. Each book begins with children coming from outside Narnia to an unknown point in its history: a good part of each story involves familiarising oneself with the people and the surroundings, so that the effect is one of an expanding network of relationships. In both *The Lion, the Witch and the Wardrobe* and *Prince Caspian*, one meeting leads to others and so to the waking of a whole frozen people. The journey of *The Voyage of the 'Dawn Treader'* brings encounters with ever-new islands and the stories of their various inhabitants, until the hoped-for meeting with Aslan himself, in the Uttermost east. Shasta's journey in *The Horse and His Boy* is marked by developing relationships, with the young princess Aravis, also escaping, with the Talking Horses that carry them, and most of all with Aslan, in whose nature and presence he has to learn to trust. The great relationship, throughout all the books, is with Aslan, who evokes love and awe in his presence, and asks trust and belief in his absence. This relationship is the Christian one, and underpins all the others. In the Narnia books Lewis is less interested in society for its own sake than in society for Aslan's sake. Growth, expansion and freedom are not merely so that one may realise the self to the uttermost, but so that one may do so in the knowledge of the divine society of which that self is a created part.

That is the frame, the pattern, the love, in which all individual impulses are set. Nothing juts out, everything fits in, is part of a larger whole. The Pevensie children in *The Lion* find that their arrival is not an accident, but part of an old prophecy; Shasta in *The Horse and His Boy* is prompted to escape Calormen not just by his wretched life there, but through a larger design of Aslan's by which he will prove to be the long-lost heir of Archenland. Several of the stories involve restorations, by which displaced leaders are returned, or 'fitted back' to their thrones – *Prince Caspian* and *The Silver Chair* also show this, and in *The Lion* the usurper Witch is overthrown. Even the strangeness of the fantasy itself may be no mere arbitrary invention, for Lewis believed that what was myth in one world might be fact in some other.[6]

On the surface the Narnia books embody many of the characteristics of 1950s children's fantasy. They are, with qualifications, interested in children's different natures – something almost entirely absent since E. Nesbit; they are centrally concerned with growth; one of their recurrent ideas is escape from confinement; they emphasise relationships, and 'fitting in.' To which one would add that in a 'demythologising' decade they seek to portray Christian reality in a new 'non-spiritual' mode.[7] About the only features they do not highlight are empiricism and science. But every one of these characteristics is turned from a secular to a sacred purpose. The books are in the end less concerned with reality than with Reality; less with good living than with good dying. As such they are a complete anomaly in their time. And yet they were to prove the most widely read of all children's fantasies.

One is left wondering what led Lewis to write for children in the first place. Doubtless one can point to Lewis's own boyishness of nature, and perhaps also to a love of innocence that comes out in *Out of the Silent Planet* (1938) or *Perelandra* (1943). But if anything, Lewis's fiction had got more 'adult,' less disengaged, in the 1940s, in such books as *The Screwtape Letters* (1942) or *That Hideous Strength* (1945), not to mention his wartime broadcast theology. There is scarcely a word about children in his essays until the 1950s, when there are a great many. The answer seems most likely to be the growing importance of childhood after the war. Some science fiction writers in the 1950s such as Arthur C. Clarke in *Childhood's End* (1953) and John Wyndham in *The Chrysalids* (1955) and *The Midwich Cuckoos* (1956) portray children of phenomenal mental powers. Probably it was to counter the weight of new expectation with children that William Golding wrote his *Lord of the Flies* (1954).

If one might term Lewis's Narnia books 'high' fantasy, in the sense of their being about great matters, the *Borrowers* books of Mary Norton, which appeared from 1952, could almost have been written to go to the opposite extreme. They describe the domestic life and adventures of a family of three tiny people who are at first found living in a house under the floor behind the kitchen stove, but have to leave when discovered. *The Borrowers* was followed by three books describing the adventures of the uprooted family in search of a new home in the outside world, *The Borrowers Afield* (1955), *The Borrowers Afloat* (1959) and *The Borrowers Aloft* (1961); a final volume followed in 1978, *The Borrowers Avenged*. These books involve a much closer engagement than the Narnia books with our world and with people's characters – even if the world is seen from a Lilliputian perspective and the people are the size of mice.

In keeping with its empiricist decade, the world of the Borrowers is a very solid and physical one – if the postulate of the fantasy, namely that human houses are packed with undiscovered tribes of parasitic mini-men living within the walls, is absurd (though were we to translate 'Borrowers' as 'our children,' it might be all too true). There is nothing of the fairy about the Borrowers, as the boy who finds them at first thinks (*The Borrowers*, 12–13, 67–8): they are hard-headed and practical, continually having to shape a resistant world for their survival. We are caught up in the frequent improvisations and the struggle to make a home, and in the way the Borrowers have both to fit in with and to use their surroundings to live. An ethic of realism is very much behind the story. Increasingly we are brought to see the Borrowers not as freaks who stand out but as creatures fitted or adapted to their environments.

As in the Narnia stories the theme is growth and expansion, but here growth relates to the self in this world, not as part of a divine purpose. Collectively the books are a 'coming out' story, in which the family are expelled from their relatively safe but isolated and paranoid underfloor life, to an existence of much greater threat and risk in the world, and also of more involvement in it. This new life is also one without rest, for they are constantly having to move on, like refugees, in defiance of their own Borrower love of security. Eventually, however, they begin to choose to do so themselves. They leave a family of their relatives who find them a burden, and later quit the safe model village of Little Fordham because it makes them the pets of humans. By the end they are more aligned to the houseless adventurer Spiller they meet, and he in turn to them: both see that home is not a place, but where the heart is, and the family here constitutes a travelling home. Effectively they have moved away from civilisation and back to nature.

At the same time they have become less shut in on themselves. Their lively teenage daughter Arietty has lost some of her rebelliousness, her father Pod has learned humility before Spiller's resourcefulness, and Homily his wife has become less fearful and neurotic, more open-hearted and happy. Just as the Borrowers have changed from narrow and enclosed places to more and more open ones – from Afield to Afloat to Aloft – so they have come out of the narrower places of their own hearts.

Effectively, too, the Borrowers have grown out of their dependency on humans, and to that extent have stopped being borrowers (maybe a symbol of growing prosperity as the postwar stringencies eased?). They have had to learn to live in the open country, surviving on whatever they can find, living in an old boot, a kettle, or a model village. And they need to be ever alert to new situations and how they can be turned to their advantage, rather than being able to live by routine as before. The ideals of 'back to basics,' living by one's wits and not veg-etating, are all very much of their time. Exactly the same values are behind John Wyndham's famous contemporary science fiction novel about a Britain forced back to subsistence living by a plague, *The Day of the Triffids* (1951).

The *Borrowers* books look both forward and back: forward in that the nar-rative focuses on the child, the spear-point of the future; and back in that they highlight the non-human, like the Little Grey Men, or White's Lilliputians or Rumer Godden's dolls. The stories are unique in their decade in not having human children as the centre of consciousness. Essentially they assume a semi-satiric relation to human affairs, and we are made to see our world afresh, from a different perspective. Tolkien called the process 'Recovery,' whereby the familiar is made new, but it could just as easily be called alienation. To Borrowers, torn-up letters and used stamps can make admirable wallpaper and pictures, and red blotting paper a carpet, while human beings are a gross waste of the planet's resources (*The Borrowers*, 68–9). And Borrowers do not think of themselves as stealing from humans: rather they are taking what is rightfully theirs, because, as Arietty says, '"We're part of the house. You might as well say that the fire-grate steals the coal from the coal-scuttle"' (73). Human beings are not the Borrowers' superiors, but their slaves, '"Human beans are for Borrowers – like bread's for butter!"' This recalls some of the inversions of *Gulliver's Travels*. And we certainly learn during the story to take the Borrowers as being fully human in nature, even while minute in size. This implicitly satirises both contemporary class prejudice and the patronising attitudes to children still prevalent in the 1950s.

The war had for some older writers cut them off from a world with which they had been familiar, and placed them in a new and strange one. It is not surprising therefore to find the first five of C. S. Lewis's Narnia books, like Tolkien's *The Lord of the Rings*, describing restorations of the past, whether of a land or a lost king. The 62 year-old Lucy Boston might have been one of these, but she came fresh to writing when she started her semi-autobiographical *Green Knowe* books in 1954, and wrote them partly in order to bridge the gap between different times. Mrs Oldknow (old-know), owner of the thousand year-old house and garden of Green Knowe, has numbers of child visitors, English, German and Chinese, to stay, and while they enter her world, she can enter theirs. Such a commerce across time is made easy in a house where times past can be felt to be continuously present, and in a work of fantasy by a relatively old writer for children.

Just as in the *Borrowers* books, a central theme is growing and widening one's horizons. The house in *Green Knowe* is ever open to new experiences.[8] Its inhab-itants are not only its family owner, but its past peoples, and its present diverse visitors; and it has been continually changed in shape throughout its history. It is a sort of expanding bag: it even takes in the gorilla Hanno, who finds freedom in its garden after escaping from the zoo (*A Stranger at Green Knowe*). In its hospitality it recalls – perhaps even subsumes – the seventeenth-century celebrations of country houses by Ben Jonson, Robert Herrick or Andrew Marvell, and the more recent one by Alison Uttwell. But the larger reference is to the house that is Britain, now becoming more open to immigrants and multiculturalism.

However the books are not quite as open-spirited as this would suggest. Mrs Oldknow also sees the house more nostalgically, as a lonely survival which may not long endure in this age; and she is concerned that her great-grandson Toseland should both understand the house and take on its preservation after she is gone. Like C. S. Lewis or Tolkien, Lucy Boston clings to the old; and looks to the old's survival. (And of course her very writing of her books may be part of this, the hope of keeping one's own voice beyond death.) The idea is that the children who come to the house should merge themselves with it, rather than it with them. The Chinese boy Ping sinks his oriental peculiarities into those of the building (*The River at Green Knowe*). The social anthropologist Dr Maud Biggin, who refuses to believe in the present reality of giants, is mocked (*The River*). The idea that time is not absolute, that the dead and the past may live on, and that they may converse with the future yet unborn is one natural to old age. But it puts a pressure on the children in the books as the bearers of an old person's wishes.[9] Here, as in C. S. Lewis's Narnia books, we see the fantasy drawing in, rather than giving out.

Such issues however do not so much affect the Yorkshire writer William Mayne, whose books show the past more as something still existing on its own than as something to be preserved. Nor is Mayne's first fantasy, the Carnegie Medal-winning *A Grass Rope* (1957), much concerned with the 1950s topic of growth. Mayne's interest is more in what things are than in what they might become, in seeing more often than in doing (which is partly why his books can be slow to read). Relationships, yes: but his children do not change through interaction so much as gradually reveal their natures – which is what happens in general in his books. And there is little that is moral or socially conformist in his work. Indeed, his non-conformity is summed up in his fantasies being local and full of dialect. The interest of his fantasy is in tracing the metaphysical in the physical world: this topic is pursued with 1950s reserve in *A Grass Rope*.

The book describes a group of Yorkshire country children who set out to prove whether the legend of hounds and a unicorn that still run beneath a local fell is fact. Adam Forrest, head boy of the local school, uses science to try to prove it false; Mary, fanciful younger daughter of Farmer Owland, uses her active imagination to try to show it is true. There are patches of evidence that could be read either way, until Mary herself goes into the deep cave behind Yowncorn Yat and finds the nine silver collars the original hounds were supposed to have worn, and the top of an animal's skull with a long single horn in the middle of it. Adam and Mr Owland now explain the whole story as a perfectly natural event in which the running hounds fell into the shaft and were drowned, and Mr Owland even has an explanation (not given) for the 'unicorn's' horn, which had for the time shaken even Adam's scientific certainties. Yet Mary at the end remains convinced of her own truth, sufficient to preserve a measure still of doubt.

Mayne embeds his potentially supernatural tale in a description of a farming family in a particular Yorkshire landscape. The first chapter is about Mary and her sister Nan gathering hens' eggs, and Mary having a lift on Charley the farmhand's tractor; and the second portrays the construction of a wire fence to keep out foxes. The legend only comes in through some questions of Adam's, but thereafter it is a recurrent topic, though still interrupted by other events, such as a night-time fox-shoot. Throughout we are aware of the children's developing relationships – Nan's nervous admiration of Adam, Adam's patronage of young Peter, and the way Adam almost needs Mary to argue with. And beyond this are the adults and their relations with the children. Everything seems to happen quite naturally, as it might in real life, and this makes the magic, if it exists, much more credible, because it does not seem to have been shaped by fiction. That it is eventually found in a cave in the form of several bits of wire and a piece of an old skull, objects one often finds in the country, only adds to this. The magic 'fits in' to a wider fabric, that social ideal of the 1950s.

A central symbol in the book is the inn signboard which Adam spends days sanding, prior to repainting it. The sanding goes through four pictures, each from earlier in the history of the locality, and finally reveals certain facts about the legend. The same is true of the narrative, which is a continual sandpapering via discussion to arrive at truth. At the same time the process of the story involves a gradual penetration, first mental and then physical, down through the landscape itself. In the end, while the truth remains elusive, one fact is unearthed about Adam Forrest: he came to the area wholly because of the lost treasure associated with the legend. The process of the story is a finding out: as in Mayne's school story *A Swarm in May* (1954), something hidden is eventually discovered. It is a sort of analytic process, like science itself.

Solidity is Mayne's technique here, and in others of his novels. He wants to get the facts as precise as he can, so that, if they are more than physical facts, it will show.

> Charley ripped off the branches of the fallen tree, and sliced the trunk in three pieces. It bounced and leapt under the blows. The axe sounded dull if you listened only to the echo from the other trees. If you listened to the stroke itself you heard the blade gnaw and fracture the wood fibres. (5)

The sentences are short. It is the verbs that do the work, for there is scant use of adjectives or adverbs throughout, and therefore less colour or atmosphere. And when people speak, their emotions are rarely described, even at dramatic moments. There is much practicality – how a child holds on to a tractor, how a fence is dug in, a signboard cleared, a fox caught, or a child rescued from a cave. There is a sense of difficulty to the style, as though it has itself been physically worked at, like a sign stripped down or a field ploughed.

Direct physical interaction with the world – even more than in the *Borrowers* books – is often the spine of Mayne's novels, many of which concern the earth and what may emerge from it. In such a context fantasy is often a half-buried thing – an old legend of what lies beneath a crag, a lost eighteenth-century drummer-boy underground (*Earthfasts*, 1966), a long-sunk cannon in an old battlefield (*The Battlefield*, 1967). But the difference with these later novels is that in them the buried magic surfaces of its own accord, rather than being unearthed by people's investigations. That is a measure of the 1950s humanism that conditions *A Grass Rope*.

With Theresa Whistler's *The River Boy* (1955), we move from the physical to the mental world, and from solid earth to changing water. Only once reprinted (1976), this is a striking tale of a lonely country child who meets a double of himself, and finds the dry valley behind his house changed to a river. Nathaniel ('Nat') meets the river boy at random, and always further down the river. They play games, meet animals, stay at a mill and harvest corn, until eventually they come to a city by the sea, where a ship bears Nat off alone. In the 'real' world he has now chosen to leave home and go to boarding school: his life's adventure has begun.

At first the book is pastoral idyll, and this takes it back to pre-war fantasies: Theresa Whistler was the friend, and later (1993) biographer, of Walter de la Mare, and some of his visionary outlook, though not its darker side, appears in *The River Boy*. Most of the first half of the book is about the games and adventures of Nat and the river boy together. It is also scattered with moments of vision, such as that of the old white family horse walking through a waterfall in death, or the strange Miller and his dark many-windowed mill, or the golden town in the midst of the corn that Nat's heart aches in vain to reach.

But the story is also increasingly one of spiritual growth, as Nat's adventures are moved steadily downriver to the sea. The river landscape and its shifting scenery recall George Macdonald's *Phantastes* (1858), another tale of a young man's stream-borne initiation into life through his imagination. Indeed this is one of the first children's fantasies since the Victorians to concern itself with the inner landscape of a child. The river boy is partly Pan, spirit of nature, and he is also Peter Pan, child forever young and full of carefree delight, child who must finally bid Nat farewell. But in another way he is Nat's truer self too, his deeper being who is seen beneath the river's surface, ever-ready like the spirit to appear when least expected. His river-land is bi-local with Nat's home, and each can change into the other.

In the end Nat's spirit, as generous, open and pliable as the river, begins to 'harden.' He deceives the river boy in order to try to reach the town in the corn. He finds that he cannot get back to the river and eventually tries to do so by going to sleep in the snow near his home, from which he is only just rescued. When he gets at last to the river he finds himself in a deep and frozen gorge, into which the river falls in a petrified sheet from far above. This frozen landscape is an image of his soul; and the river boy is nearby, sleeping as Nat once slept in the snow of his own world. But 'hardness' is not always a bad thing: it is needed for purpose and direction in life. A strange old woman with a cart full of tools (science?) helps the boys, and then while they are asleep builds an immense aqueduct to carry the river across the gorge. After this, human constructs surround Nat on his journey. The boys follow the river to a city where Nat takes ship and leaves the river boy behind. His life has taken solid shape, and he has become fitted to the pattern of the world.

A similar strain of part-imagined magic is found in Philippa Pearce's celebrated *Tom's Midnight Garden* (1958). Here discontented Tom, bored with an enforced quarantine stay with his aunt and uncle in their flat in an old house, finds one night a strange garden at the back, in which he meets and befriends a girl called Hatty. Unknown to him he has travelled back in time to the house as it was about 1890. Tom continues to visit Hatty, night after night in his own time, but at widely scattered and often non-sequential times in hers, until she grows too old for him and he cannot get back to the garden again. The garden that Tom finds and comes to desire more than anything is like the river that Nat loves but cannot keep. Both fantasies retell the Peter Pan story: both register the pull of the old pastoral-idyllic mode from which children's fantasy is now trying to move on.

In a way the book is about that favourite 1950s theme, 'where you belong.' Tom has been displaced from his home by illness and is not happy living with his aunt and uncle in their small flat. Ironically that very place is to be his window on to a place he very much likes: magic makes a space for him and gives him a companion his own age. But to try to enter the garden world entirely is to defy the conditions of life – for the garden, whether as Victorian or as an image of Eden, is in the past. Tom finds, painfully, that you only belong where you grow, inside your time. The frozen river down which Tom and Hatty later skate to Ely symbolises the frozen time they have enjoyed: on their way back the river is thawing, symbolising their places on the flowing river of time to which Tom must now return.

Nevertheless Tom has been permitted to escape from 'where he belongs' in the first place, through the working of the magic on him. It seems in a way cruel that he has been given all this only to have to learn to do without it. This seems reflective of the strain between the old and the new impulses, pastoral and evolutionary, in children's fantasy. This is also seen in the way that the real modern world to which Tom is to commit himself is viewed as cramped, mean and dirty beside the more beautiful and ample Victorian one, with crowded houses, a now polluted river, and a narrow paved yard with dustbins in place of the garden.

Apart from Mayne's *A Grass Rope*, this is almost the first book in sixty years to describe a relationship between children, rather than between children and adults or magic. Of course the children are divided in time and they have only scattered meetings, but Tom, who is missing the company of his brother Peter and at first looks to Hatty's boy cousins for friendship, strikes up a friendship with Hatty herself as intense as any he has ever known. Yet it is not all togetherness. Hatty at first pretends she is a little princess, and is quite peremptory (like the girl in E. Nesbit's *The Enchanted Castle*); then Tom exposes some of her fables about the garden; and constantly the one slightly patronises the other, depending on who is the elder in each visit. But it is a real and growing friendship for all that, based on a shared loneliness and love of the garden. The two play hide and seek; Tom makes a bow and arrow and they shoot with it everywhere; they climb trees, hunt frogs, chase birds and try to catch fish. The bond only loosens when Hatty is an older girl who cares less for childhood things: Tom then becomes increasingly ghostly and insubstantial to her. Meanwhile however he has developed something of a calf love for her, and their skating excursion to Ely is a half romantic experience for him; while she is already looking beyond him, to sexual partners in her own world. It is all wonderfully and poignantly rendered. For all the apartness that threads it, it is the only true relationship in the book, for Hatty's aunt and cousins hate her, and Tom's aunt and uncle are opposite types in a childless marriage: the normal condition of being in the book seems to be separation and solitude.

In keeping with 1950s reticence in the use of fantasy, the attempt is made by characters in the story to dismiss the magic, and by the author to explain it as somehow 'psychological.' True, Tom's Uncle Alan is criticised for insisting on the '"laws of nature"' (60) in opposition to all Tom's assertions, and for being ready to tell Tom of the current scientific theories concerning time while denying any truth to Tom's experiences of it (162–6). But Philippa Pearce displays a certain reticence too. For most of the story we have accepted Tom's adventures as at least part-real, because he gains knowledge of the house he could not otherwise have come by. This 'reality' is admittedly not plain or simple: Tom goes into the garden only when the clock chimes thirteen at night and stops, which in some sense is a figure of dreaming. But at the end of the story, when Tom learns that Hatty of the garden is now Mrs Bartholomew the owner of the house, she tells him that she somehow incorporated him in her own dreams of the past. Tom's yearning for a friend 'beating about unhappily in the big house, must have made its entry into Mrs Bartholomew's dreaming mind and brought back to her the little Hatty of long ago. Mrs Bartholomew had gone back in time to when she was a girl, wanting to play in the garden; and Tom had been able to go back with her, to that same garden' (215). This may be an explanation that is in tune with the theme of mental kinship and sympathy that runs through the story, but it is cumbersome, and it comes after the facts.[10] Most of all it is an attempt to take back the objective reality of the story, and make it wholly subjective, a dream – which is just about where the 1950s were in relation to the 'supernatural.'

Yet at the same time, and equally '1950s', there is a penumbra of religious significance about the story. Disbelief in magic and fantasy in that decade went together with a limited readiness still to bow the knee in matters of Christian belief. The garden, the happy place, is Eden, and Tom and Hatty the originally innocent pair; there is even an apple tree, from which Hatty's cousins shake down apples, giving her one to eat. There is a gardener called Abel who is very religious and thinks Tom is a devil come to tempt Hatty. When she is older, Hatty leaves the garden with Tom on the skating expedition. The grandfather clock downstairs that sounds to admit Tom to the garden has an angel and verses from Revelation x, 1–6 on the dial, relating to the angel coming to earth at the Last Judgement and saying there should be 'Time no longer.' (Here Tom's name Tom Long is itself suggestive.) Tom dreams of the angel coming down from the clock face and barring his way back to the garden with a flaming sword (161); and later does indeed find it impossible to get back. The garden is a symbol of a past paradise we cannot have again except fleetingly and in childhood; only in the future may we see it again, at the end of the world, when we have '"exchanged Time for Eternity"' (185).

In Catherine Storr's *Marianne Dreams* (1958) we again deal with a boy and girl magically brought together, but this time across space rather than time, for both children are ill in their beds in different parts of the same town. (Both Pearce and Storr deal with that common experience of 1950s pre-vaccination children – long periods ill in bed.) Young Marianne finds a strange pencil and draws a house with a boy in it which becomes real in her dreams. The boy is Mark, very ill with polio on the other side of town, and angry at being put in such a shoddily-drawn place. Here we have the interest in telepathy, in minds interlocking over distance, that we saw in *Tom's Midnight Garden*, where old Hatty says that her dreams and Tom's desires combined to put them together in the garden.[11]

Much of the book is taken up, again like *Tom's Midnight Garden*, with a children's relationship. Mark who has all the irritability of the invalid, often treats Marianne as a silly little girl; and at first he thinks her magic pencil is a nonsense until he learns better. Marianne, who at first drew idly, gradually learns to draw more purposefully.

Marianne can alter the house by drawing more; alter it badly, too, as when in a fit of rage she scribbles bars all over the windows and draws evil eyes on the boulders around the fence. What her mind has thoughtlessly made, Marianne must then use her reason to circumvent. She improves the house as best she can, for nothing she has drawn can be rubbed out. She (over)feeds Mark and puts steps and hanging rings in the place so that he can exercise his muscles and eventually walk by himself. She helps him learn to ride a bicycle she has drawn, so that they can escape when the now menacing boulders outside press in on the house to destroy them. Marianne's dreams have as it were to struggle with Marianne's nightmares to win. However it is not only Marianne's mind that is at work, but Mark's also.

Despite the broadly optimistic end of the book, the evil boulders remain, even though the anger that produced them has gone. The reason for this is that evil has real existence outside as well as inside the self: as Storr herself says, 'of course the stones are still there: evil is still there, all around us.'[12] There may be a Christian meaning here, by which however we repent and improve, we are still creatures of sin and darkness, who would be overwhelmed but for God's grace – which may be the significance of the unintended lighthouse and of the unexpected voice bidding the children escape (171–2). When they top the last darkened hill and burst into the shining light, there is a roar of defeated hate from their pursuers, which is overwhelmed by 'the music of the light' and 'a glorious, triumphant song' (185). The tower then becomes heaven, as in some medieval allegory, so far as the children's escape is concerned. It also, incidentally, recalls the tower of Ely Cathedral that Tom and Hatty climb on their final expedition together in *Tom's Midnight Garden* (the tower from which he is sent back into the world). It says much for this book that such allegorical suggestion emerges naturally from a story about two very ordinary children trying to escape. Here as in *Tom's Midnight Garden* we have a '1950s' religious penumbra.

The book is full of images of enclosure – the two sickrooms, the iron lung, being shut in a useless body, the house, the room, the bars, the fence, the stones and the tower. All of them express variously the enclosure of the self, unable to break free of its own concerns, and unable for long to think of others. As the children progressively 'come out' or grow, so these confinements disappear. At the end, 'The tower was no longer lonely or unfriendly or frightening. Nor was it any longer a place of refuge. It was a place of departure.' From being sick, which means being cut off from the world, two children have become well and reintegrated with society – a pattern seen throughout 1950s children's fantasy, from Lewis's Edmund to Pearce's Tom.

The story is wonderfully and movingly told, and the idea behind it is novel and well worked out. It has an extreme clarity of style, even to the point of measuring distances, describing progress by increments, detecting sounds through static (this at 154–7). It depends very much on the imposition of mind on experience – something Tom in *Tom's Midnight Garden* could never do with the magic there. The less happy side of Storr's precision is the tight control she exercises over the meaning of her story.[13] As Marianne draws her world, so her author much more carefully draws her, and fits her behaviour to a pattern of moral growth away from selfishness. The freedom the characters obtain is still 'the done thing.' Daddy, Mummy and the Doctor are always right, where in *Tom's Midnight Garden* Tom's mother is uncertain in her love, his aunt and uncle are well-meaning but inept, and Hatty's aunt is coldly cruel. Another aspect of this control is that though Marianne manages Mark's rescue from the house, and from his illness, she is seen as performing more 'the woman's role' of submissive helpmeet than of moral heroine: she spends most of the story thinking of Mark and his needs, and not at all of her no doubt less urgent wants.

We end this account of the 1950s with two minor and contrastive children's fantasies, Barbara Sleigh's *Carbonel* (1955), about a modern girl who becomes the owner of a witch's black cat, and Arthur Calder-Marshall's sharp allegory, *The Fair to Middling* (1959). *Carbonel* is a wish-fulfilment fantasy for younger children, a mixture of Cinderella, Puss-in-Boots and Walt Disney magic (then at the height of its popularity). Carbonel the cat has to be freed by young Rosemary from enchantment so that he may return to being king of all the city's cats. The story thus involves a creature returning to its proper nature and society, a theme we have seen in other 1950s children's fantasies: self-expression within a social frame is the implicit ideal as the restraining force of three magic charms on Carbonel is eventually removed. At the same time, Rosemary's own nature and that of her mother come out from poverty and frustration and grow into themselves. Rosemary has unwittingly been helping a royal cat, and will receive its favour; and during her quest she has befriended the boy John, who, again unknown to her, is the son of the rich lady for whom Rosemary's mother does the cleaning. From being something of an outcast, Rosemary has come to belong. Meanwhile her mother, who is in true fairy-tale fashion poor but good, eventually wins a 'respectable' job and the domestic security she and Rosemary were initially without. In being poor, they were at the mercy of others. The book begins with Rosemary shrinking from the fact that her school friends are going abroad on holiday while she is going "'Nowhere!'" But self-gratification is not an ideal. In the cramped flat, under the gaze of the landlady, Rosemary and her mother learn to suppress their feelings to get on together. Even at the end, though they are out of the flat and with far wider horizons, they still conform to and cooperate with a hierarchic social fabric. And in a sequel to the book, *The Kingdom of Carbonel* (1960) Rosemary is asked by Carbonel to be the royal babysitter for his children while he is away.

Carbonel touches the common facts of living, integrating itself with ordinary life, symbolised in a witch who retires to become a shopkeeper, and a cat whose kingdom is scattered through the gardens of the city and whose subjects and even whose enemies sit on every hearth. But at the same time the darker sides of life are abolished, in a witch who finally turns decent, and a royal usurper who turns out to be the pampered cat belonging to John's mother. Here we see children's fantasy fitting in with the determined cheeriness of its decade.

The more repressive and still strongly moral side of that decade is seen in Arthur Calder-Marshall's Christian allegory *The Fair to Middling*. At first this story seems to describe a group of disabled orphans who are taken on an outing one day from their school to a nearby fair. But beyond the ordinary fair itself, several of the children find different booths and sideshows where they are tempted to become customers, and respond according to their natures. This is a spiritual and allegorical fair, lurking behind the physical one. One child, who has been colour-blind from birth, visits a booth where she is given magic pills to cure her. Other children however find their vanities and cruelties exposed, and two are nearly drawn into a modern consumerist hell, the shops of which promise them all they could want, in exchange for the down-payment of their souls. The reference to the 'never had it so good' society of the time, and its meaning within a Christian context, is plain.

However the real meaning of having a disability does not fit well with the allegorical meaning. The children's weaknesses are meant to figure their fallen state as human beings; but the very materialism the book attacks makes it difficult for us to move away from the physical facts of their blindness or deformity. The book ends happily enough with all morally reformed, and more accepting of their handicaps. But the moral of learning to live with oneself and put up with things, backed up by the rubber stamps of heaven or hell, seems oppressive. While it is foolish to over-sympathise with people's disabilities, it is surely just as bad to take little account of them in assessing people's merits. The book is extremely well and wittily written, but it shows the problems that face a religious allegory in a modern context.

The 1950s thus close as they began, with Christian allegory. To sum up: while the idea of growth and expansion is frequent in fantasies of this time, the idea of self-containment is strong too: growth as we have seen is still to occur within a social, educational or moral frame. Narnia blooms, and also fades, within the pattern of fallen worlds under Aslan. Arietty the Borrower, and her parents, develop right out of their early paranoid life, but they still remain a close-knit family: and while developing, Arietty is also learning the virtues of her father and mother that will make her a good wife in her turn. We saw how in *Tom's Midnight Garden* Tom learns to accept his own life, not to rebel against it; and how in *The River Boy* Nat comes to terms with the real world before leaving for boarding school. The past and the old still exert a strong hold over the present in the *Green Knowe* books, and fantasy can depend less on the discovery of some new thing than on proving the old (*A Grass Rope*), or restoring something to its former state (the Narnia books, Tolkien's *The Lord of the Rings*). While the new impulse of growth gradually displaces much of the previous fantasy of nostalgia (particularly, if regretfully, in *Tom's Midnight Garden*), the past, authority, and social conformity still exert considerable sway. Indeed children's fantasy is to remain preoccupied with the past, as the region from which magic and values arise, till the end of the 1970s.

While fantasy is the preferred children's genre of the 1950s, it is also expected to fit in with the real world: Lewis apart, there are many attempts to integrate the magic of fantasy, often by making it acceptable as a dream. This idea of 'fitting in' is also seen in the theme of things finding their proper place. In the Narnia books, Narnia itself is returned to its true nature in *The Lion, the Witch and the Wardrobe*, and we find its truest 'place' of all in the afterworld of *The Last Battle*. Meanwhile three of the intervening books portray lost or exiled princes restored to their inheritance; and throughout the children have designated roles to play in Narnia's history. The Borrowers find their proper sort of home after losing their original more parasitic one; *The Children of Green Knowe* depicts a house in which young Tolly can find his true self. In *The Lord of the Rings* an evil object must be put back where it belongs; *Tom's Midnight Garden* shows a boy having to accept his own world; *Marianne Dreams* shows two children restored to health through helping one another; Nat in *The River Boy* is readied for his place in life; Carbonel the royal cat gets back his throne.

The theme of the 'proper place' continues into the 1960s, but with diminishing force. Certainly it is still central in Pauline Clarke's Carnegie Medal-winning *The Twelve and the Genii* (1962), a tale of Branwell Brontë's supposedly long-lost toy soldiers, which have stayed alive to the present day, only to take themselves to the Haworth Museum where they belong. (Actually they were broken or lost in the young Brontës' violent moorland games with them.[14]) Given life, characters and a history by the imaginations of their past 'Genii,' the Brontës, the soldiers have retained them: all of them are loyal parts of their company while having idiosyncratic characters and a strong sense of their individual selves.

Eventually, returned to the house in which their Genii once lived, the Twelve are finally at home.

The analogy between the soldiers' lives and those of the children who find them in the attic, who are also characters made up by an author, is gently but continually present. And the larger analogy made between the Twelve and man in general is that their very Genii (or souls) may themselves be the creations of a larger and divine Genius, who inspires their inspirations. It may also be this Genius who through reason and conscience suggests courses of action, while leaving His people free to choose for themselves (*Twelve* 87, 133, 193). Thus all creations and creatures are simultaneously real and unreal, and none more real than another – save God. This book is written just within the time when belief in God could still be comfortably maintained for middle-class English children: and thus provides a substantial and final Reality for a world in which all creation would otherwise be entirely fictive and all sense of self and identity ultimately groundless. From now on such security, such a final sense of one's place in creation, is to be more rare in children's fantasy.

1960s children's fantasy is also increasingly less certain of personal identity than before. This decade began the overthrow in England of old values of any kind for the new culture of youth and freedom. The price of such liberation was the loss of that sense of belonging to a wider social and religious structure which had previously defined the self. In what John Somerville has called 'the identity crisis of our civilisation' for children, there is no longer any frame into which to fit.[15] What we often find in 1960s and later fantasy is a new search for roots, through the past, through myth, or even in the solidity of the earth itself. At the same time we also find far more wild energy in some fantasies, suggestive of previously suppressed impulses being liberated. The result is an often more tangled mode, in which the desire for a new kind of security (always important for children's literature) goes together with a measure of anarchy. Each story may end in order, with things back in their 'places,' in the happy ending of children's fantasy, but the accent throughout is now more on the state of dislocation and displacement.

Not the least form of this displacement is the way fantasy is now increasingly shown invading the 'real world,' rather than being boxed off or isolated from it. This often produces a new uncertainty as to what is 'real,' as our own world is made more fantastical. In the 1950s there was usually a separation between the magic domain and that of ordinary life: one might travel to a secondary world (Lewis's Narnia, Whistler's river, Storr's magic house) or through time (Pearce) or have to use a magnifying glass (the Borrowers) or have to see in a certain way (Mayne). In addition, in 1950s fantasy there was much emphasis on human choice and freewill in relation to magic – particularly moral choice. But the magic in 1960s fantasy is much more active and intrusive, to the point of making choice more limited and desperate. Where the 1950s emphasised discrimination between areas of reality, in the 1960s there is a much greater sense of the power of the unconscious to break down distinctions: in 1950s fantasy you went to your dream world, but now the dream world comes to you. A whole way of thinking about the world in terms of reason, order, hierarchy and analysis is replaced by the instinctual, the emotional and the superstitious.

Of this the 1960s produce an early and abrupt instance in Alan Garner's strange tale about wild doings beneath Alderley Edge in Cheshire, *The Weirdstone of Brisingamen* (1960). In this story various legendary races beneath the earth are stumbled on by two modern children on holiday, who then become caught up in a centuries-old struggle to recover the long-lost magic Weirdstone. This stone, so long as it remains undestroyed, preserves a company of sleeping knights for a great task of rescue when the world will be in danger. Here fantasy and reality have begun to come together: and neither is any longer 'safe.' What Garner is exploring here is his idea of the roots of English culture.

In this first book the children are not defined, as they might be in 1950s fantasy, by society, family, or home, but rather by their discovered roles in the great matters stirring under the Edge. Garner's story goes beneath the surface, into the depths of the world itself, travelling down to find caves hiding things good and evil – partly an image of the unconscious, no doubt, but for Garner rather more the collective or race unconscious than the individual and Freudian one.[16] Most of all there is a sense of rootedness, increased by the setting of Alderley Edge itself, where the Garner family had long lived.

Garner is also – like William Mayne – fascinated by the earth itself. Both *The Weirdstone* and its companion book *The Moon of Gomrath* (1963) are set in the very earthy world of Alderley Edge, where we move through woods and fields and rocky slopes, and travel underground. One of the most vivid episodes in all Garner's writing is the desperate journey in *The Weirdstone* through narrow and half-flooded tunnels deep underground to escape the evil swarts (chs.13,14), which only someone with a knowledge of pot-holing could have told. In *Elidor* (1965) the magic treasures of Elidor must be buried in the family garden: and the unicorn Findhorn is able to enter the world because of a picture of it on a broken clay pot the children find when they are digging the hole. There is much in this story about electricity and magic, and the need for them to be 'earthed.' In *The Owl Service* (1967), too, the three children together earth the magic (again there is much of electricity and wiring), and the magic plates are made of earthenware. All Garner's fantasy has an acute sense of places and their buried pasts, and of stone too, as in his *Stone Book* quartet (1976–8): it has an obsession with matter, as a testament to spirit, and with the living past as a guarantee of the present day's solidity.

INTO A NEW WORLD: 1950–1970

Garner is again like William Mayne in his assertive regionalism. From *The Weirdstone* through *Elidor* to *The Owl Service* we move from rural Cheshire to slum-clearance Manchester to a Welsh valley near Aberystwyth. Even the fantasy peoples have their localities in Britain, such as the *lios-alfar* or elves of *The Moon of Gomrath* who come from Prydein, or the dwarfs of Minith Bannawg. They all have their own languages, and Garner is liberal in his use of dialect. He is against all norms and standard usages, something that marks him out at once from earlier writers. His children are not asked to behave morally or to fit into any larger human society: they are simply to deal with magic, with their environment, and (in *The Owl Service*) with themselves.

But Garner's localism also goes with his sense that magic focuses on small areas. All his children's fantasies deal with peculiar concentrations of magic, so much that it begins to overflow into reality, whether as electrostatic energy or as mythic owls.[17] In every story one gets the sense that the children are catalysts or lightning rods, suddenly releasing the pent-up forces focused on the area. In that sense it is somewhat more than coincidence that Susan in *The Weirdstone* should unknowingly be wearing the magic stone when she and Colin come to stay at Alderley Edge; or that the derelict church the four children in Elidor come upon should then become a gateway to Elidor. And in *The Owl Service* the children are the conduits for the release of the recurrent story that is part of the valley.

Garner's fantasy changes considerably in character from *The Weirdstone* to *The Owl Service*. First, he brings the magic more and more into our world. The wizards, dwarfs and Elves of the Edge have their own history and problems that have little to do with man, except insofar as man gets in the way of them. They may live in the same place as men, but they pass unnoticed except by the children or country folk who accept that they are there but have no concern with them. But in *Elidor* the magic does begin to impact on man in the shape of the electric energy of the treasures of Elidor and the disturbances caused by the soldiers of Elidor who want to seize them. Further, the children here are really needed by the magic to save it. In *The Owl Service* magic, which was kept out of the house in *Elidor* (though it continually rattled at the door) gets inside in the form of the plates in the attic and the 'lady of flowers' walled in with weakening pebble dash in the hall. And here the magic gets inside the children themselves: they become the characters in the old *Mabinogion* myth, re-enacting the tale of doomed love. The fantasy in the story is muted and almost continuous with ordinary experience, where in the earlier books there was a sudden jerk as it was introduced. Throughout his fantasy Garner is moving away from the dualistic mode of 1950s fantasy, where the fantastic experience is separated from everyday reality, to a much more immanentist view that sees the fantastic as part of human life.

The journey Garner follows is in part a political one. In choosing Tolkienian 'high epic' fantasy for *The Weirdstone*, Garner had chosen simultaneously what was to become part of the new wave of literary rebellion against the literature of the 1950s, and a hierarchic, reactionary, authoritarian mode. In moving away from this into other forms of fantasy, Garner's work becomes more fully democratic. By the time of *Elidor* the forelock-touching Gowther Mossock of *The Weirdstone* and *The Moon*, and the high (and mighty) people of Alderley Edge have gone, and we are in a city setting and a suburban home with some bored teenagers, while the big fantasy people live in a world of their own. And when we reach *The Owl Service* we find the ancient myth's magical power confined within a dinner service, and its human agents changed from the old heroes to some Welsh peasants and three school children. Garner's fantasy now includes all reality as equal – a drunken Irish labourer with the Lord Malebron in *Elidor*, the high magic of Elidor with a dustbin in a Manchester back-garden, the legendary killing spear of Lleu with a teenage put-down in *The Owl Service*. And in his later *Red Shift* (1976), the lives of three young men, one a Roman legionary, another a Puritan in the Civil War and the third a young Hamlet figure of the twentieth century, are interwoven across time. The vision has become one in which all the people who have ever lived in a particular place can meet as equals in each other's lives; Garner gives his Roman soldiers the language of U.S. Vietnam war 'grunts' to underline the point.

This 'democratic' impulse is also seen in the increasing challenges to authority across Garner's fantasy. It is partly a matter of his child characters getting progressively older and therefore more rebellious. But then it is interesting that Garner is among the first of many children's fantasy writers to do this: in 1950s and earlier children's fantasies the characters tend to be younger, around ten to twelve. This is about the age of Colin and Susan in *The Weirdstone* and *The Moon*, who both follow the wishes of Cadellin and the magic people without question. But in *Elidor*, while young Roland still (rightly) believes in the reality of Elidor, his teenage brothers, particularly Nicholas, do not, and do not see why they should follow the behests of Malebron. Moreover they amiably tolerate their parents, who are seen as suburban and stuck in their ways. In *The Owl Service* we find the fantastic finally opposed and cast out by the now 16–18 year-old 'children,' who will not let it or the adults it has influenced bend them to its purposes. In this story Gwyn regularly criticises his mother, and Alison is seen as weak in always doing what her own mother says.

However another reason for resistance to the magic is that it gets increasingly uncertain in character. In the first two books the issues are plain, for the good are unambiguously so and the alternative in the shapes of the svarts, the Morrigan, the Mara or the Brollachan are made simply hostile and repulsive. In *Elidor* however things are not so clear-cut. Three of the four children doubt their fantastic experiences in Elidor when they are back in Manchester. Nor is 'good' so certain: Malebron (the name itself is dubious) lays on the children the preservation of four treasures to protect Elidor, but they know little of him or his purposes, and he is quite capable of putting them in great danger to get what he wants, when he sends them into the Mound of Vanwy for the treasures – as Nicholas points out (88–9). And somehow, though shown to be 'real,' Malebron and Elidor remain doubtful to the end, in the uncertainty as to whether the dying song of Findhorn the unicorn has been able to save them.

By *The Owl Service* we know still less of what is going on. Here the issue is not so much whether one believes the fantastic events, or whether they are certain in character, but whether they are noticeable in the first place. This is far more a work of psychological realism, in which we are most plainly presented with an English family in a Welsh house interacting with the housekeeper's intelligent son Gwyn and his mother. There is no clear narrative as in the previous fantasies to direct and order events, and make us readily able to relate one thing to another – only people talking, and the occasional odd happening. It takes at least two readings of the story to understand the relation of the dinner service to the myth and to the children, and for much of the time we are left to guess when the children are acting as themselves, and when under the compulsion of the old story. The magic itself is only gradually noticed, and partially understood, as the owls made from the design on the plates disappear in preparation for 'the woman's punishment.' Further, we have to understand its workings at a deeper level, since the sexuality of the original legend in the *Mabinogion* is not overt here, and there are no deaths. This may be part of an intention on Garner's part to force his readers out of easy certainties and on to a more primal level of understanding.

Throughout the four fantasies identity becomes progressively more indefinite. In *The Weirdstone* the magic and the children are real enough, and both are quite separate. But in *The Moon* we find Susan's nature taken over by the Brollachan, which has to be cast out and magic means found to restore Susan to herself. The treasures of Elidor assume the shapes of rubbish in our world, and Elidor and the purposes of Malebron are often uncertain. And in *The Owl Service* shapeshifting is a leitmotif of the book, whether in the continually mutating natures of the characters themselves, in the changes from owls to flowers in the myth and the plates, or in the shimmering record of the warrior Lleu on Roger's camera film. In parallel with this, the relations of the stories to their sources grow more intimate and complex. Tolkien and W. Croft Dickinson's *Borrobil* are simply drawn on in the first two books, but the *Mabinogion* tale in *The Owl Service* also 'draws on' the lives of the characters in Garner's own story. And in the interim the characters in *Elidor* have re-enacted the story of Childe Roland and the legend of the Grail.[18] This progressive blurring of identity in Garner's work will be seen to be part of a growing theme of uncertain selfhood in later 1960s English children's fantasy.

Besides Alan Garner, the other best-known, and even more rebellious, children's fantasy writer of the 1960s – and later – is the Anglo-Norwegian Roald Dahl, so popular that in 2000, ten years after his death, he was voted Britain's favourite author.[19] In some ways Dahl's 1960s fantasy is expressive of the released energies of the decade, and belongs with the Beatles, the New Wave, and hip culture, which may explain why his first books *James and the Giant Peach* and *Charlie and the Chocolate Factory*, published in America in 1961 and 1964, and successful there, had to wait until 1967 to find a publisher in Dahl's more staid homeland. Yet Dahl's energies also suffered confinement in writing children's fantasy, because he had hoped to become a famous novelist and short story writer, so that effectively he is a 'displaced' author. Herein lies a measure of the creative rage we find in his fantasy.

James and the Giant Peach tells how its young hero, a wretched orphan brought up by tyrannical aunts, is rescued by magic and their power overthrown. Right away Dahl rejects the 1950s idea of one's elders being one's betters; and he cares so little for formalities that he can casually tell us that James's parents were eaten by a rhinoceros. Everything Dahl describes has touches of the savage, the amazing, or the grotesque. James one day meets a sinister little man behind the laurel bushes, who invites him to '"Come right up close to me and I will show you something wonderful"' (13), which paederastic suggestion becomes the gift of a bag of wriggling little green things, which James then drops and loses beneath a peach tree. Within minutes the tree grows an enormous fruit which soon eclipses it, and which contains giant versions of insects that have found their way inside – an earthworm, spider, centipede, grasshopper, ladybird and glow-worm. When James first meets these creatures, they announce their hunger, and stare at him fixedly: but then they tell him they do not want to eat him, and all become friends. Every new development confounds expectation, 'displaces' the last. The plot now begins literally to move. The peach is bitten from its tree by the centipede, and then rolls downhill, squashing the aunts in its way, with a crunching noise which James is ever afterwards to relish. Everything then becomes wildly unpredictable, as the peach bounds through the country and rushes into the sea, where it is attacked by sharks, saved by a flock of seagulls tethered to the balloon by spider silk, and peppered with hailstones by a crowd of irate cloud-people, before eventually arriving in New York to universal acclaim.

There is plenty of horror and disgust mixed in with the story, which is as new – and rebellious – in children's fantasy as the idea of the giant fruit itself.[20] The aunts Sponge and Spiker are respectively grossly fleshly and as dried-up as death: Dahl homes in on the nauseating about them, not least in the little dribble of spit that trails from Sponge's mouth as she surveys the peach (24). The peach has Freudian suggestions of the womb when James first enters the hole in it: but at the centre he finds the at first repellent insects that devour it.[21] Dahl depicts the true monsters as those supposedly made in the image of God. Eating imagery also pervades this story, as it does in *Charlie and the Chocolate Factory*: only James and Charlie eat modestly, everything else is voracity.

Above all there is the fantasy itself. Dahl is implicitly saying that if things do not behave like this, then they ought to. James is a challenge to conventional ways of thinking, as well as to authority. The book so violently upsets what we know as reality, so continually thrusts its absurdity before us, as to open the question of whether our own regulated world is not still more absurd. Dahl is here a pre-Beatles revolutionary, writing his own 'Yellow Submarine,' asking us to launch our own peach-like imaginations on the wildest of seas. This first children's story is Dahl's happiest and most continuously inventive.

By contrast, *Charlie and the Chocolate Factory*, while it has the same fairy tale plot of the wretched child made the cynosure of the world, is much more concerned with the urban and the manufactured. Where James eats a peach and travels over the sea, here Charlie eats chocolate and goes round Mr Wonka's factory. The narrative, directed by Mr Wonka, is much more controlled and structured, whereas the peach floats where it will. The chocolate bar is an image of the consumer society (then newly actualised in the factories of the 1960s turning out ever-new and exciting goods). Quite what Dahl's view of it is, is not clear. There is the moral of modest consumption, certainly, and the greed and selfishness of the other children who have winning tickets is spectacularly condemned. But Wonka as factory owner is a paradox. Those who chose his product, chocolate, above all else are damned; he whose factory stimulates greed denounces it. And he, the successful capitalist, is about to give his factory away to an open-hearted simpleton who could not run it for a day. Wonka's dual role as chocolate-maker and moral-maker are not compatible, unless we allegorise him as God, his factory as heaven raining blessings on mankind and the chocolate bars as human talents.

The dominant tone of the book is one of hectoring sadism, the other side of Dahl's wild energy. The great reward of having a winning ticket is not a gift, but admission to a series of tests, which serve as devices for harshly exposing the unfit: the whole story becomes a kind of moral knock-out competition. Yet it is not so much the morality that comes across as the glee of watching the nasty consumerist children suffer. Augustus Gloop is sucked up a pipe to the fudge-making machine, Violet Beauregarde is inflated to a giant blueberry ready to be crushed for juice, Veruca Salt is thrown down a rubbish chute into the main factory disposal pipe, and Steve Teavee is shrunk to a midget by Mr Wonka's magic television, and restored only by putting him in a stretching machine. This directly recalls Victorian torment fantasies from *Struwwelpeter* to *Speaking Likenesses*. The weaker sequel to *Charlie and the Chocolate Factory*, *Charlie and the Great Glass Elevator* (1973), in which Charlie follows – with his family – a rather roundabout route to his factory inheritance, lacks tension. Without antagonists on whom to exercise his sadistic and even misanthropic tendencies, Dahl languishes.

These two fantasies really cover Dahl's emotional range: later offerings, many of them highly popular, such as *The BFG* (1982), *The Witches* (1983) or *Matilda* (1988), veer rather more plainly to the savage side (particularly in the latter two). They are paranoid narratives, dealing throughout with monstrous people who are threats to children – horrible giants, a conspiracy of witches, a bullying headmistress – and who are all to be removed. Dahl's view of fantasy here is often that it is part of ordinary life: 'The most important fact you should know about REAL WITCHES is this... *REAL WITCHES dress in ordinary clothes and look very much like ordinary women. They live in ordinary houses and they work in ORDINARY JOBS.*' Where titles of Dahl's fantasy were previously 'James and the...' or 'Charlie and the...', now they are no longer two terms, for the real and the fantastic have fused. It is fair to say that by the 1980s Dahl's theme has altered from the 1960s expression of one's full abilities or enjoyment of the world to confronting one's most terrible fears, in the form of giants, witches and ogresses – fears which, though externalised in the opposition between these horrors and the children who see them, are nevertheless also expressions of a darker world within. Dahl's devils of the 1980s tap a strain of fantasy then becoming increasingly popular – that based on horror and paranoia.

A minor fantasy of the time that has proved enduringly popular is Clive King's *Stig of the Dump* (1963), about a little boy's discovery of a Stone Age boy[22] living in a nearby dump in a chalk-pit. Stig is displaced from his own time, though able to revisit it. Like other 1960s fantasies this has the idea of magic as coming out of the earth: we see the same thing in Alan Garner's books, in Dahl's *James and the Giant Peach*, Penelope Farmer's *The Magic Stone* (1964) and William Mayne's *Earthfasts* (1966) and *The Battlefield* (1967). King's particular interest here is in survival techniques and in exploiting and adapting one's physical environment. The two boys, who are soon friends, although Stig does not speak but only grunts or grins, spend their time in such pursuits as chopping and sawing a tree, making a chimney for Stig's cave out of tin cans, or hunting birds. In part Barney's meeting with Stig is an image of the bourgeois desire to rough it with the vulgar; but really, one of the truths that King has hit on is that little boys are perfect friends for Stone Agers, because their interests very often coincide. Of course, Barney goes home to his grandmother's comfortable modern house to eat and sleep, while Stig remains in his cave: whether Barney would really like to stay all the time in the wild is another matter. But the story may be partly responding to the national fear of nuclear holocaust, then at its height, and the emphasis on civil defence and survival.

Another theme of the book is the relativist one that people from the past are as intelligent as we are: Stig is continually thinking of uses for things that Barney could not have imagined, such as turning the struts of an umbrella into needles or using the cat-gut from an old tennis racket to string his bow; Barney may introduce Stig to the idea of a chimney for his choking fire, but it is not something he himself invented. In the end Barney is able to visit Stig's time in prehistoric Kent, and is impressed both by the people's manners and by their scientific abilities in moving large megaliths. The book's concern with the past makes it very 1960s, especially its presentation of the past turning up in the present, and the idea that one time is not finally separate from another.

In later 1960s children's fantasy a frequent theme is uncertain identity. In the 1950s the emphasis was on the conscious self, but that self could inhabit two different realities, whether Narnia, or Tom's Midnight Garden or Marianne's drawing of a house; and exceptionally in *The River Boy* the self was double and a function of the unconscious. In 1950s fantasy children broadly know and choose who they are, and the narratives are comparatively strongly directed and empirical. But the children of 1960s fantasy are far more passive, and the stories are – excluding Dahl – often more limp or dissipated or obscure. The fantastic side does most of the acting: the children react to it. One reason for this is that the fantasy is no longer based on moral growth, which presupposes responsibility for one's actions. It is rather about the nature of the self, often showing how people can exist in more than one mode, or how one reality may be penetrated by another – something rarely possible in 1950s fantasy where the fantastic was generally separated from the real. This interrogation of the self prepares the way for the presentation of the unconscious self in 1970s children's fantasy.

This can be seen in the fantasies of Penelope Farmer – *The Summer Birds* (1962), *The Magic Stone* (1964), *Emma in Winter* (1966), *Charlotte Sometimes* (1969) and *A Castle of Bone* (1972). These books are about children's experiences at home or at school, and involve them trying to make sense of their lives – a process in which fantasy is made to act as a catalyst rather than being of interest in itself. What is often portrayed is a change or a loss of self, in part reflective of children's uncertain grasp on their lives. But for the first time in such domestic fantasy the children's self-discovery is conducted without reference to parents, or to any ethic of fitting in with the family or society. This leaves the self more open to instability.

These books are often about children making friendships, as a symbol of how far they can make friends with themselves. In *The Summer Birds* a strange boy comes to school and befriends the children by teaching them to fly. *The Magic Stone* describes the meetings of bourgeois Caroline and spiky working-class Alice, each of them missing something the other has. Emma in *Emma in Winter* gradually comes to value and care for the initially repulsive Bobby Fumpkins. In *Charlotte Sometimes* the heroine is transported back fifty years to her school as it was in 1918, and has to make friends with girls who will in her own time be senior citizens. In *A Castle of Bone* by contrast a group of close friends fall out through their adventures with a magic cupboard, which is in one sense a symbol of the unconscious.

Farmer's protagonists are often unsure of themselves. Emma is continually guilty at her mockery of Bobby Fumpkins, Caroline is made perpetually uneasy by Alice's directness, Hugh in *A Castle of Bone* is a gawky adolescent who only finally learns to accept himself and enter his own 'castle of bone.' And a constant theme is the number of possible selves we have. This is seen in the relationships themselves, where each absorbs something of the other. At the end of *Charlotte Sometimes* Charlotte realises that 'she could never escape from being Clare. The memory of it, if nothing else, was rooted in her mind. What had happened to her would go on mattering.' Often children are shown lapsing out of themselves, to become one with the earth or sea (*The Magic Stone*, 45–9, 95–6, 107–11, 132–8), the evolution of life (*Emma in Winter*) or with the air (*The Summer Birds*). In *Charlotte Sometimes* Charlotte becomes Clare and vice versa, and in *A Castle of Bone* the boy Penn is magically transformed to the infant he once was. In the later *Year King* (1977) one identical twin keeps finding himself shut in the person of his brother, who wants to kill him; and later still in *Penelope* (1994) a modern girl finds her self being taken over by an eighteenth-century relation.

Identity is further made unstable to us by the way Emma and Charlotte of *The Summer Birds* reappear as separate protagonists in *Emma in Winter* and *Charlotte Sometimes*. There is also a sense in which the protagonists of different books can be seen as together making up one composite character, for Emma in *The Summer Birds* is about nine, and then twelve in *Emma in Winter*; Charlotte in the next book is around fourteen, and Hugh in the last (published three years later) is about seventeen. The same parallelism between books and character ages was observed in Alan Garner's fantasies of 1960–67, but without this implication.

A similar question of identity occurs even with the literary sources of the books – again as in Garner, though in another way. For most of them do indeed have a close literary source, so close as almost to involve what could be called an identity problem in itself. *The Summer Birds*, with its fairy boy who teaches the children to fly and then seeks to take them with him to his land of the ever-young, is a far more direct reworking of J. M. Barrie's *Peter Pan* than even

Philippa Pearce's *Tom's Midnight Garden*. *Emma in Winter* describes a dream-journey to the remote past that has H. G. Wells's *The Time Machine* as its inverse source. *Charlotte Sometimes* is closely indebted to Marghanita Laski's *The Victorian Chaise-Longue* (1953) and to Pearce's *Tom's Midnight Garden*. The magical cupboard in *A Castle of Bone* is an unashamed theft from C. S. Lewis's *The Lion, the Witch and the Wardrobe*,[23] and the idea of a teenager being transformed into his baby self comes (in reverse again) from E. Nesbit's *Five Children and It*, where the baby Lamb is turned into himself as a young man. *William and Mary* (1974), the story of two children with a magic half-talisman who travel to Atlantis or the deeps of the Pacific Ocean in search of the other half, comes straight from E. Nesbit's *The Story of the Amulet* (1906). Most writers either conceal or modify their debts when they are so great, but Farmer leaves them obvious. And this may be because she is showing that her texts do not have sufficient identity to stand on their own.

There is also a certain random and directionless character to the books, which furthers this sense of insecurity. The children in *The Summer Birds* eventually learn to fly, but the strange boy leaves and their skill is lost. The boy himself appears out of nowhere, and only at the end does he say he is the last surviving fairy boy looking for recruits. The magical separation of the piece of metal from the rock in *The Magic Stone* has no evident magic effect. Why in *Emma in Winter* Emma Makepeace and Bobby Fumpkins come to share the same strange dream is left a mystery; and their flying journey in time, back through the Ice Ages and the Age of Reptiles to the beginning of life, has of itself no particular purpose, even while it may symbolise a voyage back through the subconscious. The origin of the magic bed in *Charlotte Sometimes*, and why it works only on these two particular girls is left unexplored; and Charlotte comes back from her journey to 1918 with little more than an album of memories. The cupboard in *A Castle of Bone* generally moves whatever is put into it back to an earlier point in its creation, but whether that point is very far back or less so is completely indeterminate. A brass button put in it on one occasion is turned into a pool of molten metal, and on another to the two pieces of ore from which the metal was fashioned; while at another time the process is reversed, and what were its elements are turned back to a brass button. The abrupt nature of the magic in the books, found under hedges, turning up at school, or waking one up fifty years into the past, is expressive of a world in which reality and the self are unstable.

Although the stories all end 'for the best,' we are made very aware of how contingent that end may be. Mere chance allowed Charlotte to sleep once more in the magic bed and return to our world. Penn might easily have been taken further back than babyhood by the cupboard. Emma might not have stayed true to her friendship with Bobby Fumpkins at the last. The neatnesses, the sense of cause and effect, that we usually find in children's fantasy, are here challenged. The characters may develop, but it is also possible that they do not, as in *The Summer Birds* or *Charlotte Sometimes*. Nor even can we be sure that there really is a learning process in the other three, when we see how the plots of the stories often do not go anywhere in particular. In *A Castle of Bone*, exciting magical events are often dropped for the banal, as when Penn's transformation to a baby is followed by long accounts of the girls' looking after him and of Hugh's embarrassed visits to the chemist's for a bottle-teat. The castle of bone is pregnant with meaning, but it may at the same time have no meaning at all.[24]

Further uncertainty is caused by the only tentative identification of the magic with a larger and more mythic reality. Much exciting suggestion, for instance, is created from the magic cupboard's supposed construction out of apple-wood from the Garden of Eden (again drawing on C. S. Lewis, this time *The Magician's Nephew*); but there is no certainty. The strange rock in *The Magic Stone* is often linked with the one from which Arthur drew Excalibur (33, 37, 60, 91–2, 117); yet the identification is rather more surmised than proved. The journey back to the beginning of time in *Emma in Winter* is a shared dream, but it also seems watched by a supernatural reality, in the form of a satanic pair of gigantic eyes.

We find this theme of uncertain identity also in the 1960s children's fantasies of William Mayne, here more in relation to time. Mayne portrays the present as a mere surface through which the past may burst at seeming random, and time itself as no more securely linear than coiled in series. Like Garner's and Farmer's books, each of his novels shows the fantastic invading our world. In *Earthfasts* (1966), an eighteenth-century drummer-boy who has lost his way underground suddenly appears on the moor to two Yorkshire boys, who befriend him and try without success to return him to his own time. In addition, a number of ancient British giants and even the army of King Arthur also surface. *The Battlefield* (1967) portrays an old mud-filled battlefield that has supernatural legends attached to it: two children discover an old cannon buried there, and have it pulled up with a tractor, after which the field floods the nearby village. The implication is that the past still lives in the present, and the supernatural aura of the field gains a certain reality. *Over the Hills and Far Away* (1968) describes a temporary time-change between a Romano-British witch and three modern children. In all these stories we find that the past is constantly transgressive, that it no longer keeps to its 'proper place' (as, say, in *Tom's Midnight Garden*).

Mayne's vision is also a seemingly relativist one, an overcoming of temporal provincialism. We are led to see that the past has its own independent concerns, is not merely a stage in the process of producing us. The forces that lie beneath the ground in *Earthfasts* are greater than any that we know. Nellie Jack John the drummer-boy was spurred by his eighteenth-century friends to go and look for

King Arthur's treasure, and unwittingly loosed these forces when, in the dark, he took away a burning candle he found there. The three children who go back to the Britain of A.D. 450 in *Over the Hills and Far Away* have no conception of the different culture in which they find themselves, or of their significance to it, and are saved from destruction only by the devotion and self-sacrifice of a man they know only as 'Bayhead.' The whole idea of the past as something discarded is questioned by having so many meetings between it and our world. Indeed, by having not one but several layers of the past which come to life in *Earthfasts*, this mixing of times is more fully accomplished.

But Mayne's relativist vision is more functional than final: it is part of a constantly widening perspective leading in the end to a form of absolute reality. In this vision, we are all parts of a history in which the various members can still speak to and address one another, with or without pleasure. It is in fact a history of the living community that is England, and particularly Yorkshire, in which the connections are all made through the earth of the country. It is a strange red stone found in a cave that opens the gateway between old and modern Yorkshire in *Over the Hills*; a rock that holds or releases the mud slide in *The Battlefield*; and a cave in a rock that houses England's promise, King Arthur, in *Earthfasts*.

Mayne's fantasy contrasts with that of Penelope Farmer, where the relation with time is more exclusively personal. Charlotte's travel to the past in *Charlotte Sometimes* simply relates to her, and the time journey of the two children in *Emma in Winter* is quite arbitrary. Mayne's 1960s books deal not just with individual children, but with whole communities, both in the present and across time. Again, the magic in Farmer's books comes from no consistent source: now it is a flying boy, now a stone, now a shared dream, a dormitory bed, a clothes cupboard. That is part of her vision of the frequent indeterminacy of the world. By contrast Mayne is here much more of a writer of metaphysical fantasy, in which the universe is made to seem ultimately ordered and even purposeful.

In *Earthfasts*, Mayne has changed the debate between scientific scepticism and belief regarding the supernatural that we saw suspended in *A Grass Rope*. Here the ever-burning candle that Nellie Jack John brings up with him from the earth is unresponsive to any scientific test; here a doctor is prepared to believe in the existence of a family goblin, or boggart; and a boy who comes back from the dead confounds a coroner's verdict. Here the magic is strained through a large number of forensic filter papers, and still emerges unchanged. This demonstrates the greater confidence of the fantastic in the 1960s: but it also suggests a readiness to believe on Mayne's own part.[25]

Mayne's work exemplifies the way in which 1960s children's fantasy is concerned with the past, whereas in the 1950s it was also directed to the present or the future. Apart from Roald Dahl, there is hardly any 1960s writer who does not introduce a journey to the near or far past, or who does not have the past intruding on the present, whether in the form of an old myth of tragic love, a boy from the Stone Age, or a schoolgirl from 1918. This is not true just of fantasy: the 1960s are marked by a large amount of historical fiction for children. This has much to do with the already-mentioned search for roots in this decade. It has an effect on the nature of fantastic narrative. In the 1950s when the accent was as much on growth and futurity, we find the fantasy story often dominated by a single idea and forward movement: save Narnia, find a new home, prove a unicorn real, help a sick child, restore a cat. But in 1960s fantasy, again with the exception of Roald Dahl, we find a more ruminative mode. It is partly that the characters are much more acted on by the magic than acting and choosing as in 1950s fantasy: events pour in at seeming random and one can only struggle to make sense of them, as in *Earthfasts* or *The Owl Service*. But it is also quite simply that the gaze is much more backwards. So it is that in *Charlotte Sometimes* or *Over the Hills and Far Away* the interest is as much being in 1918 or 450 as in trying to get back to one's own time; or in *The Owl Service* we watch the day-to-day relations of three children and only gradually learn that they form a pattern based on an old story. In short, 1960s narratives are characterised by an interest in 'being' rather than in 'becoming.'

Other minor time fantasies of this period include Joan G. Robinson's *When Marnie Was There* (1967), in which lonely foster-child Anna unknowingly makes friends with her grandmother as a Victorian child; and Ruth Arthur's *The Whistling Boy* (1969), in which young Kirsty befriends a boy who is under a magic spell from the past. Unlike other 1960s children's fantasies, both these books are about putting the past aside and accepting oneself; *Marnie* recalls *Tom's Midnight Garden*. When Anna learns her true family identity – in this fantasy there is one – she becomes reconciled to her own time. In *The Whistling Boy* Kirsty helps Jake find the magic pipe which has nearly driven him to drowning in the sea, while she learns to overcome her long objection to her father's second wife. Here the past can sap rather than strengthen the self, and is rejected. While these books have the 1960s interest in identity, their moral message of accepting oneself and the world looks back a decade.

Wholly different kinds of past are depicted in the fantasies of Joan Aiken and Rosemary Harris. In *The Wolves of Willoughby Chase* (1962) Aiken sets us in an alternative England where James III has recently succeeded to the throne in 1832. Were we not supplied with the brief 'Note' that tells us this, we would not know where or when we are, as young Sylvia travels in winter from London to Willoughby Chase by a train and coach incessantly pestered by wolves. And even with it, we are rarely in this book given any further historical identification, since the main concern is with the doings at the hall, in which the evil governess Miss

Slighcarp tries to seize young Bonnie's inheritance while her parents are missing. For long stretches we are tempted to think of the setting as being 'our' England of about the 1840s. Furthermore, the whole narrative reads as a pastiche of *Oliver Twist* and *Jane Eyre*, not to mention being indebted for its entire plot to T. H. White's *Mistress Masham's Repose*, so that our experience is one simultaneously of the familiar and the alien, and of the fictive and the 'real.' The identity of the material is thus uncertain, and we have a continual sense of displacement.

Joan Aiken's books have little fantasy in the sense of magic: indeed what is often more magical for her is human nature itself.[26] Sometimes she plays with the possibility of the supernatural, as in *The Whispering Mountain* (1968), where an ancient prophecy concerning the mountain 'screaming' comes true: but this is explained as an escape of hot vapour from the depths of what is in fact a latent volcano. In *Night Birds on Nantucket* (1966) a pink whale appears, and a giant Hanoverian cannon is aimed at King James III from across the Atlantic; in *The Cuckoo Tree* (1971) several schemers move St Paul's Cathedral towards the Thames on rollers; and in *The Stolen Lake* (1981) a missing lake has to be recovered from Roman South America. What rather interests Aiken is subverting what we take to be real or unreal, so that we never know quite where we are or what is possible. Indeed the image conveyed by her books is one of wildly jostling planes of being. In *The Whispering Mountain* a whole series of preposterous Welsh characters is thrown together with a loquacious Sultan, a vicious Marquess, an incompetent pair of Cockney thieves and a lost race of dwarfs. In her love of playing with reality Aiken anticipates something of the character of 1980s children's fantasy.

The sense of contingency is added to by our sense that the alternative past of Aiken's fiction is just one of the many possible outcomes of history, and one chosen by nothing more significant than the author's taste in times. It is also continually on the verge of changing into a past world nearer to our own, with a fresh Hanoverian plot in each book to remove the Stuart James and replace him with a George. Reflecting this, there is a recurrent theme of hidden or mistaken identity, where people either hide their true nature from others, or do not know it. Miss Slighcarp the governess of *The Wolves*, Mr and Mrs Twite in *Black Hearts in Battersea*, Slighcarp the mate in *Night Birds*, and Colonel Fitzpatrick in *The Cuckoo Tree* are all deceiving plotters; while Sylvia and Simon of the first two books, Justin in the second, and the Pit People in *The Whispering Mountain* are all people who have lost touch with their identity.

This theme of uncertain identity is also seen, this time as imitation, in Rosemary Harris's reworking of the biblical story of Noah and the Flood, *The Moon in the Cloud* (1968). Here Harris turns myth into pseudo-history: God's purpose for mankind is not mentioned, and He is humanised to the level of a tetchy farmer who feels like shooting a few crows. The Ark and the Flood scarcely feature, and the Flood itself covers only Canaan, Egypt (Kemi) being left wholly unscathed. This makes the whole exercise of saving an example of every species somewhat pointless. Much of the story is set in Kemi, in the court of a king, whither the animal-trainer Reuben is sent in search of a sacred cat and two lions for the Ark. Throughout, we are made to feel displaced, at both a literary and a narrative level. However, at the centre of the story is a delight in the relationships among a variety of characters,[27] which Harris has preserved as in an Ark of her own. The cat Cefalu, the dog Benoni, the surly camel Anak, and young Reuben, together form an amusing group as they squabble their way over the desert; and later, in Kemi, the growing friendship between Reuben and the young king Merenkere is subtly portrayed, as are the machinations around the king of his vizier and rival high priests. A further two much less fantastic books, *The Shadow on the Sun* (1970) and *Bright and Morning Star* (1972), trace Reuben's later adventures in Kemi with the king.

Like Harris's *The Moon in the Cloud*, the ghost stories of Leon Garfield - *Mr Corbett's Ghost* (1968) and *The Ghost Downstairs* (1972) - are also imitations, this time of Dickens, particularly of his *A Christmas Carol* (1843) and 'The Signal-Man' (1866). Each is set in an imaginary London (à la Aiken), and each involves a crime and (an induced) repentance; each in a way is an imitation of the other. In *Mr Corbett's Ghost*, the apothecary's assistant Partridge is given supernatural help in taking away the life of his oppressive master, whose ghost then accompanies him through a phantasmal metropolitan landscape, until Partridge comes to realise that it has more piteous humanity in it than he ever suspected. Both repent, and Mr Corbett's ghost is once more returned to life. *The Ghost Downstairs* is a not dissimilar tale of a rapacious solicitor's clerk, Mr Fast, who makes a Faustian bargain: Fast learns humanity through his pain, and dies trying to stop a train he believes is about to be wrecked.

Though these stories end happily, with reassurance and the triumph of goodness, we feel how easily they could have finished otherwise. Only the transformations of the supernatural monster who collects lives in *Mr Corbett's Ghost*, and of the hitherto entirely vicious Mr Fast, serve to bring about these outcomes. Most of the narratives are filled with images of unreality. Ghosts are at the centre; and the characters move through a night-time or fog-bound city which is not any historical London. The ghost of Mr Corbett insists to Partridge, "'I'll not betray ... not I'" so often that the 'not I' begins to take on a meaning of its own: the ghost, in being a ghost, is a 'not I,' but Partridge, having himself made it a ghost, is also a 'not I,' a not-self too, and wanders for much of the story through a phantasmagoric land on the frontiers between life and death.[28] In *The Ghost Downstairs*, Mr Fast meets and talks with himself as a child, and realises that his supposed cunning in tricking Mr Fishbane in his bargain has cut him off from the springs of his own life – a life which he can only recover by ending it.[21]

But the sense of unreality in these stories also comes, as in Penelope Farmer's novels, from their proximity to literary sources. So close are they to Dickens's idiom and the plots of particular stories, that they begin to become almost an apocryphal part of his œuvre. Garfield has found himself only by losing himself – apt enough parallel, doubtless, with the spiritual patterns of his own stories, but still a startling literary self-surrender. We may explain this in terms of the needs of his individual tales, but the likeness to other authors of the decade, with their prominent literary indebtednesses, is more significant. Here it would seem that these authors are not confident enough of their own visions to present them on their own, but prefer to filter them through more celebrated voices and texts.

But it seems insufficient simply to personalise it. It is just as likely that this 'cross-dressing' reflects something in the world itself. For in many 1960s children's fantasies we have seen a loss of the authority that was expressed in the fantasy of the previous decade. Parents are sometimes less present, or less reliable; children can be orphans, or their fathers and mothers may marry again, or they are fostered, or they simply quarrel with their 'betters.' Children are more challenged and challenging than before. The result of such alienation is inevitably self-doubt, as we see it in some of these fantasies. In such a context it might not be surprising that other 'authorities' should be invoked to exert control – the past, literary sources and old myths. And indeed across the 1950s and 1960s we have seen the gradual replacement of the pastoral with the past, as a value in children's fantasy. Pastoral was a sign of adult dissatisfaction with the present, a longing to get back to a better and simpler world, but in the new children's fantasy the past comes into the present and gives meaning to it, even while its arrival may disrupt it.

Yet while authority still exists in these (unstated) forms, there is much more democracy in the fantasy of this decade. Alan Garner puts high magic in the middle of a Manchester slum, and has Welsh and English children clash over their social and national differences. Roald Dahl has a poor boy made prodigiously rich. Penelope Farmer has snobbish physical beauty befriend physical ungainliness (*Emma in Winter*), a bourgeois girl make friends with a lower-class one (*The Magic Stone*), and time itself turn into a medium of exchange (*Charlotte Sometimes*). In William Mayne's *Earthfasts*, the drummer-boy and the giants who arrive in the modern world in part represent a new earthiness in the lives of the middle-class boy protagonists; so too with the journey back of the children in *Over the Hills and Far Away* to the 'barbaric' English Dark Ages. The same process is at work in Clive King's *Stig of the Dump*, in the friendship of modern

5 REBELLION AND REACTION: THE 1970s

In the 1950s and 1960s, English children's fantasy was often social in tendency, in that the story involved either fitting in with a given collective or, in the more secure and conformist 1960s, making friends with often very different people or creatures. Lewis's children found their allotted roles in Narnia; Tom of *Tom's Midnight Garden* became reconciled to living in his own time; Dahl's James shared the giant peach with a group of huge insects; Farmer's Emma slowly overcame her repugnance at Bobby Fumpkins; and an eighteenth-century drummer-boy gradually became friends with two modern Yorkshire teenagers. But in the 1970s, children's fantasies are often without this social impulse. Their protagonists are frequently the outsider or the rebel. They question the family or society much more, and sometimes they even undermine the certainties of the reader. Because of their individualism, their fantasy is often that of the inner world, the psyche, unintegrated with the world outside; and they are full of images of self-enclosure and paranoia. As a result, the problem of identity in these fantasies becomes much more acute.

At the same time, however, there is still a strong conservative impulse at work in several writers, a desire to reconnect with a past and traditional values that are now more distant. Here identity can still find metaphysical assurance, if sometimes no other, in being caught up into larger mythical narratives and trans-temporal societies. Nevertheless, the fact that such reassurance has now become a primary aim, as we will see in the fantasies of Penelope Lively, is a sign of increased desperation.

Thus the fantasy writers of the 1970s tend to be mainly either revolutionary against perceived tyranny, or reactionary towards diminishing values. The one results in protagonists who insist on themselves or are rebellious against convention, and the other on those who give the self up to a larger system. On occasion, however, both impulses may be seen in different areas of the same work. And most of the writers, however anarchic their outlooks, are in the end conservative enough within the genre to create relatively ordered fantastic worlds with happy outcomes.

William Mayne's fantasies of the 1970s, *A Game of Dark* (1971) and *It* (1975) are more on the side of rejection of the past than were, say, his *A Grass Rope* (1955) or *Earthfasts* (1966). In *A Game of Dark* a boy is rebelling against the crushing influence of his cold Nonconformist parents, and particularly against his dying father, who will not give him any love. The boy, Donald Jackson, also inhabits as 'Jackson' a fantastic-seeming world ravaged by a hideous worm, of which he is elected the latest in a line of doomed knightly opponents. Mayne's fantasy has always suggested the unconscious mind, in its use of the underground or the hidden or pent-up past (*The Battlefield*), but in *A Game of Dark* this comes into prominence. In the end Jackson kills the dragon and then, as his father dies, has to choose which world to live in, that of the dubious hero or that of the ruined teenager.

By interweaving the two worlds more and more closely through the narrative, until Donald's switches from one to another occur within a sentence (125), the story suggests that they reflect one another. The huge, phallic white worm with its terrible stench can be seen as Donald's dream-image of his father, viewed as the tyrant, the Nobodaddy, that Freud says every son must kill. The city, which has to feed the worm with cattle and even humans to keep it from breaking in, represents the desperate forces of reason and civility against chaos and death. And in the end it is the methods not of the civilised hero but of the trickster that kill the worm. Jackson does not feel he has killed it properly; and in the modern world, though he has 'killed' his own evil self and learned, briefly, to love his father, he has done so without having to show it, for this father is dead. 'There was no more breathing. Donald lay and listened to the quiet, and went to sleep, consolate.'

However, there remain two worlds side by side: the one does not exist simply to reflect the other, indeed each is so vivid that it cannot finally be said *which* of them reflects the other.[1] The story is also a search for reality, since Donald's problem is also that nothing is real to him. He does not know who his real parents are or what world he belongs to, because he has had no love, and therefore no home. '"Who am I, who are you? Are you the man lying in the bed? Is the man in the bed you? Who is my mother? Where did I come from?"' (123). It is only when he lives by his own lights in killing the dragon, and not by any knightly code, nor by his parents' imposed Christianity, that Jackson and Donald come to know who they are, and can choose which world to live in. At that point the protagonist gains his full name: he becomes Donald Jackson, rather than the two divided.

A striking feature of the novel is how much Mayne addresses children, while at the same time dealing with themes and topics which would normally be found in adult fiction. Hatred of one's parents, death of people close to one, terrible fears from the night-side of life, decay, corruption, stench, hostility to religion and the very nature of being itself, all these exist without strain in the book, and never quite go away. Here we have a children's fantasy that does not simply have a happy ending: Donald is only 'consolate.' In *A Game of Dark* Mayne shows us a world with which we cannot easily be integrated.

Alienation, living inside one's head, and loneliness are also portrayed throughout the 1970s children's fantasy of Helen Cresswell. *The Outlanders* (1970) is set in another world, where a family leave a city to search for a strange golden boy who once stayed with them. (The very use of secondary worlds with an uneasy relation to our own is a sign of alienation, of displacement, characteristic of much fantasy of this decade. Our reality is still the main one, but it is beginning to leach away into others with as much ontological weight. This is later to go the whole distance with 1980s 'postmodernism.') The golden boy, for whom the family search, was driven out by the townsfolk, who also follow in the hope of being led to gold. This journey is like one into the mind,[2] while at the same time recalling the American Dream: the family cross the Dry Mountains into the Mid-Lands by covered wagon, and thence to the sea, where they find the boy and their desire – for the boy gives back the father his lost gift of poetry and song. The more material gold that the townspeople seek is not there.

The book sometimes reads like a young person's version of Angela Carter's 'way-out' *Heroes and Villains* (1969) or *The Passion of New Eve* (1977). A similar creative anarchy is espoused, and an attack on all social barriers. The town shuts the family in, and so does its bigotry, until they leave it. The family is held together by love rather than rules, and can welcome the stowaway girl Emily. Their journey is away from the built self and the collective into the deconstructed wilderness, to find a new vision. In part it is a journey into the imagination. Each of the characters in the end journeys alone, and meets the golden boy separately; and he gives each his or her own secret name, or true identity. When this happens, an old townswoman, who has for long repressed her secret desire to be a witch, lest the people kill her, throws off her fear and enters on her wild vocation.

This love of the anarchic is at the heart of Helen Cresswell's 1970s fantasies. In her Carnegie-honoured *The Night-Watchmen* (1969) she deals with a pair of visionary tramps, outsiders who inhabit a wider and more dangerous supernatural world than we know, but still one immensely fascinating to the boy protagonist Henry. Her *Up the Pier* (1967) is at first a picture of the imagination gone repressive and wrong, in an old man so possessive of his memories that he has imprisoned the 'ghosts' of his long-past family on the pier he owns. In the end, however, the heroine Carrie sets them all free. Yet even then she herself has become in a way possessive of them: the story partly symbolises a writer's love of his or her characters, and reluctance to part with them.

Enthusiasm for the wild and uncontrolled is also seen in *The Bongleweed* (1975), which, following the gigantic precedent of Cresswell's *The Piemakers* (1967), describes the chance growth of an immense but beautiful plant in a compost heap. Most people want to kill it, but the gardener, who is continually patronised by his bourgeois employer, lets '"nature take its course"'. The wild and exuberant Bongleweed, whose nature is mirrored in the gardener's rebellious daughter Becky, is in effect a critique of repressive English society. It is also the unconscious imagination that breaks down the rules of the conscious self. Similarly Cresswell's next fantasy, *The Winter of the Birds* (1975), portrays the transformation of the lonely and fearful people of an urban street by the electrifying presence of a semi-angelic Irishman called Finn. The story ends, 'Anything can happen, from now on.'[3]

In Helen Cresswell's later fantasies, however, the imagination and the wildness outside society are seen as more of a threat: early radicalism has turned to a more conservative view. *The Secret World of Polly Flint* (1983), *Moondial* (1987), *The Watchers* (1993) and *Stonestruck* (1995) are increasingly concerned with the terror of lost security rather than with self-expressive freedom. In all four books, parents who have been sick, disabled, absent or negligent, are cured and reunited with their children in the end, but not before the children have been exposed to a world of threat. Liberation is still a theme of these books, but now it is more liberation from abnormal entrapment than from social convention – from being stuck in time or preyed on by an evil human monster. The theme is partly anticipated in *Up the Pier*, but there it is more the breakdown of possessive habits of mind that is asked, than the overthrow of an external enemy.

Fantasy, for Helen Cresswell in the 1970s, is on the whole 'inside one's head,' and her characters are on their own. This does not mean it has only mental existence: it means that it comes into its own in the mind, where alone one can be free and rebellious.[4] Young Harry in *The Night-Watchmen* realises at the end he has no proof of his fantastic experience, but for him it continues to live in his memory:

> In the end there was really only one thing of which he could be quite certain.
> That whenever he heard a train hooting in the night, whenever he saw a tunnel or a hole in the road, he would think of Josh and Caleb, and remember that once, at any rate, they had been as real to him as the fingers on his own hand. (124)

The 'golden boy' in *The Outlanders* is in effect a part of the mind itself, the imagination. Carrie in *Up the Pier* realises that her own mind has been partly responsible for the wrenching of the family out of their time, and says, '"You're mine. All of you. And I set you free!"' (143). *The Bongleweed* ends with Becky telling the benighted boy Jason that all is not finished, that there will be another kind of Bongleweed, and what kind '"I haven't decided yet!"' The world may be without the Bongleweed, 'But now it was a world where the Bongleweed had been, and that would make all the difference.'

The Winter of the Birds is perhaps the most elaborate picture of this idea. Old Mr Rudge in his house has visions of steel birds that move on wires and hiss, and which menace the lives of people in the street below. Living as he does, cut off from society and even from time and space, he is considered mad: and certainly his view of himself, as custodian of the awful truth and prophet to the world, recalls the insane astronomer in Samuel Johnson's *Rasselas* (1759). But for Helen Cresswell Mr Rudge's vision is both imagination and truth. The birds, with their awful mechanical regularity, are in a sense symbols of 'our' regulated and spiritually frozen lives;[5] but at the same time they are real horrors of the sort we often find in Helen Cresswell's work, whether it is the haunting 'Greeneyes' in *The Night-Watchmen*, the menacing Miss Raven in *Moondial*, or the demonic Enemy in *The Watchers* – figures of nightmare, images of trauma, but also real, though invisible. Though they never appear, they are always there, until the sky is cleaned of them by love. The whole novel is founded on this fusion of what is in one's head with what is in the outer world, by a narrative method which is divided between the narrator and two of the protagonists, the boy Edward and Mr Rudge, writing down their own parts of the story. Living solely in one's head is dangerous, Edward comes to see: but it can allow you to see truth, if sometimes one-sidedly (177).

The theme of 'inside one's head' is less pronounced in Helen Cresswell's books of the 1980s and 1990s, where the fantastic is given more objective reality. There is no sense that Minty in *Moondial* dreamt the strange children she meets, and Miss Raven's arrival and interest in them supports this. The 'time-gypsies' in *Polly Flint* are real enough, both to the child and to 'Old Mazy': in contrast to the vagrants of *The Night-Watchmen*, there is clear evidence of their presence, in the tree with Polly's initials carved on it. And in *The Watchers* there 'really' is a devil, in the form of the leather-jacketed enemy, and a kind of heaven guarded by the angelic Quantum and the angelic bag-lady. The change is partly due to postmodernism and the idea of the multiverse – of our world no longer being as the primary reality, but existing side by side with other worlds with equal claim.

Nevertheless the inner world of the authoress herself does seem to be displayed throughout her fantasy, in the constant sense of threat, of approaching horror, which gives her books an air of paranoia. People are often being watched: watching and waiting is one of Helen Cresswell's recurrent themes. Despite the social rebelliousness of her 1970s books, there remains a certain helplessness about them, a feeling of being up against forces that can be defeated only within fantasy. And this sense of helplessness is furthered by the way that the freedom reached by the characters is largely 'inside the head.' In this Cresswell may be reflecting the comparative political cynicism of the 1970s after the heady idealism of the 1960s; this was a decade marked by an increased sense that politics, economics and society were beyond the power of revolutionary change, having become the tools of political tyrannies and global monopolies.

Individualism and rebellion against systems is more unambiguously portrayed in Richard Adams's *Watership Down* (1972). Told originally by Adams to his two young daughters, this is his only children's book,[6] yet from the outset it challenges the comfortable pastoral assumptions and the frequent anthropomorphism of children's animal fantasy. Adams gives us a group of wild animals gripped by the imperative of survival, and a pastoral landscape bristling with threats, mostly from man. Death is always close, and reproduction its only answer: both these topics were unusual in children's fiction before this time.[7]

The book is full of a sense of the individual, even down to making its land-scape a very particular one near Newbury in Wiltshire, so that we can follow the rabbits' journey to find a new warren across the Ordnance Survey map for the district. This landscape has sharply distinguished soils, smells, weather and crea-tures, and all of them are seen from a rabbit's point of view. Each of the rabbits is a unique character, from the prophetic Fiver to the sturdy leader Bigwig; nor are they our idea of rabbits, for they have lives, behaviour and language of which we know nothing. Indeed Adams increases their difference by allowing them to show qualities we would otherwise assign to humans. There is scarcely a moment early in the book when the reader, having been inclined to see the rabbits as humans in rabbit clothes, is not pulled up short by their sheer peculiarity. Man cannot, as it were, take them over, cannot monopolise what they are. The rabbits have no history; nor has their society evolved. They make no mention of a rabbit past outside that of their own lives. What they have is a mythology, but it is a mythology not about a god but about a rabbit trickster, a Brer Rabbit, who con-tinually sets his wits against a god, who in turn secretly enjoys the challenge.

The individualism in *Watership Down* is also seen in its opposition to societies that tyrannise or impede thought. The book starts with visionary Fiver's intuition of a horror about to befall the Sandleford warren (it will be gassed by humans before being levelled for building). But the leader of the warren, the Threarah, rejects the warning, and later pays the price. The band who leave encounter on their journey a group of well-fed rabbits who, in return for rich food, have made themselves the 'cattle' of a farmer who can snare them when he will for their meat. These rabbits have the fatalistic emptiness of those who have given them-selves away. At another farm the band release four caged rabbits that are too used to captivity to escape. Later, they come upon a crowded warren ruled by a huge rabbit called General Woundwort, a sort of rabbit Stalin, who runs a totalitarian and highly secretive society. All these failed rabbit societies are characterised by rigidities of thought that shut them off from truth. In the end Woundwort is overthrown, and a new lapine democracy is set up in Watership Down.

The mythic figure who is the ideal of the travelling band, the Ulyssean trickster El-ahrairah, is the archetypal outsider. He lives by his wits, and takes pleasure in showing he can outwit anyone else. Most of his tricks involve escaping people's clutches so that he can remain himself. He is the rabbit who defies walls, both in escaping over them and in penetrating them to steal. He lives by no-one's standards but his own. This is not quite the situation of the wanderer-rabbits, for they have to cooperate as a society, but their bottom line is this challenge to convention and to static thought or control from outside – indeed to the whole apparatus of what we know as civilisation.

Adams even has a place for a mind that can defy the laws of time and space. Fiver the rabbit-seer can perceive disaster coming to Sandleford warren; he senses that the well-fed rabbits of Frith Copse have death hanging over them; he can send out his mind to pinpoint the wounded Hazel stuck in a pipe; and he has dreadful premonitions about General Woundwort. At first thought of as a freak, Fiver is gradually consulted as a prophet, and has something of the place of a shaman in the group.[8] But his is an instinctual intelligence, derived from his sense of smell and from so close an intimacy with the world that he is part of it.

The other reality behind the book, however, is that rabbits as we know them would be helpless before the approaching destruction of their warren – quite unable to foresee it, and even if they did, to act on the knowledge. In our understanding of them, rabbits do not have intelligent choice. Indeed they go into states of paralysis at danger – we all know the results on country roads. Adams calls it *tharn*. In *Watership Down*, however, it comes not just from terror, but from a failure of will, ranging from the complacent Threarah of Sandleford Warren to the passive subjects of Woundwort's dictatorship. By contrast, Adams's band of survivor rabbits defy events and impose their wills on the world, shaping a course to their own Canaan.[9] The book thus plays our 'knowledge' of rabbits against a possible alternative, to put over the more strongly its ethic of self-determination.

But if such individualism has a happy outcome in *Watership Down*, this is less the case in Adams's subsequent 1970s animal books – *Shardik* (1974) and *The Plague Dogs* (1977). Here the societies and systems fled by the escaping beasts do not remain passive but hunt them down. These books are narratives of pursuit, pictures of wild and 'dangerous' individuality driven by society into a corner or else torn down. Clearly Adams moves from an optimistic to a more pessimistic view of the possibilities of individual freedom symbolised in his animal characters.

Watership Down differs from earlier animal books in that Adams is describing a largely alien society living within our own. Apart from Walter de la Mare's *The Three Mulla-Mulgars* – to which Adams is indebted – most previous animal stories did not have such independent reality in our world. They might awaken nostalgia for pastoral (*The Wind in the Willows*), or for human communication with the wild (*The Jungle Books, Doctor Dolittle*), or make animal worlds that partly imitate ours (Beatrix Potter), or provide amusement (the *Pooh* books). But to make something independent of human desire, an animal society standing on its own inside ours, upsets this convention. And Adams's book is followed by others doing the same, such as Colin Dann's *The Animals of Farthing Wood* (1979), William Horwood's *Duncton Wood* (1980), W. J. Corbett's *The Song of Pentecost* (1982), and their various sequels. Such a secondary reality made out of creatures within our world, living right under our feet, can rival our own reality in a way that a wholly alternative world in another dimension, such as Narnia or Middle-earth, does not. And this too is part of the individualism in Adams's work.

So far we have been dealing with the fantasy of rebellion. In the other 1970s stream, of reaction, occasional scepticism and conservatism, we find individualism challenged much more radically. These fantasies often deal with time and the past, seeing individualism itself as the problem, whereby lack of humility or myopia prevents us from seeing ourselves as parts of larger societies or natural processes or societies beyond the self. Such fantasy questions self-assertiveness, often by blurring the boundaries between the self and the world, or between one time and another. In this sense it takes us back to the 1950s.

An instance is Richard Parker's *The Old Powder Line* (1971), a story of journeys from a strange extra platform in a station, where a steam train takes people to their pasts.[10] On one trip teenage Brian meets himself as a baby, and finds his mother half-recognising him. This is not quite the same as the baby the teenager Penn turns into in Penelope Farmer's *A Castle of Bone* (1972), for in Parker's book both boy and baby self exist at the same moment. The whole time business is given a pseudo-scientific explanation by Brian, by analogy with the polarising of light, but is really left a mystery – as, particularly, is the railway porter who is custodian of these time-visits. Nor is it a dream, for three people make the journeys, and material evidence is found. The book interweaves the past and present lives of the characters so that they begin to shift into one another. Here the very notion of 'oneself' and 'one's own time' are thrown into question.

For the 'point' made by the book is that all linear time, symbolised by the old railway line itself, is still potentially 'there,' still joined up and alive, and that our habit of making the present our sole window on reality is only a habit. The book is close to a vision of the multiple character of reality, by which not only is the past as 'real' as the present, but in some other dimension goes on alongside it, on a parallel track – except that the view is ultimately as much a moral one involving humility, as a philosophical one concerning reality. Although the book ends with the line closed and the characters all restored to the present, we are left to think of a series of them at different ages from babyhood on, continuing in different time worlds. This decentering, or 'non-privileging' of our reality works against human pride (while on another level it looks to the 'multiple world' fantasy of the 1980s). Incidentally, the blending of the real with the fantastic, and the management of a complex theme clearly without forfeiting the vividness of the characters or of the growing romance of Brian and his girlfriend Wendy, are very well handled.

The time-fantasies of Penelope Lively undermine the self-sufficiency of the present from another and more specifically conservative point of view, by reconnecting the present with its history. In Lively's work, unusually, the past is often shown invading our own times, and not often pleasantly. *Astercote* (1970) describes how the experience of a buried medieval plague village begins to resurface in the people of the modern village nearby, when an old chalice is stolen from its hallowed secret place. In *The Wild Hunt of Hagworthy* (1971) the ignorant revival of an ancient and savage dance, originating ultimately in the Old People, the fairies, comes into terrifying reality in the midst of a village fête. A children's game of spell-making in *The Whispering Knights* (1971) brings the appearance in their time of the evil Queen Morgan Le Fay, who takes the guise of a local businessman's wife. In *The Ghost of Thomas Kempe* (1973) we have a truant sorcerer ghost from the seventeenth century who breaks into the present of an English village and tries to take over the life of a schoolboy.

More recent pasts feature in two books by Lively for older children, *The House in Norham Gardens* (1974) and *A Stitch in Time* (1976). Here, however, we also deal with the opposite, and more divisive, effects of the present on the past. In *The House* a tamburan, or sacred shield taken from a New Guinea tribe in 1905 by the explorer great-grandfather of the heroine Clare, is for a time the object of the tribe's desire across the years, until modernity wears both the desire and the shield's meaning to them away. *A Stitch in Time* (which won the Whitbread Award) is different, portraying a girl who tries – and fails – to shape the life of a nineteenth-century girl to her wishes. Across her fiction Lively moves her pasts nearer and nearer to the present; and as she does so, her work becomes less fantastic, more akin to the psychological novel.

The best of Lively's books in the fantastical vein is *The Ghost of Thomas Kempe*, which won her the Carnegie Medal. This novel, possibly indebted to Kingsley Amis's *The Green Man* (1969), deals with an unnatural survival from the past, in the form of a ghost. The invisible Kempe has chosen to outlive his allotted time, and in the book's view it is not choice, but change and nature alone, that can join different times. Some of the comedy of the book comes from the myopic Kempe's dealings with the very resilient boy James (modelled on Richmal Crompton's William); and some from the attempted imposition of his sorcerer's beliefs (altering a chemist's prescription, enjoining certain directions for study on the local school blackboard, even trying to burn down an old woman's cottage in the belief that she is a witch). A strength of the book is that the humour accommodates a more serious note, as Kempe finally accepts his mortality and irrelevance, and is helped into his grave. Though his sorcery enables him to survive beyond his own time, his mind has not made the journey with him, and he has, so far as his attitudes are concerned, remained in the bottle from which he emerged. The book ends with a meditative passage on time which is to form the idiom of Lively's later novels, as James walks home through the churchyard, beneath autumnal trees on which the buds of next year are already showing:

> Time reached away behind and ahead: back to the crusading knight, and Thomas Kempe, and Aunt Fanny, and Arnold [two people from the nineteenth-century whom James came to know]: forward to other people who would leave their names in this place, look with different eyes on the same streets, rooftops, trees. And somewhere in the middle there was James, walking home for tea. ... (159)

In the end the stream of time is seen back in the natural channel to which it belongs. Time may short-circuit in Lively's work, but it returns in the end to travel along its more linear course.

Nevertheless Penelope Lively has, like Richard Parker, a deep feeling that the present is not an island, but part of a continent of time, and this is reflected in the invasions from the past in her stories; and however the intrusions are in the end removed, their appearance assures us that the past is never wholly dead or finished with. Lively even theorises about the matter in her more discursive novel *The Driftway* (1972), where it is asserted that certain powerful people, or moments of intense experience or emotion, so imprint themselves on time that they can recur. (This is not wholly unlike the idea in Garner's *The Owl Service*.) Young Paul and his sister, runaways from home and their father's new wife, meet an old man with a caravan, who takes the ancient and 'haunted' way across country. For the rest of the novel he reveals to them how much wider life is than their own concerns. On the old Driftway they meet the shadows of a prehistoric scout, an Anglo-Saxon warrior, an English Parliamentary soldier in the Civil War battle of Edgehill, an inn-boy, a highwayman and a nineteenth-century poacher. Each of these wordlessly imparts his story, à la Kipling's *Puck*. The old man explains the appearances as being particular travellers on the road who did "'an extra hard bit of living, as you might call it. That'll leave a shadow on the road, won't it?'" (27). These shadows are not ghosts, but time-transcending spirits. This is basically what is shown at work in Lively's fantasy, where a sacred talisman, a spell, a wild dance or even a sewing sampler, can transmit across time the energies that went into their making.

Seen in this way, Lively can be called a 'psychological' fantasist. In her fantasy the world is a fabric of spiritual and mental communication, a sort of great brain which has imprinted on its synapses all the spiritual crises of the past. And with better mental reception, presumably, we might well detect all the hosts of other less intense lives beyond, all calling across time with the passions of the passing minute.

Such a fabric establishes the sense of continuity – almost the key value for Lively[11] – but it cannot silence her equally strong sense of the transience and mortality of all things, or her growing feeling that of all times the modern one is particularly divorced from its past. This is seen in her later children's fantasies, particularly *The House in Norham Gardens* and *A Stitch in Time*. Here for the first time Lively confronts the death of old values and attempts a new kind of accommodation with the present-day world.

The Driftway and *The House* are still full of the impulse to preserve, and yet are shot through with a sense of elegy and loss. The long-gone showed their lives in *The Driftway*, but it was like a camcorder film, a section of their life severed from the rest of their living process. In *The House*, a passage in italics at the beginning of each chapter records how the impact of modern civilisation on the primitive New Guinea tribe since their discovery in 1905 has eroded their belief in spiritual things. The tamburan or sacred shield taken from them by young Clare's great-grandfather contains within it the tribe's spirit, and at first they call through it to Clare to take it back to them.[12] But as the story and their larger history proceed, the calls grow fainter, reflecting the gradual loss of spiritual value to twentieth-century materialism. In the end, in Clare's own day, there are no living tribes-people to whom the sacred shield can mean anything, and Clare gives it to the dead, in the shape of the Pitt Rivers Museum in Oxford.

At this point Clare comes to a sense of how everything passes. Her beloved aunts will die, and their house, so long preserved unchanged, will one day also be modernised out of all recognition, or else bulldozed. Here the past is not something that survives, but is killed by the wilting action of the present, against which the only weapon is the lonely mind, committing the past to memory. At the end, 'She looked at ... [her aunts], intently, at their faces and their hands and the shape of them. I'm learning them by heart, she thought, that's what I'm doing, that's all I can do, only that.' This is what happens in Penelope Lively's *Going Back* (1975), a detailed picture of an imagined Somerset childhood, which is in effect a 'learning by heart' by the central character of her own past, so that it may outlive time. In a sense it is what Lively is doing as a fiction-writer, for her books are talismans, tamburans, or samplers of her own spiritual life.

In this strain of elegy and mental resolve, Lively shows a certain dislike of the modern world, an English preference for the relatively unchanging countryside, where continuity between past and present finds favourable soil. In *The Driftway*, the modern speed of travel that has no time for the scenery is deplored. Morgan le Fay in *The Whispering Knights* is the sophisticated power-wife of a factory owner who wants to drive a motorway through the nearby village. There is a marked partiality for old people and for children, who, unlike 'adults,' do not make the world what it is. Most of the books are set in relatively unchanging country villages with links to the past. All these locations are founded on real – and memorable – places. Astercote is based on the buried village of Hampton Gay near Oxford, the Whispering Knights were suggested by the ancient Rollright Stones in Oxfordshire, Hagworthy is Rodhuish near Washford in Somerset, and the Driftway takes us E.N.E. from Banbury along the ancient trackway to the village of Cold Higham near Northampton.[13] Behind all this pastoralism lies a feeling that the modern present is cut off from the past as never before.

In Lively's last children's fantasy, *A Stitch in Time*, we deal not just with the human past, but with the aeons of geological time behind it. Unlike human history, those times are nameless and unidentifiable, rearing like the cliff of blue Lias at Charmouth on the Dorset coast, and topped with a little fringe of living grass. Looking at the stray ammonites she finds in sheaves in a rock, young Maria is possessed by a sense of universal waste, of the freakish, random character of the present (29).[14] Later on in her dreams, 'things were not as they should be, the world became an unstable and uncertain place, nothing could be relied upon. She walked across a green and solid lawn, but the lawn collapsed beneath her feet...' (117). This larger sense of incoherence cannot easily be wished away.

'Things were not as they should be': Maria is to find this all too true as she tries to shape the past to her own unhappy fancy. A shy and lonely child, on holiday with her prim parents and ill at ease with herself, she forms a mute relationship across time with a girl called Harriet, who lived in the same cottage a century earlier. She has visions of Harriet through the latter's unfinished sampler, and also by the sea beneath the cliffs. Unlike Clare of *The House in Norham Gardens*, Maria has little inbred sense of the past, having been brought up in a modern house, not one like the cottage, which has had generations of children in it. For her the past is a wonder, which, as with the local fossils she begins to collect, she seeks to possess. Alienated from herself, she talks to herself as though she were someone else, and has conversations with the cottage cat, in which she gives the cat speech which criticises herself. She becomes convinced from stray pieces of information that Harriet died young in a cliff fall of 1865. Maria once harboured pictures of herself dying young, and of her grieving parents at last taking notice of her (65): she has the nervous imagination of a Catherine Morland. To some extent she does not want her human specimen to have grown into an adult (56)

– not least because most of the adults she has met are genuinely unpleasant. But by the end of the story she has learned that it was Harriet's dog, not she, that was killed in the fall, and that Harriet went on to marry and have children. Harriet becomes independent of Maria's imagination, and lives on in her own time.[15] Here we see that the past has an integrity of its own.

Maria imagines that Harriet was killed because she is herself cut off from the flow of life. She is an only child whose parents live a life of ordered timidity, holding rigidly to the proprieties, keeping themselves to themselves. But it is Harriet's spirit that gives Maria a new appetite for life, Harriet the supposed dead girl whose more vital nature, across a century, enters and transforms Maria's heart. Her dark illusions removed, Maria is ready, like Harriet, to grow up herself. She takes away the cat's voice, for her self is now at home. It is still a home on a frail beach of the present, washed by huge seas of time, but now she can live to herself without that larger annihilating perspective. There is no philosophical answer here, only a spiritual self-sealing.[16]

The advance in *A Stitch in Time* is that it has a very particular child character, whose view of the past is partly coloured by her own personality. In Lively's previous books the view of time presented was almost solely objective, but here we have the mind shaping what it sees, which is more subtly true. Maria's personality, moreover, is both a very individual and a representative one. In some sense she is the modern child, cut off from the past and history, and trying to re-learn them.[17] In this book Penelope Lively does not move away from the modern world as in most of her earlier books, but tries to understand and accommodate it. The greater degree of engagement is seen in its symbolism, too, which is far more complexly expressive than in earlier fantasies.[18]

At the other end of the fantastic scale from these books is Susan Cooper's five-book 'The Dark is Rising' sequence (1965–77), written at the height of the popularity of Tolkien and secondary world fantasy. In these books, huge metaphysical opposites, Dark and Light, engage in final war, the primal elements of the cosmos are awakened, great gulfs of time are traversed with ease, and wondrous realms visited. This sequence is in the tradition of 'High' or heroic-epic fantasy, and has its sources most immediately in Tolkien, Alan Garner and the American fantasy writer Ursula Le Guin. The first book, however, *Over Sea, Over Stone* (1965), gives little inkling of this, being a somewhat Blytonesque tale of three children on holiday in Cornwall who find a lost grail associated with King Arthur. At this stage Cooper had little thought of a sequel.[19] It was only in the four remaining books, published from 1973 to 1977, eight years after she had moved with her American husband to the United States – the adoptive home of High fantasy – that the Dark versus Light theme really appeared, and with it the supernatural and the fantastic.

These books have been very popular with children, and have a certain celebrity in the fantasy genre. Their attempt to show ordinary childhood life suddenly being brought up against figures of universal power is hugely exciting. Their plots have the primal narrative attraction of being treasure-hunts, with strange objects having to be found in order to proceed further. The idea of an eventual goal of final overthrow of the Dark is a great pull, heightened by the constant fear that it may not succeed. Each adventure is married to a particular English or Welsh landscape and people – Cornwall, the Thames valley, the Lleyn Peninsula, Cardigan – lending the magic events immediacy and (varying) credibility. Indeed Susan Cooper's sense of place is one of her strongest suits: her fantasy is continually bound up with geography. This makes it more objective and 'out there', and the conflicts it portrays more with the other than with the self.. Here we do not often look within people's minds, or even at their individual characters, except in the fourth book, *The Grey King* (1973).

In the tradition of conservative fantasy, Cooper joins the present to the past, to reconnect it with traditional values: but her primary concern is to recharge her fictive modern universe with numinous meaning. Great spiritual forces fill her books, lurking within people's everyday lives and demanding of them at any instant the most momentous decisions and the most heroic deeds. One cannot go for an ordinary walk in the country without meeting some emissary of the absolute. And all the tasks and quests in the narratives are parts of a growing pattern through which the Dark will be overthrown. The world is seen as both ordered and significant, in consoling contrast to the way it is increasingly appearing outside the circle of fantasy.

But this conservative vision requires the interconnection of all things, in contrast to individualism's stress on the singular. And here Cooper's books fail the vision, for, despite all their emphasis on spiritual matters, they show little interest in metaphysics.[20] So long as the Light defeats the Dark, that is for her enough: no god or theology is adumbrated, and in consequence the epic vision of history becomes somewhat rootless and insubstantial. Each, Dark and Light, exists primarily for its emotional value of shuddering rejection or intense desire; and affords the pleasure of moral simplicities. This lack of a rationale removes certainty from the supernatural happenings. It is not clear why, as we are told, the Dark has risen only twice in human 'history'; nor why the first occasion was in the time of Arthur, and its second, despite all the intervening horrors of history with which it could have been identified, is in 1970s England amongst a few children. Nor is any significance given to the various magic objects that have to be obtained by the Light in order to prevail, whether it is six strange Signs, a long-lost Welsh harp, or a sword: exciting and mysterious though they are, they gradually become a collection of individual trophies.[21] Further, since at the end the Dark has finally been overthrown, it is hard to understand how there is any place remaining for human evil in the world, as the last book maintains (282–3).

Just as the history lacks coherence, so does the sequence of the narrative. The general objective is always clear enough: find a grail, a scroll, six signs, a harp, a sword. But all sorts of other requirements are thrust in later. In the second book, *The Dark is Rising*, the boy-hero Will Stanton is constantly being told of fresh tasks, or of new twists to the present one. When he has the Six Signs, he learns that "'they are not yet joined. If the Dark can take you now, they take all that they need to rise to power'" (240). Meanwhile, the plots of the stories constantly veer in different directions. As revealed 'Old One,' Will has continually to flicker between his life as an English child and his role as heroic saviour of the Light, and to travel through time in the blink of an eye, so that both his identity and the contexts of his actions become rather evanescent. This is better handled in *The Grey King*, where we stay in one place and time throughout, and Dark and Light appear solely in the forms of ordinary Welsh people and their behaviour; here, however, the opposite happens, and human jealousy and sexual passion compromise the easy categories of quasi-theological fantasy. Divided spheres of action return in the next book, *Silver on the Tree* (1977), where the first half of the story is spent in our world, and the remainder in a secondary one remote from our own. This comes near saying that victories over the Dark can happen only in a wholly fantastic world. And throughout the five books locations shift, from Cornwall to Berkshire to Wales, and back, for no particular reason, for there is no hidden 'British' theme. The three children we meet in the first book are wholly absent from the second; then they reappear and meet Will in the third, are replaced again by Will and a new boy character Bran in the fourth, and return in a subordinate role in the fifth: it is as though they became something of an embarrassment. All these shifts and insubstantialities take away from the visionary certainties of the books.[22]

By contrast with Cooper, a 1970s writer of children's fantasy who deliberately welcomes such dislocations is Diana Wynne Jones. Perhaps the most able, inventive and prolific of modern children's fantasy writers, Jones has written some thirty highly various fantasies since *Wilkin's Tooth* in 1973, all of them marked by an individualist, 'rebellious' vision. Currently enjoying a revival of interest, her work demands attention and intelligence from her readers, who are rewarded with her brilliant inventiveness, her wit, and her insight into human nature. At first often comic in character, her fantasies have latterly been more serious and speculative: but no trend can be read into this, for Jones loves trying anything new and reversing the old. Her later *The Tough Guide to Fantasyland* (1996) is a gentle mockery of the often clichéd nature of modern fantasy: between 1974 and

1979 she wrote four different types of fantasy. All her books however show a love of clashing one reality with another: with her comic vision, Jones revels in the very insecurities of being that bedevil Susan Cooper's more conservative books.

Jones is at first very much in the tradition of E. Nesbit, in the way that she plays reality against fantasy: but she is more transgressive. The children in her 1970s books are often rebels struggling against adult authority, her magic is less controlled by rules than Nesbit's, and she so frequently alters 'reality' that we often lose touch with it. In *Power of Three* (1975), the setting is at first a swamp where two primitive races live surrounded by giants: but when the giants turn out to be a modern boy and girl, we are shaken into our own time. David in *Eight Days of Luke* (1975) accidentally brings Luke – who is actually the Norse god Loki in the shape of a modern boy – to life through a curse he utters against his unpleasant aunt and uncle. Further Norse gods then appear, in the form of village locals, to deal with their escaped compeer. There is similar humour in *Dogsbody* (1975) which has the star king Sirius punished by being shut within the body of a family dog.

Jones is much happier than Susan Cooper with fantasy that undermines assumptions and switches between worlds. The people of *Power of Three* turn out to be midgets, while the 'Giants' are a boy and girl.[23] The true wizard in *Charmed Life* (1977) proves to be the dull boy Cat, not his precocious sister. Our own world may be seen through the eyes of a dog, a midget or a ghost.[24] Across Jones's three books about the secondary world of Dalemark – *Cart and Cwidder* (1975), *Drowned Ammet* (1977) and *Spellcoats* (1979) – she tells no continuous story, but visits a series of times, places and peoples in Dalemark, one of them far back in its prehistory, and all so distinctive that each almost constitutes a separate secondary world in itself. And in *Charmed Life*, the world we are in turns out to be a fantastic one, from which the wicked sister Gwendolen escapes to our own – which itself proves one of an infinite series of alternate worlds.

The delight is in multiplication, in making one world generate a thousand others. The chemistry set in *The Ogre Downstairs* (1974) contains a powder called 'Animal Spirits,' which brings to sentient life everything it chances to touch – which includes the plastic bricks in a boxed construction set, twelve bars of toffee, several pieces of fluff, the wooden people in a dolls' house, and the stepfather the Ogre's pipe. All of these have to be fed, and live in their own peculiar little worlds. In *Charmed Life*, Gwendolen animates the people in the stained-glass windows of a church during a boring sermon, whereupon 'Almost every saint turned and fought the one next to him' (81). In Nesbit's work, while one thing may turn into another – as children may be given wings, a prince be turned to a hedgehog, or the population of an entire country be transformed to mussels[25] – there is not the sense of having created a new little world that then gets on with itself. Both Jones's and Nesbit's fantasies to some extent reflect the craziness of children, turning the world upside-down, and both love the sheer variety of people and things (packing their fantasies with domestic objects); but Jones always goes further. To some degree the wicked Gwendolen of *Charmed Life* is needed to enliven a world in which – perhaps satirising Ursula Le Guin's conservative wizards in her 'Earthsea' books – the object of the ruling magician, Chrestomanci, is precisely not to do marvels, but to keep an unstable universe in balance.

While Jones approves of Chrestomanci's governance, her work is full of rebellions against the family, society and authority. Luke/Loki in *Dogsbody* is seen as right to challenge the complacent gods and their heavy social norms. The children's assault on their stepfather in *The Ogre Downstairs* transforms a situation of frozen animosity for the good; and the protagonists of the Dalemark books have left society, family or tribe, to change the world. The family itself is often under question. The one in *The Ogre Downstairs* is at first a wreck. Sirius's stellar mate in *Dogsbody* proves his enemy, and the sun his new friend. David in *Eight Days of Luke* becomes friends with his detested sister Astrid and learns the full fraudulence of his harsh aunt and uncle. The children in *Cart and Cwidder* discover the unpleasant truth about their father; and after they have left their cold mother, they have to make a new family themselves. Mitt in *Drowned Ammet* also finds out about his father's treacherous life as a state spy, and leaves home; later he also leaves his shallow mother, and begins to learn to relate to people quite different from himself. (Eventually this streetwise enemy of the state is to become the restored king of all Dalemark.[26])

Mitt is Jones's only proletarian hero, but at the same time he makes good by hacking out a place for himself among his social betters: he is both a Machiavellian revolutionary and a classic example of free enterprise. As has been said, most children's fantasies confine themselves to middle-class characters. However Helen Cresswell has already shown herself an exception: and other rebels against the dominance of the bourgeois come in on a wave of more 'socially aware' children's fantasy in the Labourite Britain of the later 1970s. Such writers include Robert Westall, Andrew Davies, Jill Paton Walsh and even Michael de Larrabeiti, whose *Borribles* books are a proletarian parody of the earlier bourgeois *Wombles*. But the most striking is the Newcastle writer Robert Westall.

Westall introduces a new note of stark, often urban realism into children's fantasy. He challenges class complacency and uproots the secure worlds of his child characters, forcing them to confront new selves. One motif that runs through his work is the overthrowing of set ideas about the world or the self. Another is the evil of power. Both involve repression, whether of the self by itself or of the self by another. The power motif is most commonly seen in terms of control exercised by the past and the dead over the present and the living, which often symbolises the tyranny of old values versus the freedom of individual choice. This inverts the view of time in Lively and Cooper.

Westall's children's fantasies often deal with adult problems. The children of *The Wind Eye* (1976) are faced with their parents' dissolving marriage. There is a failed mother and family disputes in *The Watch House* (1977). A nineteen year-old biker is the hero of *The Devil on the Road* (1978). In *The Scarecrows* (1981), which won the Carnegie Medal, the relative marital merits of a boy's dead father and his new stepfather are canvassed. We also often have a sense of a wider society and more 'public' matters: jobs, cars, cities; Tyneside in *The Watch House*; an atavistic Suffolk village just off an 'A' road in *The Devil on the Road*; and a stepfather in *The Scarecrows* who is a left-wing cartoonist for the *Observer*. Themes concerning adults are brought in that we have not much seen before: class, sex, divorce, poverty, drink, war. In doing all this, it must be said, Westall is partly reflecting contemporary changes in the lives of children themselves, who were being exposed much more to adult concerns, through both the breakdown of previous parental distance and the influence of television. The admission by Westall of more of the outside world into the protected enclosure of children's fantasy is parallel to the breaking down of self-protective enclosures in his own characters.

All Westall's fantasy stories portray time-shifts and the (usually) malign influence of the past on the present, and involve individuals who in some way go on living beyond the time of their deaths. In *The Wind Eye*, a modern family holidaying near the Farne Islands encounters the seventh-century Saint Cuthbert, and all its members have variously to come to new terms with themselves. *The Watch House* has the malignant ghost of a murdered criminal exerting power over the living a century later; and in *The Devil on the Road*, a witch executed in the seventeenth century seeks to control a modern day biker and make him her route back to life. *The Scarecrows* portrays a boy whose rejection of his stepfather for his idolised dead father turns into an evil supernatural force, with the potential to destroy his mother's new happiness. In all the stories the time-shifts are just that – the slipping of one reality into another in a way that had not yet been seen in children's fantasy. St Cuthbert, and a ship-full of marauding Vikings, are met in a strange fog-bank amid modern seaside holidaymakers. A girl on a holiday job in an old Tyneside watch-house sees its former inhabitants go to and fro in the place, a century ago and now. John Webster the biker slides in and out of the seventeenth century as he moves about a modern Suffolk village. A small boy finds three scarecrows in a field at the wrong time of year.

So far as the theme of being open to new realities is concerned, the first and fourth books portray refusals that must be broken down, and the other two a too-passive acceptance that must become more resistant. In *The Wind Eye*, St

Cuthbert ('Cuddy') lives alone on his rock stubbornly rejecting his passions in the hope of reaching God, and surrounded by his rejections in the shape of little devils on goats that seek to do him harm. Meanwhile Bertrand Studdard, father of the holidaying family, and an academic, is a man who prides himself on knowing and being able to do anything by reason and will; and his stepson Michael follows him. But Madeleine, Bertrand's second wife, and Beth, Bertrand's daughter, are people of passion and warmth, In Madeleine's case, the warmth has gone too far because of Bertrand's cool rationalism (the book is quite schematic as well as human), and she has become something of an exhibitionist, seeking attention and passion wherever she goes. Beth, however, is without Madeleine's pain: and she is able to give St Cuthbert an understanding of the worth of women, and of the rightness of the affections, which he has so long refused. Bertrand, who is so like Cuthbert that he never meets him, is broken down by other means, and becomes the astonished guardian of the ancient gateway to the saint, as he now finds his ancestors have been ever since Cuthbert's time. He has opened himself to a Christian reality, as Cuthbert has to a human one.

In *The Watch House*, by contrast, young Anne has long been passive before her mother's will, and it is her passivity, her lack of a solid self, that exposes her to the influence of the ghosts in the story. The ghost of the long-dead criminal Major Hague owes its force to the weakness of men, on which it feeds. Anne, whose much-loved but weak father has been deserted by her mother, is left with her Tyneside grandparents, who look after the former watch house of the Life Brigade. The Life Brigade was long ago founded by Henry Cookson, a guilty witness of the shipwrecked Hague's murder for his money: but Cookson's continual guilt, instead of propitiating the dead, gave the ghost of Hague increasing power over him. Alison, longing for her father, is at first uncertainly addressed in the watch house by Cookson's ghost, and then feels beyond that the manipulative power and malignity of Hague. As she tries to find out about Cookson, and is drawn into his story, so he and his companion are increasingly drawn from the grave, to the point where Hague's ghost threatens the living with harm.

So far in the story Alison has given away her power, whether to her mother or to the ghosts: symbolically she best communicates with the ghosts when under hypnosis and passive. She is able to put both in their proper places when she asserts herself, and when she refuses to go back south with her mother. As her friend the boy Timmo says, when Alison wonders where her mother got her power over her, "'*You* gave it to her; and your father gave it to her. The more you gave it to her, the bigger and more awful she got ... '" (179). Even the dead may be awakened if the living give up their wills to them.

The idea that the dead hand of the past can drain the life from us is also central in Westall's next two novels. In *Devil on the Road* the biker John Webster's lazy self-abandonment, his belief in chance, and the hypnotic effect of the Suffolk countryside he is passing through, together bring him to stop near Basingtree at a barn which was the site of a seventeenth-century witch trial. The same spiritual inertia then leads him to allow the owner of the barn to use him to travel back in time to save the witch Joanna Vavasour from execution. He succeeds in this task, his physical prowess being in inverse proportion to his strength of will: but his success is itself circumscribed by the plan of the local villagers to have him marry the witch and make her a part of their time, so that her magic may be restored to them. When Webster realises this, he at last has to exercise his will and escape; and the witch returns to her own time, to await the next passing fly to enter the village web. In this book Westall explores the kind of moral weakness that can be found in the 'tough guy,' 'man of action' hero. Webster's rootless travelling is a symbol of his not being rooted, or having a home, in himself.[27] The theme of true 'manliness' is a frequent theme in Westall's work.

In *The Wind Eye* and *Devil on the Road*, Westall deals with sexual relations, in which first the man, and then the woman is dominant; and in *The Watch House* he portrays a parental relation in which a mother dominates her daughter: now, in his next fantasy *The Scarecrows*, he gives us a son who is dominated by his father, even beyond the grave (though not as a ghost). Simon's obsession with his hero father leads him to reject that father's opposite in his mother's new man Joe, who is left-wing, casual, easy and loving. One of the things Simon cannot bear is that Joe should be at the centre of his mother's attention, and this is height-ened to the point of mania when he sees them making love. Simon's hostility eventually awakens the destructive rage of a long-past murder of passion in the nearby water-mill and attracts it towards him and his home: it is only when he sees the horror of what he has been doing that Simon can, with difficulty, put his personal wishes aside and stop it. Here being manly is not being cold and hard, which is often a sign of continued childishness: rather, it is being generous and open, with oneself and with love. This aligns the book with *The Wind Eye*, also about psychological refusals; *The Watch House* and *Devil on the Road* are alike in being about psychological permissions.

Westall questions all veneration – for parents, the past, men, the romance of war. In his later fantasy *Gulf* (1992), he shows the Gulf War from the viewpoint of an Iraqi conscript watching the horrors of Western technological warfare ap-proach him. And he challenges old assumptions about parental roles, the 'roles' of boy and girl. His novels do not suppose that such old power-centres are easily challenged, or that they are always wrong. It takes supernatural intervention to overthrow Bertrand's mania for perfection in *The Wind Eye*, and other novels show battles only just won, or at considerable cost. People have to see through themselves, to the passivity that lets others take them over. And on the other side, the desire to possess others is not easily relinquished either. In the making and unmaking of selves lies the field of moral energy in Westall's books.

Another author questioning such rigidities is Andrew Davies, in his Guardian Award-winning and largely comic *Conrad's War* (1978), about a boy obsessed with the Second World War, who eventually finds himself magically transported to the middle of it with his writer father. There is much heroic-comic action, with Conrad and his 'Dad' bombing wartime Nuremberg from an enlarged version of a plastic model Lancaster of Conrad's, and then being shot down, imprisoned in Colditz and escaping via a glider. But the turning point comes when Conrad, who has commandeered a German tank, finds an ambulance full of wounded people, and has an emotional crisis: this image of people suffering was not part of Conrad's clichéd view of war. Magically returned to his home, he resolves to abandon his war craze and take up electricity instead. The novel is full of slippages between Conrad the modern family boy and Conrad the bomber-ace tank commander, mirroring the way he has let fiction rule his life, as even his Dad, who is a writer, has not. The book suggests that if you believe your own fiction or fantasy, you may in some sense find yourself inside it.

A third male writer of 1970s children's fantasy who also writes against power-lust and false veneration of the past, is Peter Dickinson in his (also Guardian Award-winning) *The Blue Hawk* (1976), a story of the revolutionary struggles of a king against a priesthood in a god-filled ancient land. Images of escape fill the book, which begins with the flight of a young priest with a sacred sacrificial hawk, in the midst of a royal ritual. We learn that the kingdom has long been closed from the outer world by the priesthood, who wish to preserve both their dominance and the order of their rituals against change. The new king, however, seeks to break out into the world outside. And the gods, who, aeons previously, were drawn into this world by the desires and the wiles of men, wish to leave it. Symbol of it all is the hawk, a bird which, however trained and controlled, remains savage, and will break loose if given the chance. Whoever tries to fit life to his own wishes does wrong: the book is about a reality far wider and more complex than the one we think we know. Men think they direct their own fates, but the actions they choose may be part of some larger manipulation and purpose beyond them. This is also the idea behind Dickinson's *The Changes* trilogy (1968–71). The gods, it is surmised, organised a means of escape by creating so 'pressurised' a kingdom, and such individual characters within it as would produce an outcome that would release them from the earth (211–13). What we call history on earth is, in the heavens, prearrangement. This book is very well imagined and controlled – perhaps in the very end too well controlled – and richly deserved the Carnegie commendation it also received.

If *The Blue Hawk* is about letting things go free, William Mayne's more conservative *It* (1975) portrays the shutting away of something that has been free for far too long. A spirit from the dark medieval past of a town inhabits the mind of a young Yorkshire girl, Alice, and she has to find the right way of 'laying' it, and the vexed spirits of all the dead of that time, finally to rest in their correct places. To do this, a circular route must be walked round the town, through the sites of four crosses, one of which has long ago been obliterated and its cross removed. Once again Mayne returns to his interests in the half-buried and the earth which, as in *Earthfasts*, is disturbed and unquiet.

Nevertheless displacement is a central motif in *It* – as in many children's fantasies of the 1970s, from the time-shifts of Penelope Lively's novels to the homelessness or exile experienced by Richard Adams's or Diana Wynne Jones's characters. Expressing the displacements the spirit causes, the language itself of the book is frequently displaced or ambiguous. When Alice says, "'I'm not acting... I'm realling"', "'I doubt you are," said Mum, and Dad said "I doubt you aren't," but they both meant exactly the same thing, only Dad used his town language and Mum used vicarage language that she had been brought up with' (18). Alice's own speech is dislocated: she uses words she did not know, and her voice is continually being interrupted by her throat, 'which seemed to be wanting to say something different, and her mind couldn't make itself up' (86). There is a newspaper reporter who speaks in shorthand to the confusion of sense, a printer's room where words are upside-down in steel. And Mayne's own style – though this is not always peculiar to this book – continually brings us up short, 'displaces' us, with its frequent oddities of syntax, uneven rhythms and mixtures of bluntness with complexity:

> Alice stood on a patch of the last sunlight to touch the ground. It was the late
> light of the end of the day, and it was coming uphill and only touched the ground
> because the cobbles sloped down the hill. She was arguing with Raddy, who stood
> a little way off towards the sunset so that red light came up her back and seemed
> to shine through her knees and make them pink, and get into her hair and make
> it scarlet. (39)

Like Alice herself, the whole book seems poised between this world and another, between physics and metaphysics. However, Mayne does not doubt 'reality': for him it is not a series of fictions, but something like a tank holding different levels of liquid that can mix.

Last here is Jill Paton Walsh, with her social-realist fantasy of displacement, *A Chance Child* (1979), about a neglected modern child 'Creep' in an industrial city, who finds his way along a canal into the England of the early nineteenth-century Industrial Revolution. There he meets people who, in a larger way than himself, have been cut off from human feeling by their lives; and after helping several wretched children, he eventually loses his invisibility to that world, and enters it fully, never to return. His brother Christopher later finds in the local library a yellowing biographical pamphlet written by his younger brother in 1831. Here, in the fading of Creep, the past devours the present.

While the book is ostensibly a picture of the horrors of human repression by 'progress,' its relevance to our own day is uncertain: there is little immediate point in calling attention to abuses that are long past, unless it is to put our own into perspective (not really Walsh's central concern[28]). But it has another, more latent, subject. Its interest is at least as much in touring an industrial wasteland to gaze on iron smelters, a foundry, a coal mine, a pottery, a canal-digging and a cotton factory. 'Plot' is relatively vestigial, a wandering from scene to scene. And while the concern with child-wretchedness is to the fore, there is a fascination with the very forces that grind them down. The preoccupation, as with Robert Westall, is with power: power, both industrial and political, is in the very breeze of the early Thatcher years. Just as the child Creep is slowly drawn into that world, so, we might say, is the author herself.

> The captive water shot from the race, and poured from above over a huge water
> wheel; the wheel turned a shaft, and cogs on the shaft caught upon two huge
> bellows, and thrust them shut, blowing them alternately. They blew from left
> and right into an arch in a bastion of blackened brick, and, fanned to fury by
> their gusts, a fire raged within, and burned in a blazing jet from the top of the
> furnace. Here was the giant breathing, the hell's mouth glow! Along a platform to
> this mouth of fire men ran with barrows, tipping into the pit loads of ironstone,
> limestone and coke. At each load the blaze dimmed briefly, and then resumed its
> fury. (49–50)

Much can be made of the way this machine operates almost independently of men, who are its mere scurrying servants; much too of the way the cause-and-effect relationships described here are much more enduring than any human ones. But the overall effect is of an energy which the creeping, ghostly boy from the twentieth century can only be sucked into, dropping out of his own time. Here in this last significant children's fantasy of the decade, just as in the first, *Astercote*, where the Black Death returned to a modern village, we see the past draining reality from the present: reality is becoming a series of fictions, each one of which may at any time turn the others to shadows.

The shifting roles of rebellion and conservatism in 1970s children's fantasy eventually result in the dominance of the former. Few fantasies of the 1980s – or indeed the 1900s – attempt any more to negotiate with the past, or to revive old values. Instead, there is a mood of radical experimentation, an eager embracing of the multi-textual worlds that had become the postmodernist idiom of the day.

As for old values, we find these exchanged for new ones such as feminism and ecology; while such sheet anchors as family life, economic stability and social cohesion come increasingly under strain. It is ironic that these changes should have come under a Conservative government, but then this was conservatism aimed at power, not preservation, the thrusting individual, not society. The postmodernism of the decade is as much the product of political rootlessness as of the exploring mind.

6 PLAYING WITH REALITY: THE 1980s

In the 1980s the issues of insecurity that became dominant in the previous decade are for the time veiled, by being treated more often metaphorically. In this decade the influence of the postmodern view of reality as a multitude of texts written by its various perceivers is dominant, in both children's and adult English fantasy.[1] The fantasy itself is often more extreme, because reality itself is seen as a series of fantasies. As a result the reference to children's real-life problems is often more indirect. Such inventions as the terrors of a walking statue, the miseries of an imprisoned Czar, or the dreams of the wizard Merlin, here do duty as metaphors for children's uncertainties about the world – uncertainties which will return more nakedly in the 1990s.

Two features recur in the children's (and the adult) fantasy of the 1980s: they are more often set within entirely fantastic worlds, and they question reality by depicting it in multiple forms. The theme of the past often disappears, for the past may be co-present in another dimension. Worlds exist in parallel rather than in sequence, and the idea of linear influence is less marked, to the point where plots often involve the discovery of why things are as they are, rather than development to something entirely new. The idea of commerce between this present world and another, as we see it in Diana Wynne Jones's *Eight Days of Luke* or *Dogsbody*, or Jill Paton Walsh's *A Chance Child*, fades. For our own world is no longer automatically given primary reality, and we may find that it is a fantastic world that is made the objective one, while ours becomes fantastic. In such a context, even such central concerns of our world as moral or social conduct, or even truth to human nature, can sometimes fade away.

Diana Wynne Jones had already touched on the topic of multiple worlds in her *Charmed Life* (1977), setting the book in an alternative version of our own world: and this is continued in her further 'Chrestomanci' novels, *The Magicians of Caprona* (1980), *Witch Week* (1982) and *The Lives of Christopher Chant* (1988). As Jones puts it in her Author's Note to *The Magicians of Caprona*,

> The world of Chrestomanci is not the same as this one. It is a world parallel to ours, where magic is as normal as mathematics, and things are generally more old-fashioned. In Chrestomanci's world, Italy is still divided into numbers of small States, each with its Duke and capital city. In our world, Italy became one united country long ago.[2]

The setting is Cinquecento, and the plot is based on Shakespeare's *Romeo and Juliet*: both render Caprona a consciously fictive world. The story involves finding out why things are as they are, and then putting them right. Two great magician-trader families of Caprona, the Montanas and the Petrocchi, have long been in dissension, the cause unknown; and it takes the entire narrative, and the near-ruin of Caprona through its treacherous Duchess, for the lovers from each family to discover the long-lost way to the saving of the state. This is for members of both families to sing together in harmony the forgotten song of the Angel of Caprona, a custom unfulfilled since the beginning of their dispute. The idea is based on the medieval and renaissance notion of the ideal commonweal being founded on a musical concord. We are left to assume that it is because of such disputes that the larger country to which Caprona belongs is still a cluster of little states: it will take many acts of harmonious singing to turn it into a unified nation.

Witch Week, the next Chrestomanci novel, is set in a boarding school in a world where witches are burnt, and there is a brutal Inquisition to find them out. The Chrestomanci, wizard overseer of worlds, describes the universe as an infinity of alternative worlds, each as real as the others; but he says that the world of this novel is imperfectly divided from another, which it is like in every respect save in persecuting witches (151–4). This explanation unravels the puzzling character of the preceding story, involving a return to origins: everyone has been so far trying to operate in a distorted medium, which is then put right by the Chrestomanci.

In the multiverse there is, as said, no before and after, for all is co-terminous. *The Lives of Christopher Chant* (1988) inverts such temporal sequence as has appeared, by taking us back 'before' the other novels, to the time when the present Chrestomanci, Christopher Chant, first realised his powers. In this story we are in a quasi-Edwardian otherworld, from which Christopher's Uncle Ralph is making plundering raids into alternative universes to enlarge his magical powers. Meanwhile from one hidden alternative realm, a cold elven people are seeking power over the Chrestomanci and his world. But in a sense these antagonisms are symbolic of the fact that, for most of the story, Christopher is not yet at home in himself as Chrestomanci: for he is continually rebelling against his position. Only when his self-discovery is complete, and he fully accepts his role, is he able to quell these invasions. Thus established, he is able to set out in the roles we have already seen him perform in the previous books.

In two other books, *The Homeward Bounders* (1981) and *Archer's Goon* (1984), the search for why things are as they are is much more complexly interwoven, involving the gradual discovery of a pattern. In *The Homeward Bounders*, protagonists from several worlds are caught up in a gigantic electronic game being played by a pitiless race of demons called 'They,' and have to find out the game's very elaborate rules and psychological deceptions. The demons have drained the realities from all worlds to themselves and their 'Real Place.' In this novel, it is argued that the concept of 'home,' which gives prime reality to one place out of many, is anathema to the idea of a multiverse, where every place has equal and democratic reality. The multiverse can only be sustained, and 'They' kept out, by the hero continually travelling among the worlds; that is, he says, the way the system works: "As long as I don't stay anywhere long, as long as I keep moving and don't think of anywhere as Home, I shall act as an anchor to keep all the worlds real"(224). This is effectively a book written against provincialism. It is such provincialism that has made the reality of the multiverse a prey to 'Them': but then they too, for all that they control all worlds, are in the end provincial also, amassing all reality to their electronic game-board in a tiny three-sided house in one corner of a municipal park. But in another way the authoress Diana Wynne Jones is describing her own life as a writer, for she too never stays in one place, but from book to book, she travels to ever different fictional worlds – and stays in one room while she does so. This novel implicitly asks certain large metaphysical questions concerning the nature of being, and about the nature of any god that governs the universe; it also explores the inhumanities of power, and the dangers of manipulating reality with machines (which could include typewriters).

Even more elaboration and complexity are found in *Archer's Goon*, a title in itself as odd as any Jones gave to her novels. Here we are set in an apparently real and normal world which turns into a fantastic one. The boy hero Howard is found to be both a boy and a god, who has pre-programmed the events of the story on a computer while he gets on with inventing a space ship that will be its solution. Throughout, the story removes one assurance after another until even our trust in the narrator is gone.

In the end it all has to do with the nature of writing. Howard's father Quentin is a writer who once, when he had writer's block, made a joking agreement with his town councillor friend Mountjoy that he would send him two thousand words a week, on penalty of having the council services to his house cut off should he fail. Recently, however, he has had writer's block again, and broken the agreement. The story begins with the arrival at his house of a huge 'heavy' called the Goon, whose boss, Archer, has replaced Mountjoy on the council, and takes the agreement seriously: if the required words are not sent, the house will lose its local services.

Gradually we come to see that Archer is not the only one on the council asking for the weekly supply of words: five other people, of increasingly sinister power, apply both blandishment and force to the same end, and fight with one

another to gain sole rights. It turns out that these people are of no less than supernatural power, but all of them believe that their existence is entirely textual,
being sustained by the words supplied by Howard's father. In the end the six
of them are seen to be the boy Howard's divine siblings, he being the missing
seventh, Venturus.

This story shows Jones's sheer ability at roccoco plotting, piling twist upon
twist while removing plank after plank, till it all fits and floats free in a wonderful sphere of self-contained logic. The last twist concerns her own fiction, this
invented story, which is made out of thousands of words. Within the story,
Quentin's words seemed increasingly powerless: the trust of Howard's siblings in
them is exposed as a trick of Howard's. Yet words remain crucial, for everything
that the six do is part of a programme of words written by the seventh: and in the
end Howard continues the programme by typing in the statement that the more
obnoxious of them left by space ship, upon which they do. And beyond that
Howard himself is caught up in a larger programme of words, the one by which
the entire story exists, the one written by the author Diana Wynne Jones. The
novel is thus 'postmodernist,' without being in any way portentous about it.

The force of the book also comes from the way that Jones has blended these
fantastical events and attenuated motivations with a very 'real' and comic world
of a human family and a bureaucratic and meddling local council. Our sense of
this very local setting never goes, whatever happens. The characters, from the
blundering Goon to Howard's 'awful' sister are alike vivid, and all have human
as much as supernatural relationships with one another. Such a beautiful integration is hard to achieve, and in others of Jones's novels it is not so readily seen.

For example, *The Time of the Ghost* (1981) is disconcerting in that its young
heroine seems to be a ghost who returns from her supposed death to watch how
her eccentric sisters behave without her. It turns out later, more reassuringly, that
she is in fact lying injured in hospital after an accident, with her spirit roaming
at large.[3] Nevertheless, for most of the story, memory loss makes her unsure of
which of the sisters she is, and even when visited by them in hospital, she is
never addressed by name. Our sense of linear time is here again subverted, for
we assume that the girl-spirit and her young teenage sisters are close in age, but
as the story goes on, it emerges that she is in fact seven years older than she was
then, and what she is visiting is a picture of them all in the past. These is all very
dramatic, but it often feels like legerdemain, as *Archer's Goon* does not.

And there is more.... The girl-spirit and her sisters used to play a game of
worshipping a dark goddess they called the Monigan (compare Morrigan or
Morgan), but when she began to offer herself to Monigan, the game turned real
and the goddess came. Despite the girl's retraction, Monigan has promised to
return after seven years for her pledge, and the seven years are almost up. The

Monigan is brought in to provide supernatural explanations for events in the novel that should have been accounted for in their own terms. This has not apparently stopped it from being one of the more popular of Jones's books among children.[4]

The story involves finding out why the world is so strange, who one is, and how one has got to the present state of affairs: and this sense of unravelling something, of going backwards from the first page (rather as in a detective novel) is seen in many of Jones's novels of the 1980s. In *Howl's Moving Castle* (1985), the plot involves young Sophie in finding out the precise contract between the wizard Howl and Calcifer the fire demon who keeps the castle moving. *Fire and Hemlock* (1985), another complex novel, describes the gradual discovery of the true relation between the orchestral musician Thomas Lynn and his ex-wife Laurel Leroy. This hardly sounds the usual material of a children's novel: and the book also involves an unloving mother and a feckless father who variously betray the girl-heroine Polly, who herself grows up into sexual awareness in the course of the story. The ballad quotations at the head of each chapter may give us clues, but Polly has to find out for herself that Thomas Lynn 'is' Tam Lynn and Thomas Rhymer of the ballads, who fell in love with the Fairy Queen and became trapped in fairyland till a mortal woman rescued him. Polly re-enacts the old story and wins her modern Tom, in what is now an inter-textual narrative.

However Jones gives a modern twist of vampirism to the old story, in that her King and Queen of Faerie must renew themselves by feeding on a younger life at regular intervals, or else die. This is the additional fate from which Polly saves Tom. The repulsive man Leroy ('the king') himself dies finally. But at the same time the novel is the picture of a girl who, rejected by her parents and loved too little rather than too much, has the grace and self-sufficiency of a true queen. Indeed the novel could be said to be about love, love which at its best endures without hope, and gives without thought of self. But it is also, like all Jones's books, about the nature of reality. For unlike earlier fantasy stories which show a fairy tale or a myth happening again at a later time – Katherine Briggs's *Kate Crackernuts* (1963), Alan Garner's *The Owl Service* (1967) or Penelope Lively's *The Wild Hunt of Hagworthy* (1971) – *Fire and Hemlock* is about how all experience is potentially 'literary' or textual, and thus 'simultaneous.'

Jones's *A Tale of Time City* (1987) is a weaker affair, in which Vivian Smith, a child of the 1939 evacuation from London, is mistakenly transported by two young brothers to a future place outside history, called Time City. Time City and all history are under threat from a female renegade who is gradually removing the four buried 'polarities' that uphold the order of this world. Here again we are with the theme of contingent reality. Vivian was mistaken for this fugitive incendiary and abducted, in the hope of persuading her to put things back. But with the error realised, the story becomes a tour of Time City, and a series of pursuits into the past, to find the times and places where the founder of the city hid the several caskets containing the polarities. The characterisation is flat, and the story rather fumbled, perhaps because here the situation is resolved early; mental finding-out matters more than physical finding, as in many of Jones's novels of the 1980s.

In the progressive decay of the city, the book exhibits that favoured theme of its time: entropy. "'This patch of time and space here is almost worn out. The City is going to crumble away'"(14), says one of its young citizens, and later the process approaches final collapse:

> Time City was in upheaval all round. ... The steps heaved under them with long shudders and cracks appeared under their feet. ... A particularly grinding shudder produced a long crashing, over to her [Vivian's] right. She looked in time to see the golden dome of The Years slide away sideways and disappear in a great billow of dust. One of the metal arches in the Avenue tipped crooked and, beyond that, with a mighty tinkling, the blue glass dome of Millennium crumbled down on itself and poured blue shards into the River Time. (272–3)

However, this is a children's, not an adult, fantasy such as M. J. Harrison's contemporary 'Viriconium' sequence, and all is put right to produce the happy ending.[5] That ending is, as in much fantasy, a return to beginnings and a restoration of the *status quo ante* – but here with a difference, for history is seen as circular, following the stellar Great Year, and is renewed by the re-dedication of its founders. For all its name, Time City is finally immune to time.

Castle in the Air (1990), sequel to *Howl's Moving Castle*, is quite consciously fictive, even metafictive in one view.[6] A jolly *Arabian Nights* romp, full of comic oriental flattery and threats, it portrays the quest of the bazaar trader Abdullah with his magic carpet to recover his beloved Princess Flower-in-the-Night, abducted from her pleasure garden by a monstrous djinn. As in several of Jones's books of the 1980s, a cat plays a central part. A cross between Fieldingesque travelogue and E. Nesbit (a genie grants one wish per day),[7] the book explores an intertextual universe of exotic adventure and *Hassan*-type diction, where nothing is as it seems. Howl's castle is present as a rented location for the climax of the story, which otherwise has little in common with the earlier book. By 1990 at the end of the 1980s Jones has moved away from her 'intellectual' motif of finding out a situation, to a given situation which is resolved through action.

Jones wrote little children's fantasy in the 1990s. There is the comic-satiric *Black Maria* (1991) in which a girl has to defeat the destructive megalomania of her aunt, who is a witch; and there is the rather flat and overlong finale to the Dalemark books, *The Crown of Dalemark* (1993), in which we see the proletarian

Mitt become the new king. This continues the democratic tendency of all Jones's books. But by then Jones was turning to more adult fantasy, in *Hexwood* (1993), *A Sudden Wild Magic* (1996), *Deep Secret* (1997) and *Dark Lord of Derkholm* (1998). Here she continues to explore the idea of control of other people's lives, for good or ill, which has been the recurrent *leitmotif* of all her fiction. The upshot in each case is that we should choose our own destiny against the would-be manipulators of it – an injunction which in some faint sense makes Jones's work a parable for our times.

The range of Jones's work puts her almost in a class of her own: the only other contemporary English fantasy writer with whom she has much in common is Tanith Lee, who explores parallel and fictional universes in such stories as *East of Midnight* (1977), *The Castle of Dark* (1978), *Prince on a White Horse* (1982), *Sung in Shadow* (1983), *A Heroine of the World* (1989) and *Black Unicorn* (1991). Nevertheless the idea that we make reality, and that the world is much less certain than we suppose, is behind much other English children's fantasy of the 1980s.

The fantasies of Dick King-Smith might not immediately seem candidates for this sort of description: after all they are on the face of it simply comic tales of precocious animals. *Daggie Dogfoot* (1980) and *The Sheep-Pig* (1983) portray intelligent pigs, and *Harry's Mad* (1984) a parrot linguist. Aside from these classics, much of King-Smith's oeuvre concerns intellectual animals – chickens in *The Fox-Busters* (1978) and *Pretty Polly* (1982), cats in *The Mouse-Butcher* (1981) and *Martin's Mice* (1988), mice in *Magnus Powermouse* (1982), a guinea-pig in *The Jenius* (1988), a donkey in *The Toby Man* (1989) and another pig in *Ace* (1990). As in Jones's books, however, many of them involve the discovery of the true, and truly fantastic, nature of a thing.

In *Daggie Dogfoot*, for instance, a pig is born with wit and a dog's feet, which enable it to swim through a flood to find help for its marooned fellows, and rescue their guardian pig-man from drowning in a pool. The characterisation is well-handled, with an amiable mother-pig, an imposing father called the Squire, and a trogloditic pig-man, whom all the pigs regard as their servant. Daggie's world, like that of the pig Wilbur in E. B. White's *Charlotte's Web* (1952),[8] is surrounded by the threat of butchery, yet he is able to enjoy an aquatic idyll, being taught to swim by a duck and an otter. At first Daggie is to be killed off as a mutant, but the dread event is kept at bay, and his very peculiarity, his dog-feet, help him to swim in an element closed to all other pigs. At the end, when he is rescued by a helicopter, he even turns the adage 'pigs might fly' on its head. And there are several other inversions in the story. The pig-man, who gazes on the world with 'little piggy eyes' is more porcine than his charges, beside whose eloquence he is almost inarticulate, frequently resorting to expletives. The Squire regards him as stupid, and Daggie and Felicity the duck talk of him as '"making a pig of himself"' (122). Comical though this is, it does just touch on the issue of who might master whom, and of whether beasts have an intelligence of a sort that narrow and ignorant humans cannot conceive – an idea earlier entertained in the pigs of George Orwell's *Animal Farm* (1945).

This idea is further developed in *The Sheep-Pig*, where another forward pig is so astute as to become an expert sheep dog, and wins the national championship trials – which British readers know of from the TV programme 'One Man and his Dog.' Babe the pig's master is called Farmer Hogget. Speech and words as indicators of intelligence are more of an issue in this tale. Farmer Hogget says very little, while his wife talks a stream of disorganised domestic detail.

> 'Well, will you look at that!' said Mrs Hogget. 'That old Fly [the collie], she'll mother anything, kittens, ducklings, baby chicks, she's looked after all of they, now 'tis a pig, in't he lovely, what a picture, good job he don't know where he'll finish up, but he'll be big then and we'll be glad to see the back of him, or the ham's of him, I should say, shan't us, wonder how I shall get it all in the freezer?'
> 'Pity. Really,' said Farmer Hogget absently. (21–22)

Babe uses mannered and polite language to the sheep and succeeds with them, where Fly the collie simply orders them about as doltish inferiors. Because of Babe's kindness to them, the sheep give him the ovine 'password' by which he can be accepted by the sheep he has to drive in the trials.

Of course it is a fantasy and a joke, but King-Smith makes us just consider that some animals might be brighter than others, or that what we humans appropriate as 'reality' might be quite other than we know. What the story gets at is the habit of seeing things by preconceptions. Babe alone goes out of himself and sees the world from the sheep's point of view, and this makes them more responsive and less stupid-seeming. For if Fly considers sheep stupid, that is also what sheep think of dogs (or 'wolves' as they call them). In exactly the same way the Squire and the pig-man in Daggie Dogfoot thought each other dim. Kindness and consideration nourish intelligence which contempt and patronage freeze: there might be a moral here to apply to human society, were the context not so ludicrous as to blunt it.

The habit of categorisation is also mocked in the images of a pig that crosses species, whether in having a dog's feet and swimming, or in having more than canine intelligence and aptitude. It is not a question of King-Smith asking us to believe that such things could happen, rather of his mocking the habit of mind that says they could not – and thereby, as in Swift, man's pride in himself as the sole rational species.

He goes a step further in *Harry's Mad*, where a bird communicates directly with humans. Madison the African grey parrot has lived for many years with Harry's Great-Uncle George, a professor of linguistics in America, and has been left on the uncle's death to Harry's family in Britain. We learn that 'Forty years in the company of Professor George Holdsworth had given Madison a great liking for the art of conversation' (27). This parrot can help Harry's father when he is stuck for a complex crossword clue, adding, '" You want I should spell it for you?"' Madison ('Mad') cracks jokes, talking about his learning having been acquired '"parrot fashion"' or his having to act the '"dumb cluck"' in front of Harry's parents. He even sells himself as a parrot on the phone, mimicking the way a normal parrot might speak, '"God save the Queen! Rule Britannia! Land of Hope and Glory! You've got a face like a chicken's bum!"'(68–9). Here reality is turned inside out, as a parrot mimics the cliché humans have made of it. When Madison has been stolen, Harry is given another parrot they call Fweddy, who lisps a much more limited and imitative vocabulary – as when the phone rings it says, '"Answer the wetched thing, dahling, I'm too weawy to lift the weceiver"' (91). Harry and Madison enjoy playing with words and making puns, in a way that Babe the pig, who could not distinguish between 'you' and 'ewe,' could not.

In a way, though, King-Smith has steadily 'come out.' Daggie and the animals in *Daggie Dogfoot* had a community of intelligence closed to the pig-man; Babe climbed the evolutionary ladder with his apparent canine abilities, while the source of his power over sheep remained hidden; while Madison, as a parrot supposed to mimic intelligence with speech, actually mimics speech with intelligence, which he reveals to his owners. But of course, none of it is meant as anything but a joke . . . .

Consideration of Diana Wynne Jones and Dick King-Smith has given an idea of the range of explorations of reality in 1980s children's fantasy. Jones's eye is on the multiverse and the infinite possibilities of being, whereas King-Smith considers rather the contingency of this world. The one explores a different universe from fiction to fiction, while the other keeps to the animal world, steadily increasing its differences from the one we think we know.

But there are many other forms of the multiple reality theme in children's fantasies of the 1980s. Some of them explore the contingency of time. Others play fiction against reality, through such motifs as lying, dreaming, or story-making. Some use secondary worlds to create a sense of multiple possibility. Still others even evacuate our own world of meaning. Taken together they subvert any clear, single or fixed view of the universe. They will be our concern for most of the rest of this chapter.

PLAYING WITH REALITY: THE 1980s

First, time. A recurrent motif in 1980s fantasy is the past re-entering the present, not to suggest continuity, as for example in the 1970s fantasies of Penelope Lively, but to show our reality no longer the only one. Our first example is Joan Aiken's *The Shadow Guests* (1981). In a sense this fantasy follows on from Aiken's alternative world stories from *The Wolves of Willoughby Chase* (1962) to *The Stolen Lake* (1981). But those books propose only one historical alternative world, which is so thickened through novel after novel that we forget its contingency: indeed there Aiken is more interested in the romantic possibilities of the past than in its alterity. It is the contingency, the insubstantiality, of what we take to be reality, that is more at the forefront in *The Shadow Guests*. During the book the appropriately-named boy-protagonist Cosmo is reading E. A. Abbott's *Flatland: A Romance of Many Dimensions* (1884).

Cosmo's family Curtis (from the Latin for 'short'), have been subject to a two thousand year-old curse by which the eldest son of the family is always killed and his mother then dies of grief: he himself has already thus lost his brother and his mother. In this the book reflects the theme of the stranglehold of the past over the present that we saw in 1970s children's fantasy: "'you can't get away from your ancestors'" Cosmo is told (49). But the book conceives of the past not only as historical, but as recurrent through a fold in time. For two centuries a strange coach-and-six has visited Cosmo's family at full moon. He wonders whether "'that couldn't be something that's happening in another dimension. ... We just happen to see it because there's a fold in space at that point – or in time – it happened a couple of hundred years ago, but because of the fold it keeps coming back again'" (71).

Cosmo lives with a cousin called Eunice who is a professor of mathematics at Oxford, and has written a book called *Man and Measurement*. Eunice sees it as the distinction of man that he is "'the only animal that has taken to measuring'" (95). Yet if measurement alone were involved, no-one could apprehend the possibility of another dimension or a fold in time. Indeed it is precisely outside measure that Cousin Eunice works: her book is "'a kind of mathematical judo. Wriggling about, coming out in unexpected places. Trying to get the best result with the least effort'" (95). Only by leaving our categories of reality behind is the truth found. Cosmo himself lives two lives: one, at his weekday Oxford boarding school, where his fellows try to make him fit their measure, and when he does not, exclude him; and two, his weekend life, where he is allowed to be himself, and is visited by strange people from the past. Cousin Eunice tells him of the 'Irregulars' in Abbott's *Flatland*, and says, "'The author is making fun of the way that society as a whole turns against people who don't conform to all its rules'" (71); so with Cosmo. He lives a supernatural experience beyond most people's measure, for which his school friends think him a liar. But in the end they come to accept him, and to read Abbott's *Flatland* with him. However the book ends, too, without the comfortable 'measure' of fantasy whereby justice is done and good rewarded. Cosmo may now have friends, but his mother and elder brother remain forever lost to him, and he himself is fundamentally alone, with the curse still hanging over his own future family.

Such 'bi-temporalism' is also seen in David Wiseman's *The Fate of Jeremy Visick* (1981), which on the face of it is also a 1970s-type story of the influence of the past on the present. It tells how a modern Cornish schoolboy Matthew Clemens becomes influenced by the spirit of an unburied child lost long ago in a copper mine disaster, and experiences with him the struggle to find a way out after the explosion. The influence of dead Jeremy Visick on Matthew results from the fact that the Clemens house is built next to the shed in which the Visicks once lived. The story recalls Jill Paton Walsh's *A Chance Child*, with its tale of young Creep wandering back along a canal from a modern city to a landscape of the industrial revolution, never to return.

However Wiseman's novel alternates chapters of Matthew's present-day life with accounts of his dealings with Jeremy, so that he moves in and out of two worlds and begins to lose hold of his identity. The past does not merely influence the present, nor is it a place one moves to through time or space: it is bi-local and bi-temporal. One of the subjects of the book is history, which Matthew dislikes at school, but comes to find has a power over the present and over himself which he could never have suspected. And he is brought to realise that the past is no completed thing, but something that the present can still alter and help, as he relieved Jeremy Visick's fear and exhaustion in the mine. Beyond this, Matthew finds in Jeremy a boy very like himself, whose life could have been his own but for the accident of time. But such messages are well bedded in the reality of the book, a reality which has happy, often unthinking, Matthew come largely to forget his experience with Jeremy. Till that point, however, Matthew has not been sure of his own reality, nor of who or where or when he is.

Other kinds of 'reality-questioning' through time are found in Penelope Lively's *The Revenge of Samuel Stokes* (1981), Mary Wesley's *Haphazard House* (1983), Tim Kennemore's *Changing Times* (1984), Nicholas Wilde's *Into the Dark* (1987) and Jane Gardam's *Through the Dolls' House Door* (1987). *The Revenge of Samuel Stokes* portrays an irrepressible eighteenth-century architect who cannot bear a modern housing estate being built on the site of his former landscape garden, and keeps sending shoots of eighteenth-century architecture and herbage up from underground to cause ruin. *Haphazard House*, at first a would-be humorous story of an eccentric artist and his family who settle in an old country house, becomes increasingly ambiguous as to what time they are living in, and under what conditions: for people sometimes seem much younger, and nobody save an old couple is ever seen in the nearby village. This is a complex and moving tale, in which the characters increasingly become part of the spiritual world of the village when it was depopulated at the time of the Great Plague of 1665. They are, effectively, at one with the dead – who are, for them, part of the everlastingly alive. Having mastered travel within time, they have moved out of it. Yet they remain just as real and idiosyncratic as people for all that.

Changing Times, by contrast, gives us an often brilliantly comic story of an alienated fifteen year old schoolgirl, Victoria, with a singular line in backchat, who acquires a clock that proves magical, and sends her into various times in her past, including her helpless infancy. In the past she finds the sordid truth about her father's faithlessness, and her mother's subsequent limpet-like behaviour to him. Unable to change the past, Victoria resolves to leave her parents and set up with her boyfriend David, but a glance at the future shows the appalling outcome of their relationship, and she goes to her grandmother's instead. A rather inappropriate moral conclusion about coming to terms with things follows: we are left adding the rider, 'Only make terms with what you cannot avoid.' But the starkness of the contrasts between what Victoria believed and what her time-trips reveal to her leaves us wondering whether she did right to accept them as true, and whether her trips may not have been to *the* past and future but to one of several possible pasts and futures.

Nicholas Wilde's *Into the Dark* rather portrays time as a circle, by which the present may of itself return to the past. On holiday with his mother in a cottage on a country estate, Matthew, who is blind, meets and befriends a boy called Roly, who gradually turns out to be the child Rupert who lived in the big house a hundred years earlier. This child, who was spoilt, dragged his only friend Tom to death with him; Matthew, it transpires, is the now living form of Tom. Matthew eventually forgives Roly by retracing the events up to his death, and Roly can then rest in peace. The story says that imprints on time are always there (compare Penelope Lively), and it frequently mentions there always being two points of view in life: and certainly the reliving of the death time is part of this. But it also says that as well as moving, time stays forever still. Matthew has only four days' holiday, but those days are part of eternity. It is a story which, like Wesley's *Haphazard House*, disorients us: and this is one symbolic significance of Matthew's blindness, which leaves him uncertain of the identity of Roly and of where he is.

Jane Gardam's *Through the Dolls' House Door* presents us with two different species' times – doll time and human time. The humans move the dolls about, making their environment better (girls) or worse (boys); but they themselves are moved by time. They move to new houses, as the dolls never do; they grow, have another generation of children, and then age: a constant air of evanescence surrounds them. Doll time is much longer: the china cat tells a tale of how she lived in ancient Egypt, a plastic Trojan recounts the fall of Troy, the wooden Dutch doll tells how she was the constant companion of a medieval master craftsman. There is however also an invisible doll called Sigger, who is fading, and who represents the spirit of the dolls' house. When 'by chance' the now grown-up human children are reminded of their long-lost dolls' house, and reclaim and repair it, Sigger, who was on the point of expiry, revives; and they all 'sat smiling at the new day.' Time is seen here from two points of view, as in Wilde's *Into the Dark*; and neither is more real, for if the humans are evanescent, the dolls are static and passive. The unanswerable question by the end is, who are the real dolls?

'Dolls' who come alive, and time, also feature in Lynne Reid Banks's *Indian Trilogy* - *The Indian in the Cupboard* (1981), *Return of the Indian* (1986) and *The Secret of the Indian* (1989). Here two boys gain access to different parts of the past, which they then begin to cross with one another. But it is not just different times, but games and 'realities,' fictions and 'truths,' which are made to interact here. Young Omri (= *omniae rei* = all things = God?) is given a plastic toy Indian and a little white bathroom cupboard for his birthday, by his friend Patrick and his penniless brother. He also finds a strange little key on his mother's key-ring that fits the cupboard door. One night, he puts the plastic Indian into the cupboard and locks the door, and when he wakes up finds that it has come to miniature and irascible life.[9] The process is reversed when the door is locked again. Patrick eventually has to be let into the secret, and himself activates a plastic cowboy called Boone from the late 1880s, whom he adopts as his own. Each of these figures is enlivened by the spirit of a real being from the past. Various accidents suffered by the mannikins, who can travel back to their own times, are remedied by a plastic First World War medical orderly, then by a modern staff nurse, and finally by a toy modern surgical team. The Indian, Little Bull, who is an eighteenth-century Iroquois chief, is determined to make war on his French and Indian enemies, even with dangerous modern weapons. He also chooses a wife from Omri's plastic collection, and eventually has a son. Boone is a comic cowboy with a passion for whisky, and a sentimental side that makes him continually burst into tears; he is finally married to an intelligent whore with a heart of gold. The interactions of these characters and their different-natured boy creators produce great humour and life. And of course beyond them is the author herself, whose talent is the key that brings to life all the figures in her cupboard of fiction. And beyond her. ... What is fiction, what truth? Are we not ourselves little plastic figures enlivened by souls? (And other such large questions.)

Especially in the third book there is much exploration of the theme of fiction and truth, or plastic representation and living reality. By the end of the second volume the reality contained within the fiction, or the magic world of which the boys are custodians, begins to break out from its safe confines. Numbers of the Indians are killed when they take modern weapons back into the past, and a late nineteenth-century tornado bursts into our world and becomes the 1987 English hurricane. The rules of the magic grow more complicated as the boys explore them, and they make mistakes. They themselves find out how to travel back in time with the small people, but only in such a way as to be present as part of the design on a tepee, or, Swift-like, to be themselves small beside the now giant figures of the erstwhile Lilliputians. They begin to lose their grip on events, which also threaten to be revealed to the world outside. Meanwhile Omri has written a story about 'his' Indian for a national story-writing competition, and has won it, to great acclaim: he has passed off truth as fiction, but in so doing has opened himself to questions concerning certain things he has let slip in the past. The upshot is that the 'story' must end, and the enlivening souls of the various plastic figures must be returned to their own times.

Omri realises that he has been wrong to go on considering the little people partly as animated toys: 'They were flesh and blood, with their own characters, their own lives and destinies' (*Secret*, 28; see also 30). At the same time the spirits that are brought to animate the little models have to accept that this new world in which they find themselves is not an illusion or a game, but hard truth. These are real people who happen to be in little bodies, and their relationships with one another and with their boy-creators are almost as idiosyncratic and individual as with people in real life – one says 'almost' because some of them do tend to act according to stereotypes, particularly the staff nurse, the whore, and an N.C.O. Yet they are in one sense indeed an illusion, for their existence in these little forms depends both on the workings of a very peculiar magic apparatus, and on the often misguided manipulations of two boys. The relations of fiction and reality, of play and truth, are finally left teasingly indefinite. This contrasts significantly with Pauline Clarke's story of children and little people, *The Twelve and the Genii* (1962), for there there is an ultimate divine reality beyond all uncertainties.

Much 1980s children's fantasy plays fiction against reality, exploring the nature of illusion, dreams or lies – in short, any mode in which mind reshapes the world, including that of writing fantasy itself. This is quite different from most previous fantasy, which assumes some form of ultimate reality – whether that of our own world outside the fantastic one, or the truth within and beyond the fantastic world, as with Narnia or the 'back' of the North Wind. The children's fantasies of the 1870s might question the truth of the imagination's pictures, but that was by the yardstick of a settled external reality. The children's fantasies of the 1980s pose the possibility that there is no settled reality or truth anywhere.

To start with the topic of fiction versus truth, first in relation to the use of lies. The *Pentecost* animal stories of W. J. Corbett, for example – *The Song of Pentecost* (1982), *Pentecost and the Chosen One* (1984) and *Pentecost of Lickey Top* (1987) – explore the problematic character of reality through this theme; here, though, it is a reality made more problematic for many of the characters than it really is. Many of the characters in the books spend their lives deceiving others. Indeed *The Song of Pentecost* portrays one long series of lies. First, the character Snake is chased from his home on Lickey Top when his cousin appears claiming it as the gift of Snake's late father's will, and produces a lying frog as witness. Then, the perfectly healthy old Uncle mouse continually pleads ill health to have a life of luxury on the backs of his fellows. The frog lies so continually that the mice learn to derive truth from what he says by reversing it; until one day the frog finds himself uttering a truth, and likes it so much that he instantly resolves to reform. The pert orange bug, the cockle-snorkle, lies to everyone in sight, to make mischief among them: he is a sort of Sporus figure (Pope). The Fox uses his skill as a trickster to draw the hounds and frighten the weasels into their holes, so that the mice can pass safely through a wood.

By the end the journey has become not only a physical one to the goal of Lickey Top, à la *Watership Down*, but a spiritual one through delusion to possible truth. Reality is so frequently reshaped, particularly by 'story-tellers,' that its discovery requires continual vigilance. Snake is a sucker, the Owl is flattered by the bug, Uncle plays on his fellows' good nature. The mice move through a landscape of deception. They have to trust the Snake, the river is wider than it seems, and they get through the wood by disguising themselves with leaves. The frog lives by self-deception, ignoring the foul landscape of Pentecost Farm, with its rubbish, its stagnant stream and its scum: 'He had convinced himself that this place was a little paradise' (17). Even the mouse Pentecost lives by two selves, an inner and an outer. In the end it is only by luck that the mice reach their destination and are allowed to settle.

Cheats litter the *Pentecost* books. The leader of the town mice in *Pentecost and the Chosen One* is a swindling tyrant appropriately named Zero.[10] This book is to some extent about the nature of true leadership, which the new Pentecost has to discover. It is a political book, full of machination, intrigue and crowd-manipulation. Pentecost learns that you cannot live alone and for yourself, as he does at first: he is introduced to a much more chaotic 'real world' than he has known. That also applies to megalomaniacs like Zero, who rule only to tread others down. Pentecost is a true leader and hero when he shows kindness even to his enemies. People here live by subtleties and end by deceiving only themselves, like Sneak the city mouse, or the cockle-snorkle with its endless schemes of mischief. The cockle-snorkle reaches an ecstatic pitch of deception in *Pentecost at Lickey*

Top, continually weaving fresh lying tales for each character until everything blows up in his face. It is clear that, like the novelist Henry Fielding, Corbett is fascinated by the hypocrite, against whom he cannot warn us too much. For the hypocrite twists reality into destructive illusion. Lying assumes its opposite, truth: in these books, altering reality is being seen as a vice.

If the *Pentecost* books are often about political lies, lying to others, Michael Morpurgo's *King of the Cloud Forests* (1987), the story of a boy who has a paradisal sojourn with the mythical Yeti in the Himalayas, is as much about lying to oneself. Fourteen year-old Ashley has been sent by his missionary father under trusted protection to escape from China to India during the Japanese invasion of 1937. He has to live a lie – to be disguised, and to pretend to be dumb and Chinese – to pass through China and Tibet; and his subsequent life with the Yeti is burdened by his having to live up to their false view of him as a miracle-worker and a god. Later, he has to conceal from the Yeti his inadvertent part in the death of one of them. The strain of continuous deception brings Ashley at length to leave his strange hosts. Back in England, he meets another man who once stayed with the Yeti, but who, as a leading scientist, was persuaded not to publish an account of this lest it compromise his reputation as a scholar. Ashley, with less to lose, 'has written' the book we now read – another 'untruth.' We are left to tease out the relation between his fiction and any reality, and to chew on the view of the characters that '"anything's possible"' (121). Ashley at least resolves to go back to the Yeti after writing this book: whether they, who loved him as a lie, will ever welcome him as he is in truth, remains untold.

Lying is found as a theme in other books of the 1980s, particularly Vivien Alcock's *The Stonewalkers*, where the protagonist Poppy is known as a liar and is therefore not believed by her mother when she describes a walking statue she encounters in a park. Similarly, in Joan Aiken's *The Shadow Guests*, Cosmo is put 'in Coventry' by his school mates for supposedly being a liar. And in 1988 two titles, *A Pack of Lies* by Geraldine McCaughrean and *A Pack of Liars* by Anne Fine, appeared independently of one another. It is just possible that this in some way reflects the new society of the 1980s, in which ambition and greed, and the compromises needed to satisfy them, became more prominent. But certainly it seems to reflect the generalised 'postmodernism' of the time: 'lying' is another word for turning reality into a series of fictions – though it involves a much less disinterested attitude towards doing so.

This is precisely what happens in Geraldine McCaughrean's *A Pack of Lies*, where the strange new assistant in a second-hand shop, MCC Berkshire, weaves such amazing stories around ten pieces of junk that they sell for far more than their value to enthralled customers.[11] Whether the stories about them are true or false we never learn, and in the end the objects are no more real as they 'are' in the shop, than as they are in the 'fictions' about them: in short, in postmodernist terms, they acquire a textual reality. Whether they become '*inter*-textual,' that is, whether the stories partake in one another's natures, is another matter. Certainly they are inter-textual in that they are all literary, and probably derived from MCC Berkshire's prodigious appetite for fiction. They include such genres as the murder story, the Chinese fairy tale, the pirate romance, the detective story, the Irish tall tale, the Kiplingesque story and the tale of the supernatural – all of them 'sensational' fiction. They are so interwoven with the story of MCC Berkshire and the shop as to be parts or extensions of it. Indeed, at one point one of the characters in the shop is found to have been part of one story; and several supposed inventions concerning objects for sale are found to be 'true.'

Also, at the beginning and end, there is a series of metafictional skips and jumps. The girl Ailsa meets MCC Berkshire in the local library, at a point where she has put a microfiche the wrong way round in a reader, and is trying to decipher, from upside-down and back-to-front, the title of a book called 'A Pack of Lies, Oxford University Press, 1988.' And at the end the MCC Berkshire who finally walks out of the shop and the lives of Ailsa and her mother, is suddenly presented as a recluse writer who made up the whole story we have just read, and is now looking for a way to end it. He had to leave his own fiction because the characters started getting too real for him (166–7). Again he changes the ending, this time to remove himself from the world altogether, and his mother, coming up with some sandwiches for him, finds only his spectacles left in the room. The ending is reminiscent of Diana Wynne Jones's *Archer's Goon*: all reality becomes literary and textual. And beyond the story that MCC Berkshire 'makes'(?), there is the story of MCC Berkshire that a writer called Geraldine McCaughrean makes: and so on. The whole thing is literally 'a pack of lies,' in the sense that fiction is shuffled with fiction in bewildering variety. As for lies, fictions and truths, who finally knows the difference? The book is a series of games that never forfeit the chance of being earnest. Every one of the stories told by MCC Berkshire is a joke; yet at the same time many of them are strictly moral and 'proportionate,' involving punishment (or unmasking) of the wicked, reward of the innocent, and exposure of the stupid.

Similarly made up of nine stories interwoven with the context of their making, but here based on dreaming, is Peter Dickinson's *Merlin Dreams* (1988). 'Merlin' here – he is never named – is dreaming under his moorland rock, where he has long been buried at his own wish. This is not the Merlin of Arthurian chivalry, nor the peevish Merlin of Dickinson's earlier *Changes* trilogy (1967), but the shaman of a prehistoric British kingdom, who oversaw the building of Stonehenge and the cutting of the White Horse of Uffington in Downland chalk. Again, no names are used in his narrative, whether of people or events. Remembering his past life, this Merlin's mind drifts associationally into nine dreams. What he dreams are mostly tales in the style of medieval romance, involving knights and damsels, enchantresses and warlocks, castles and palaces, and magical beasts. Merlin is not dreaming future history, for these are stories only: but he is dreaming medieval culture. That he will himself become seen as one of its prime actors, in the Arthurian story, is an irony which perhaps belongs to time. But the implication of the entire book is that we may ourselves be both dreaming and dreamt.[12]

The stories themselves are mostly about deception – the overarching one being the self-deception that makes medievalism a cliché of nobility and courtesy.[13] There are tales about swindling, as in 'Stone,' where a travelling cheat who deceives villagers with a fake cockatrice is himself tricked into gazing at a real basilisk, and so turned to stone (see also 'Hermit'). Then there are stories of betrayal, such as 'Unicorn,' where a baron who has blackmailed a girl into trapping her friend, a young unicorn, for him, is himself killed by the unicorn's hidden parents (see also 'Sword,' 'Damsel'). Or there is concealment, as in 'Sciopod,' where a freak creature is hidden by villagers from its cruel owners. And there are several stories concerning hidden abilities, or discrepancies, such as 'Knight Errant,' about an apparently degenerate knight, who is yet able to overthrow great opponents by cunning; or 'Enchantress,' where a witch who feeds on children's beauty is defeated by the ugliest boy in the village (see also 'King'). The suggestion behind all the stories is that the world is a bewildering series of appearances, each of them as real as any another. The basilisk in the mountebank's box is first a fake, and then a reality; the man who turns into a dog in 'Damsel' is no less dog than man. When the ugly boy defeats the enchantress, her castle is ruined and the impenetrable woods around its people are laid open; but when the villagers go back to their old ways, the evil magic returns.

Nevertheless, many of the stories involve exposure of illusion or trickery for what is 'true.' In 'Knight Errant' the dread invisible black knight, who is last on Sir Tremalin's list of opponents, turns out to be an old man; and Sir Tremalin begins to surmise that his quest has actually been arranged so that he may succeed, and either replace the black knight or destroy the enchantment of the town for ever. So too the cunning mountebank, the stepmother-dragon and the lying retainer of other stories have their schemes laid bare. But more than this, in weaving nine enchanted pictures of the high Middle Ages, the dreamer both propounds and exposes the courtly and aristocratic civilisation on which such stories depend. Sir Tremalin is a cynic, who abuses the knightly code to achieve his ends by trickery. In 'Stone' the traditionally exotic nature of a basilisk is enmeshed with a fraudster, and in 'Sciopod,' a single-legged human wonder is part of a dingy travelling circus. The high kingly language of Sir Hugh in 'Damsel' is undercut by the direct Scottish tongue of a Highland chieftainess. '"Madam," … [Sir Hugh] said, "what would you of me, for my sword and my arm are yours and your enemy is mine?"', to which comes the answer, '"I dinna talk sic speech.… But you'll be hungered?"' (82). There is a certain democracy here, which marries coarseness and grandeur, just as Hugh and the Highland lady come to marry. And Merlin the primitive wizard is also the dreamer of Arthurian civilisation. Such a mixture of wilderness and civility, of high and low, is also seen in Dickinson's *The Blue Hawk*, where the king and the common boy must act together to defeat the dangerous over-sophistication of religious ritual on the one hand and the savagery of barbarian invaders on the other. And in the *Changes* trilogy, humanity can learn true culture only by being thrown into near-barbarity by the destruction of civilisation.

But in the end, for Dickinson, all reality is dreamt. In 'Dreams,' the poetic coda to the book, Merlin is vainly sought by the agents of a king whose ordered realm is about to be swept away: 'Wolves [are] in the roadways, brothers at war,/ The sword a tool to be bought and sold,/ Savages raiding the eastern shore/ And the King old, old.' But like the king, Merlin too is dying. And yet Merlin's mind, which held the imagined lives of others across time, will itself be renewed in future imaginations. The knight searching for Merlin dies knowing that the tale of the great wizard sleeping beneath the stone 'Was a lie, but true': a lie, because Merlin will not act to help the king; true, because the king will be saved in his dreams. The whole story is a magic nine-tale charm, a spell for lasting life and perpetual renewal. Merlin has shut himself beneath the rock so that he may do nothing physically, and yet do everything.

The 1980s fantasies of William Mayne, 'Boy to Island' (1982) and *Kelpie* (1987) are also about the shifting borders of illusion and truth, but here more in relation to the deceptiveness of the outside world than to that of the perceiver. Mayne's vision is always outward-looking, and ultimately metaphysical, except perhaps in *A Game of Dark*: in his 1950s fantasy the concern was with the empirical truth of a legend of a unicorn; in the 1960s it was the rootedness of magic in the earth; in the 1970s it was the displacement of the self or of time. 'Boy to Island' is a story of a Highland boy Colin who is kept for years on a fairy island; and *Kelpie* portrays the relationship between some Yorkshire children on holiday and a Scottish kelpie, or great water-horse, which is trying to show one of them how she can give it its freedom. 'Boy to Island' is about continued illusion or 'glamour.' Once caught by the fairies, Colin can no longer distinguish time or place. In attempting to escape, he all too often thinks mistakenly that he has broken out of the bubble of faërian unreality into his own world. Mayne conveys the uncertainty through shifting syntax:

> The world in a bubble or drop of dew is sharp and curved. Being here was like being outside the bubble looking in, as well as being inside, part of the curving flatness, the sea sloping away to the edges of what could be seen, the sky a tight curve overhead, the beach of white sand being a bay and at the same time sloping back, the white rocks in the shining water tilted away yet showing their tops. (111)

Colin does not know whether he is alive or dead, or whether what he sees is there, or a picture in his head, or a memory.

Even at the end, the long-lost Janet, whom Colin rescues and brings back home, is another illusion, for she turns to dust. 'He saw that the reality of her was not here in the village, that the shape he saw was of someone in another place, that he was seeing through her the land of the fairy people still' (125). As for himself, his vision of his own world is increasingly obscured by that of fairy-land, which in the end finally reclaims him. '"I am dizzy with coming home," said Colin; and he thought it might be so, but it was his seeing that troubled him, with a patch down the world now as if the middle of a page were torn out and the next showed through, reading no sense' (127). This story is a contrast to Mayne's earlier *A Year and a Day* (1976), in which a naked fairy boy is found and temporarily made part of a human family: there the fairy is domesticated – so far as possible, for it reverts in the end. But in 'Boy to Island' the fairies like spiders capture mortals, and so stung are they with the poison of enchantment that they never finally escape; nor do they any longer know what is real.

In *Kelpie* the fairy beast in question is at first denied as an illusion by the boys and the adults; but later they admit that it is a question of how you see. 'Not seeing' is related not only to the Kelpie but to the little girl Lucy, who is continually passed over by everybody as though she does not exist. It is a question not just of some seeing what others of a different disposition do not – though rational adults and 'practical' boys cannot for long see the Kelpie. It also involves an angle of vision, by which the Kelpie makes itself visible only on certain planes of light (59, 64). The neglected Lucy, whose name means 'light,' is the first to see the Kelpie, because she exists on a similar plane of (in)visibility. The Kelpie can appear as rocks or islands that suddenly come alive. And if it can seem a delusion to some people, our own world is a mere appearance to it, for it walks through walls and dams as if they were not there. At the end, when everyone has learned to see the Kelpie, they have also learned to take notice of Lucy (who alone drew the creature to her and could give it freedom). But the photographs of the Kelpie all have a blank where it should be. Lucy catches the duality of truth and illusion when she says '"It was as true as sums.... As true as taking nine from eight, and you know that's impossible"' (81). Aside from these continual speculations, the book is a beautiful picture of young primary school children and their world, which in another angle of light is as fantastic – and as fleeting – as that of the Kelpie.

Another fantasy dealing with the mind's constructions of reality is Jan Mark's *Aquarius* (1983). The hero, a water-diviner, is driven out by his tribe, who live in a too-frequently flooded area. He travels far to a drought-stricken kingdom whose king, a supposed rain-maker, has been unsuccessful. The water-diviner's science supplies what superstitious belief has not – or so we are led to assume – and the rains come. After this the water-diviner befriends and eventually abducts the now weakened king and takes him back to his own homeland – why, we do not know. There the king realises his true abilities: he is in fact not a rain-maker, but a rain-stopper. At once reality becomes magical again, as well as being 'rational'; and our assumptions about the king as a failed water-bringer are reversed. We also see that reality is multiple enough for failure in one place to be success in another. One of the strengths of this story is that this pattern emerges quite naturally from a vivid narrative of human intrigue.

In the 1980s there are a large number of such 'secondary world' children's fantasies, especially as seen in the work of Diana Wynne Jones. The reason for this is precisely the postmodernism of the decade, and the multiplication of realities, whether temporal or spatial. In John Gordon's *The Edge of the World* (1983) for example, our world is shown increasingly supplanted by the reality of the secondary one until that other is finally overcome. A sexually jealous witch has imprisoned her sister in the other world. This world shoots up within the known one whenever a disk of bog-oak is turned over in sunlight, and is suggestive of the unconscious or 'dark side' of the self. Two children (natives of the unconscious?) enter it, and after unbelievably heroic exploits eventually rescue the lost sister and return her to her now aged lover. The secondary world is more real than the known one, being a brilliantly-imagined landscape of red desert plateau, huge cliff and swampy grassland, ending in a colossal glass palace. Guardian horrors from this land are from time to time summoned into our world, where they are no nebulous threats, but are very solidly-pictured skeletal horse-heads on human bodies: when one of them climbs a slope in pursuit, the children can hear how 'between clawed toes, bristles scratched the ground' (27).

The secondary world in Catherine Storr's *The Castle Boy* (1983) is founded not on magic but on the human spirit. It is in part a symbol of how reality can become indefinite when we are uncertain of our own lives. Young Robert is staying with his parents and sister in a Northumberland hotel which was once the site of a Borders castle. Whenever Robert touches a stone from the old castle, he finds himself transported back to the castle in its medieval heyday. 'From whatever part of the hotel he started on his journey into the past, he would find himself in that place in the Castle which had once occupied the same space' (79). Though

Robert is subject to epileptic fits, the castle is not altogether a piece of imagining, for he has always pictured himself as the centre of his fantasy worlds, and here he is peripheral, spurned and largely ignored by all the castle's inhabitants. Because of his desperate desire to fit into society, only added to by his hero-worship for his wartime pilot father (60), this is peculiarly painful for him. Yet his epilepsy and the fact that 'his' medieval family apparently disowned him, have there made him outcast as an idiot. And even when he hears of a plot that will overthrow the castle, his halting words telling of this are rejected by the people there. Only in the end is he able to carry out a successful heroic act, in giving his life in a vain attempt to protect another deformed outcast in the burning castle. Returned to his own world, Robert finds that the hotel has had a fire in which his father has lost his life trying to rescue a trapped maid. This is partly symbolic of Robert's no longer needing his father. In a sense he will not return to the castle because it has taught him to accept himself for what he is. Like him, his world has become more certain and substantial. In some ways the book recalls William Mayne's *A Game of Dark*. It contrasts however with Storr's own earlier *Marianne Dreams* (1958): that was concerned more directly with moral behaviour between two children, whereas this deals with the more 'ontological' issue of one child coming to terms with his own reality.

In Susan Cooper's *Seaward* (1983) the secondary world is much more of a dream. In American fashion (Cooper had lived in America since 1965), it prefers its secondary world to be separate from ours, to which it gives primary reality; and it portrays the other world as only a symbolic version of events going on in our own. Here we move away altogether from the bilocalism of other 1980s English children's fantasies. A bourgeois girl Calliope, and a rougher boy, Westerly, have lost their parents and entered a strange world, where they believe they will find them again by journeying westwards to the sea. Their journey is a maturation quest through a kind of purgatory, during which they are pursued, until they realise their pursuers are horrors of their own making: what seemed 'real' in the physical sense, is actually mental. A hostile goddess figure, Taranis, a demonic Stonecutter, and various more helpful characters are met, in a punishing journey across deserts and mountains that takes the pair through a giant annihilating chess-game, pursuit by menacing boulders (drawn from Catherine Storr's *Marianne Dreams*), siege in a stone tower, and so on, till they come to the sea, which is death. They refuse the choice of travelling over the sea to the paradise of Tir n'An Og, preferring to return to their own worlds. Though the book's settings are finely imagined, they are not suggestive of meaning, but are there simply as fantastic inventions to give an exotic and exciting air to the plot. The journey itself seems modelled in part on George Macdonald's dream-romance *Phantastes* (1858), yet is without its symbolic resonance, and what significances there are are usually pointed out with American directness. "'Snake ... has much in common with the part of yourself which is giving you trouble at the moment ... Energy ... Enjoyment, delight, a glad fierceness'" (100). Part of the trouble is that the book is non-moral: enjoyment of life is the only notion of good, hating it the bad. "'There is no right or wrong, here. There are only different ways of living'" (168). And the book is in the end quite decided as to the true nature of reality, in contrast to most of the English fantasies considered here.

Two different realities are shown negotiating with one another in William Mayne's secondary world fantasy *Antar of the Eagles* (1989). Here a boy is stolen by great eagles and trained to fly, so that he may recover for them the lost egg of their now aged Great Eagle, and save their royal line. Eagles and boy each have to adapt to the alien reality of the other if the scheme is to succeed. The savage imperatives of the eagles make it hard for them to accommodate, particularly to a creature who is usually their enemy, and whose body seems so useless beside theirs. The book concerns the physical adjustments required to obtain a physical end (the egg), and is thus more 'solid' and narrational than *Kelpie* or 'Boy to Island' – which itself shows Mayne creating two opposite kinds of fictional reality in the 1980s. Antar's struggle with other eaglets for meat in the giant nest where he is trained, his first terrifying attempts at flight, his desperate search beneath the snow for the egg when he has lost it, all these are vivid and memorable. Mayne finely imagines the different avian characters and their more and less violent outlooks. He also continues his earlier dialogue between fantasy and the physical world – here in such terms as weight, falling, flying, striking, burial.

Another kind of interrogation of reality altogether in 1980s children's fantasy is that which confronts the void behind being, the realm of no meaning. These fantasies challenge our faith in reality at a more visceral level, posing the possibility that the world is hollow at the core and ultimately meaningless. Here the contrasts we have so far seen between different ontologies, or fiction and reality, or lying and truth, are finally evacuated, in a picture of our world as having insufficient reality to be an illusion, while containing so much substantial horror as to be beyond truth.

This is most starkly portrayed in Vivian Alcock's *The Stonewalkers* (1983). This book is a disturbing challenge to the assurances about 'real life' that almost all children's fantasies entertain – namely, that the world will ultimately smile for a child, that death, exclusion and alienation are at most what happen to other people. On the surface, however, the book tries to suppress its own darkness. Poppy, a young girl with a loveless relation with her mother, accidentally brings to life a terrifying female statue, which then wakes up many more statues in a moorland garden centre. These statues pursue Poppy and her friend Emma to the nearby moor, and seal them in an underground cave with them. At one point Poppy has the chance to escape, but stays to help Emma, who has broken her ankle. This brings her back into loving feelings towards people, and later to her mother, who has been shocked into reform. Because Poppy has selflessly loved one person, it appears, love has spread in her own heart.

That benign meaning is present in the book: and for all that the change of heart in Polly and her mother comes only at the end, it is at least partly convincing. But on the other side the book is about insecurity – not merely childhood insecurity (Belladonna the female statue is in part Poppy's cold mother), but real nightmare insecurity about the world, which perhaps only the child can see. The statues, though beautiful and even smiling, are cold and alien, Poppy's attempts to befriend the female statue meet with no clear response, and many of the other statues want to kill her and Emma on the moor:

> 'But we were *friends*! You can't have forgotten! Say something Belladonna! Say you remember me! You must understand me! You must!'
>
> Belladonna made a low, harsh, muttering sound, and waited, watching Poppy, almost as if expecting an answer. In the hollow centre of her eyes there was nothing. No kindness, no anger, no malice, just nothing! (85)

The statues are images of a world where no values prevail, where love, gratitude and justice are meaningless, and where human intellect is overwhelmed by the void. This is the world that the very young and the dying often know. Even God, whom Poppy invites to punish her if she ever again tells a lie, seems absent. Every way in which the human spirit has tried to make a home in the universe – civilisation, community, care, responsibility, religion – seems annihilated: and yet, in the face of the alien, we do not even have that certainty. The children are taken to an empty moor where they are lost, and then like wild beasts to a cave where they will be slaughtered. The vision is compelling and terrible, and itself defies the civilising and ordering power of the story. We know that Poppy has found what love is when she stays to help Emma (not a feeling, as she earlier supposed, but a bleak, hard act); we know that Poppy is learning through the statues what true lovelessness is compared to her mother's self-suppressions: yet this cannot subdue and make sense of the terrible power of the statues, through whom Poppy has a sight of a universe of utter indifference, in which as King Lear said on another houseless moor, 'As flies to wanton boys are we to th' gods: / They kill us for their sport.'

In her next fantasy, *The Monster Garden* (1988), Alcock presents a not dis-similar-seeming pattern, with a cold scientist father (whose repulsiveness is however shown at the end to be only shyness) and a daughter Frankie, who grows a monster from a slide. The monster to some extent here symbolises the father[14] since the substance from which it grows is thought to come from his supposedly sinister research institute. But Frankie (nicknamed 'Frankenstein,' because her name is Frances Stein) comes to love the shapeless monster she has nurtured, and it in turn loves her. At the symbolic level, she has domesticated the alien, and made the horrible human: the monster grows arms, legs, fingers and an expressive mouth as it becomes more attuned to its human friends, ending as a humanoid but aquatic creature. In this sense the story describes how Frankie overcomes the sense of alien coldness she has felt in her father, so that we are 'ready' at the end for this to be reduced to mere shyness, and for him to be much more loving to her. Here the organising significance of the story dominates the material, and the monstrous character of reality is tamed. Significantly, in this story the monster is opposite to the statues, though both are shaped by man: where the statues are hard and unresponsive, the monster is organic and plastic, changing through the story in both shape and disposition; and it is eminently emotional in its responses. The book works better than *The Stonewalkers*, but only because Alcock has risked less with the alien, never moving from the comfortable arena of domesticity, with the monster kept in a rabbit hutch and watered with a garden sprinkler. At the level of moral development, however, it is a companion-piece to *The Stonewalkers*, with a cold father in place of a cold mother, and another partly symbolic monster.

Alcock returns to statues in *Singer to the Sea God* (1992), which is a picture of mythic Greek civilisation. Indeed the cool vision of Greek myth lies behind her best writing.[15] Here however the statue, though created in horror, is ultimately a joyous thing. Phaidon's sister Cleo is accidentally turned to stone when Theseus uncovers the head of the Gorgon to his enemies in the royal hall where she is serving. The stone form of Cleo is later lost, and Phaidon's travels in search of it bring him at last to a beautiful seaside courtyard at Telos, where he builds a tomb for it. He is no longer sad, for he knows that his sister's spirit is now free, 'not trapped in the stone' (185). The book is on the whole an untroubled one, horror done with in the first pages and annulled through years of love and adventure. Like Frankie in *The Monster Garden*, Phaidon is not alone but always surrounded by friends. Phaidon is in a sense the author herself, chasing horror and the alien away through art, trying to cancel the stark vision of Sophocles with that of Apollonius Rhodius' *Argonautica*.

Also portraying horror at the root of life are the stories of Anthony Horowitz, *The Devil's Door-Bell* (1983), *The Night of the Scorpion* (1985) and *The Silver Citadel* (1987). These are poor stuff compared to Alcock – preposterous tales of supernaturally-endowed adolescents who single-handedly defeat national and international plots to overthrow the world order. These plots involve bringing back from the pit where they have been locked for millennia the terrible and hideous Old Ones who once held sway over the planet. There is nothing religious in the novels, though they draw on images of hell and the demonic. But they are typical of their time in continually challenging reality – here suggesting that our world is a thin fabric of defence against dark powers. In a sense they are in quest of the supernatural and the absolute. Their decrepit worlds, whether a rotting Yorkshire village, a Peruvian slum, or a run-down New York waterfront, are places of alienation, where parentless children struggle to pick up a living, while adults prey on them. In a sense the dark forces represent the decayed state of the world. But they are also far more real than it, the vortices towards which the stories drive, even while we see the unnatural powers of theologically uncertificated urchins overthrow them. That the defeat of the horrors is nebulous is implicit in their having to be frustrated three times in different stories.

In the late 1980s, a quite different kind of fantasy appeared in place of the prevailing reality-questioning mode. The postmodernist impulse in children's fantasy was fading, and was briefly taken over by a much more ontologically and morally definite kind derived from American writing. This kind promotes feminist and childist values, in almost as authoritarian a manner as the old moral values of the 1950s: only in reverse, for here the propaganda comes not from the socially powerful but from the historically marginal. Ecology is also a recurrent theme, for the exploitation of nature is seen in the same terms as that of women and children: indeed the collocation of nature with femininity is implicit.

Perhaps the best work in this vein is Susan Price's moral and symbolic reworking of Russian fairy tale, *The Ghost Drum* (1987), which won the Carnegie Medal. Portraying the training of the young witch Chingis, and her rescue of the boy-Czar Safa from the clutches of his usurping aunt Margaretta, the story is a marvellous account of stifling existence in the huge, dark palace of the tyrannical Czars, and of crippling cold in the forests about it.

The main focus is on the cruelty of power and its acceptance among most men. 'If the world were well rid of every Czar, then the most greedy, the most cruel, and the least truthful of those left would call themselves Czars, and the rest would let them do it' (160). Power brings isolation, shuts life in on itself, spreads a spiritual frost: the icy Russian setting, the darkened palace, and the room to which the young Czar is confined, all symbolise this. Meanwhile the evil wizard Kuzma sits alone in the wastes of the north, nursing jealousy of Chingis until he tries to destroy her, only in the end to be defeated, and then fittingly shut away in a bottle, in a coffin of glass, inside a cage within a cave, in a remote other world.

Against the stasis of these evil people, the story sets growth and education, as first Chingis, and then Safa, are trained to be shaman-healers. And against self-enclosure and obsession with only one thing – the self – the story sees a trained delight in the variety of all things: '[Chingis] travelled ... and saw that for every stream there are a thousand streams, all the same, and all different: that there are a thousand different trees, but that not even every birch tree is the same as another; and that nothing in the world is content to be alone' (64).

Such a theme means that this story is more concerned with true reality than with posing a multitude of possibilities, as in most other 1980s children's fantasy. The young Czar has been cut off from life and the real outer world all around him. Nevertheless, like other 1980s fantasies, the story shows an interest in lying and in fiction. Margaretta, we learn, 'never says what she means, but lies all the time' (8). The palace is an ornate shell hiding brutal realities, a fraudulent civility. And at the end the cat-teller of the story says, 'It was all true – I know it was true because I was at the Czaritsa's funeral.' It bids its readers, if they would know the truth of the story, to 'Open the windows and let the lies fly out!' This places no value on deception, and supposes truth to be something attainable; yet it also gives a place to the fiction that carries it. In 1987, the same year the book was published, Susan Price's story-collection, *Here Lies Price*, also appeared.

In the sequel to this story, *Ghost Song* (1992), we have something of a reversal of the vision of *The Ghost Drum*, for whereas that moved from conditions of imprisonment to freedom and opening of the spirit, this has the free lives of hunters and reindeer-herders restricted and strangled by the vengefulness of the wizard Kuzma. Kuzma is in search of a shaman-apprentice, so that he may be freed from his own life, but he is refused. For all his terrible punishments of them, men's wills do in the end stay free of him, and it is Kuzma who loses his chance of freedom. But the dominant feeling of the book is one of paranoia, in keeping as we shall see with its decade.

Several children's fantasy writers of the late 1980s, Ann Halam, Monica Furlong and Annie Dalton, seek to reverse false views of reality, on the assumption that there is now a true – and politically correct – one. In her 'Daymaker' trilogy – *The Daymaker* (1987), *Transformations* (1988) and *Skybreaker* (1990) – Ann Halam shows a witch-hierarchy called the Covenant healing a world ruined by technology. Technology is seen as changing reality rather than working with it, and is implicitly associated with men and power-lust. In the first book, a 'daymaker,' a machine for transforming the environment, is found, and has to be disabled, despite the temptations to knowledge that it offers. In *Transformations*, another and more obviously evil nuclear device, which mutates those living near it to bestiality, has to be turned naturally back to the 'rock and air and water' from which it originally came. However, in *Skybreaker* we find the Covenant no longer opposing but modifying science, in the form of a rocket, so that its 'brutalities' are removed. Though a space rocket does not directly alter reality, this is something of an inconsistency, a weakly liberal end to a fundamentalist manifesto. These books are rather one-sided and 'preachy' about truth; and they are concerned with making only one kind of reality.[16]

PLAYING WITH REALITY: THE 1980s

We are back with the feminist and magical-pastoral-utopian in Monica Furlong's *Wise Child* (1987) – which was 'commended' by the Carnegie Medal board – and its prequel *Juniper* (1990). The beautiful nature-witch Juniper, who thinks that "'girls can do all the things that boys can do if they try, and ... they may not wish to marry'" (214), brings up little Wise Child when her mother dies and her father is away on a voyage. The setting is a stylised – and clean – rustic village in the Dark Ages; Juniper is the local doctor, healing many ills by what we would call methods of alternative medicine. (She would be seen by the priestesses of Ann Halam's books as putting nature right, where science puts it wrong.) The local Catholic priest dislikes her powers of natural magic, and eventually enlists the villagers against her, so that she has to flee with Wise Child and take ship for Tir n'An Og. The Christians are here criticised for trying to suppress or pervert nature rather than work in harmony with it: this is just what Ann Halam's books said of science. Here too the female priest of nature defeats the male priest of super-nature. The next, and less dynamic book, *Juniper*, tells of Juniper's own early training as a 'doran' or witch. Again the feminist-magical view of reality dominates, and the alternative Christian view cannot be accommodated with it.

Annie Dalton's *Out of the Ordinary* (1988) is an over-fervent story of a girl looking after a beautiful golden-haired boy called Floris from another world presently in turmoil. As with Halam's and Furlong's books the girl Molly is an outsider, a challenge to the social norm. Women are central to the story, and males, except in the form of a pretty child, either peripheral, or hostile, or absent. The only difference is that Molly longs for another world with the same passion that the other fantasy heroines have for their own.

As if in reply to such feminist views, one of the few male writers of this time, Robert Westall, in his *The Promise* (1990), tells the tale of a female vampire from Newcastle who tries to pull her one-time boyfriend Bob into her dead world. Her father tells Bob she was always selfish, like her mother: "'Eat you body and soul'" (160). The men eventually win. The daughter retires to the dead lands, her mother ends in furious despair: but Bob comes through and goes on to university, and the fathers remain steadily heroic, and cope. That is the upshot: but it is not quite the whole truth, for the first part of the book, before the girl dies, is a moving portrayal of a relationship under the shadow of death; and the book is actually divided between two unreconciled visions. Both here and in the feminist books, we have lost the complex and subtle visions of the decade's best fantasies, for simplistic views and too-ready escapes from the harshnesses of reality. More of this is to come.

7 FRIGHTENED OF THE DARK: THE 1990s

The main writers of children's fantasy in the 1990s are Annie Dalton, Ann Halam, Sylvia Waugh, Gillian Cross, Helen Cresswell, David Almond, Philip Pullman and J. K. Rowling. The postmodernist idiom of the 1980s continues with Salman Rushdie's rather overplayed *Haroun and the Sea of Stories* (1990), but in the main we find that children's fantasies of the 1990s have moved beyond the 'literary.' Indeed, as literature, few stand out, apart from such classics as Waugh's *The Mennyms* (1993) and Pullman's *Northern Lights* (1995). One reason behind this is that many 1990s fantasies try to dispense with the adult and sophisticated voice that often gets between them and their readers. With most earlier books we feel in some degree that most awkward of facts, that children's literature is written for them by people who are no longer children. But 1990s writers often try to conceal that fact by having their stories 'told' by a child or teenage narrator with an inside view of contemporary child culture. The use of 'I' narration is more common: indeed it is hardly to be found in children's fantasy until 1987, with Michael Morpurgo's *King of the Cloud Forests*: then Vivien Alcock, Monica Furlong, Robert Westall, Ann Halam, Jan Mark, Pete Johnson and David Almond all use it.[1] And books that use the third person often get so far inside the central figure's mind that they are almost 'I' narration: one can see this, for example, in Annie Dalton's *The Alpha Box* (1991), Helen Cresswell's *Stonestruck* (1995) or Gillian Cross's *Pictures in the Dark* (1996). There is a special intimacy, a sense of the way a child actually feels things rather than an interpretation of it. This can forfeit coherence.

Few of these books have an evident shape or vision. They are addressed to children's immediate experience, which fantasy and the supernatural are often a means of both heightening and threatening. As an example take Helen Cresswell's *Stonestruck*. Whereas in the past we might have had more of an adult's controlling perspective, which would shape the material, in *Stonestruck* we have only a child's feelings, as she is evacuated away from wartime London, her bombed home and her mother, to an unknown destination, which turns out to be the still more alien country town of Welshpool, with its strange superstitions. There children form their own society, and adults play scarcely any part in the narrative – except for one, an evil Green Lady, who turns children 'stonestruck,' into zombies, who prey on others; the deadening effect of adult control over children's lives seems symbolised here. Nor is the evacuee girl Jessica left an unchallenged authority on events, for the narrative is fragmented by the later arrival of thirty more rusticated London children, most of them from much poorer homes than Jessica's. These children regard Jessica as 'lah-di-dah' (their constant refrain) and their stunted psyches and vocabularies slip aside from her continually. As Jessica's passions and frustrations at them come over, we feel her lonely selfhood keenly.

The real life and supernatural sides of the story appear to fumble against one another, never fully meshing. The jagged variety of the urban children is in sheer contrast to the empty zombies they become when they are caught by the ghost children. The eventual defeat of the ghosts is almost happened upon: all other plans by Jessica have come to grief. Plans are the imposition of reason on experience, and are parallel to adults organising children or children's fantasy stories. We will see this penchant for the unplanned again in the *Harry Potter* stories.

The story *in Stonestruck* is like a series of tentacles thrown out in all directions until something is grasped. If we ask what it *means* – what having wartime evacuee children in such a place, threatened by a predatory Green Lady *means* – we can only say it is a child's, or children's, coming-to-terms with life's horrors as symbolised by these things, with war, loss of home or family, death and non-being; and in doing so still somehow remaining a child. The end of the book, in which all the children link hands and join with the chain of the undead to save them, is a (Blakean) victory for children. And perhaps it is the sheer variety of the children, and of living, wild experience, that the book is about: the antitype then is the one dead level to which the stonestruck children have been turned. Such a motif is not unfamiliar in earlier children's fantasy, but here it is felt through a tangled form, imitating the way children respond to experiences, as well as the limitations that prevent some of them from doing so fully.

A similar child's point of view is found in Cresswell's *Snatchers* (1998), where we follow infant Ellie's every terror of being seized by a witch or a Bogey-man, right down to her thoughts while frantically sucking her thumb. So too with the tortured perspectives of the teenagers in Annie Dalton's *The Alpha Box*, Gillian Cross's *Pictures in the Dark*, and Ann Halam's *The Powerhouse* (1997) and *Crying in the Dark* (1998), with their uneven plots and shrill emotions. These are in marked contrast to two more moral and structured books of the 1990s (both, significantly, given awards by adults): Pauline Fisk's *Midnight Blue* (1990) and David Almond's *Skellig* (1995). *Midnight Blue* is about a girl who flees from her family by balloon to the other side of the sky to confront herself through a simulacrum of her family, before returning to earth to find the pastoral paradise of her travels now recreated back there. *Skellig* portrays a boy whose kindness to a tramp-like angel brings about the miraculous healing of his terminally ill baby brother, and the restoration of family harmony. Each book is closely patterned morally, and has authorial detachment (no 'I').

As seen in Cresswell's *Stonestruck*, with the accent on so much involvement with the child's mind, there is often a problem in uniting this realist vision with a fantastic one. The mystic box in Annie Dalton's *The Alpha Box* has only intermittent and strained connection with a narrative involving the developing love of a boy and girl, and the making of a musical group. The Box seems to have a pair of contrastive goddesses in it who keep changing for some reason – or so we learn, usually at second-hand, from the girl Asha. In the end it enables the musical group to defeat the mass-hypnotic powers of a rival and demonically-inspired group called the Hoarsemen, lending enormous effect to the guitar-playing of the young male hero Joss. The Hoarsemen's music is about to turn the whole world into zombies, and a giant spaceship has appeared to bear away all catatonic humanity, when the god-fuelled *Song of all Beginnings* shatters the whole evil plan in one over-lyrical and proto-orgasmic climax. The perfervid supernaturalism of the book sits poorly beside the far better-realised romantic ineptitudes of the boy and girl. In effect the Box is little more than a supernatural echo-chamber for adolescent concerns, giving them spurious cosmic depth.

A not dissimilar point might be made about Ann Halam's *The Powerhouse*, in which three children of GCSE age form a rock group and practise in a derelict powerhouse. They are however disturbed by the presence, in one part of the stage, of an evil force conjured up by an earlier group in the 1960s, several of whom paid for this invocation with their lives, and with their leader's imprisonment for their supposed murder. With the help of a nun and prayer to God, the spirit that has taken over one girl is exorcised. The book ends rather apologetically:

> I suppose the whole story could be told without the demon. I could say that I had a friend who had a sort of breakdown, and when she recovered she wasn't quite the same person. I could tell you that all the rest of it was just our imaginations. Some of the time I'm sure there was no more to it than that .... (166)

Again, most of the book has been concerned with adolescent relationships, and children beginning to make their own lives, and the demon topic does not sit very well with this.

So too with other books. Robert Westall's *The Promise* (1990), the story of a Newcastle schoolgirl who tries to draw her boyfriend to her after her early death, puts the emphasis very much on this life, and makes the supernatural a threat to it that must be removed: the book falls into two halves. In Westall's *Gulf* (1992), a boy's preternatural abilities put him inside the mind of a young Iraqi soldier during the Gulf War, after whose death he is no longer fully himself. The point of the book is to convey the experience of the coarse reality of a war we only read about, and the magical means by which this happens here is not of interest – indeed it is seen more as a random mental quirk. Gillian Cross's *Pictures in the Dark* is about a maltreated schoolboy who finds relief in turning into an otter in his local river: but most of the book is a portrait of a misfit child who is bullied both at home and at school. In David Almond's Carnegie Medal-winning *Skellig* a boy finds a half-dead angel lying in the garage of his new home: but the concern is much less with the angel's origins than with his rewarding the boy for his kindness in looking after him, through which his family's critically sick new baby is cured, and domestic bliss re-established. Such bliss seems to be a prime value in 1990s children's fantasy – perhaps because families are increasingly under threat from marital breakdown.

Rather as in the 1970s, the fantasy in these stories is often an extension of the excited mind rather than a separate existence. This can be seen in Annie Dalton's books for younger children, *Demon Spawn* (1991) and *The Dream Snatcher* (1998). The bowl of demon-spawn in the former is a projection of the frustrated anger of a submissive girl. Nina meets an old witch-ghost whose sister, like Nina's own friend Carly, dominated her. From her Nina takes cold hatred for Carly, and breaks their friendship: as she continues in this vein, so her demons come nearer hatching. But at the end she learns that the spawn could turn into angels as readily as demons, depending on the human moods with which they are fed; and when she meets the old witch again she persuades her to repent her old hatreds and thus gain rest at last. *The Dream Snatcher*[2] portrays a wizard who steals children's dreams because his father cut him off from his own when he was a child. Most of the narrative involves the characters wandering through the world of Afterdark, which is really a series of dream-projections of their own minds. The book is in effect a plea for the value of dreaming, and has something of the air of a hallucinogenic drug.

The girl Bonnie in Pauline Fisk's *Midnight Blue*, who has fled from her bullying grandmother to find a new and better version of her family on the other side of the sky, undergoes a moral transformation, and returns to earth to find all her family problems resolved; after which she realises, "'I didn't just run away from Grandbag...I ran away from hate....'"(69). Evidently the world she has been in was the soul's true country; and indeed it has its own god and goddess. And it is also the land of spiritual truth, the land where you learn what you really are inside. In these senses Bonnie's journey has been 'inside herself.' When she returns it is to find Grandbag overthrown at last by her mother Maybelle, who has married Michael the balloon man from the big house near the council flats where they live. Together they all set off for their new house in the country – which turns out to be a replica of the farm on the other side of the sky. This, while an annoyingly sentimental and escapist conclusion, does complete the circle of the spirit.

Ann Halam's *The Haunting of Jessica Raven* (1994) is another example of this 'interiorised' fantasy. It is an account of what often seems to the modern girl who experiences it a hallucination, whereby while on holiday she is given images of a Frenchman's guilt-ridden past, through which she is able both to find him his innocence, and to discover a cure for her own brother's fatal wasting illness. Halam's *Crying in the Dark* also involves the haunting of a girl, by the mind of a similarly ill-treated girl from the past with a secret to reveal.

Ian McEwan's comic *The Daydreamer* (1994) portrays a boy who likes to imagine fantastic things happening, such as his sister's many dolls coming alive, himself and the cat changing bodies, a vanishing cream making his relatives disappear, a burglar turning out to be the old lady from across the street, or himself changing places with an annoying baby in the house. The novel is written straight on so that these stories at first seem as real as Peter's other daily experiences, which to him they are. Daydreaming does have its practical side, as when he reduces a school bully to tears by telling him he is only a rather repulsive product of his own imagination; and an educative one, in his realising that when he is an adult he will not find adult interests half so dull as they seem to him as a child – in short, that all is relative (no pun).

Last, Jan Mark's *They Do Things Differently There* (1994) describes two girls who, repelled by their suburban surroundings, imagine that they live in a town called Stalemate, which has been taken over by evangelical pagans from Mars, who have turned the populace to zombies and built a factory making mermaids. Postmodernists might have it that Stalemate is no less real than the actual town of Compton Rosehay which the girls' imaginations have transformed: but the point is really the freedom from flat reality that the mind's powers can give.

The most frequent of children's emotions portrayed by this 'interiorised' fantasy of the 1990s are however insecurity and terror. There are frequent accounts of family or other relationships breaking down. Elinor in Ann Halam's *Crying in the Dark* has lost her parents, and lives with her bullying aunt and uncle, at the mercy of her fears. The hero of J. K. Rowling's *Harry Potter* books is an orphan downtrodden by his uncle's family. In Helen Cresswell's *Stonestruck*, the evacuee Jessica's mother is far away, and she believes her father dead; while in the same author's *The Watchers* (1993), both child characters have been failed by their mothers. Joss in *The Alpha Box* pines for the father his mother has left, until – rather too conveniently – the problem is solved by his learning that his supposed father was not in fact his real one (the latter having died). The boy Peter in Gillian Cross's *Pictures in the Dark* belongs to a dreadful family, where the all-dominant father hates him and continually locks him in the garden shed. In Philip Pullman's *Northern Lights*, the child Lyra's parents turn out to be enemies to her and to all children. In Pauline Fisk's *Midnight Blue* and David Almond's *Skellig*, threats to the family are central, even if they are finally overcome. Other such threats are seen in Rosemary Hayes's *Dreamchild* (1990), where the father may lose his money; and in Ann Halam's *The Haunting of Jessica Raven*, where a much-loved brother is terminally ill with myasthenia gravis. Jealously-maintained and agonisingly-lost school friendships are seen in Annie Dalton's *Demon Spawn*, Halam's *The Powerhouse* and Pete Johnson's *The Creeper* (2000). The theme of threats to family happiness has been seen before in children's fantasy, notably in E. Nesbit's books, but never so pervasively, nor in relation to the failure of parents or guardians.

There are numerous horror figures and terrors of the dark – the Hoarsemen and their demonic source in *The Alpha Box*, the hellish evil that haunts the stage in *The Powerhouse*, Vasco and the Afterdark in *The Dream Snatcher*, the vengeful ghosts in *The Haunting of Jessica Raven*, the wolf-woman from the Land of Starless Night in Cresswell's *Snatchers*, Grandbag in *Midnight Blue*, the haunted bed in *Crying in the Dark*, the dread corpse-ghost of *The Creeper*. Many of the central events occur at night or in the dark, and the idea of nightmares come true is recurrent. Much of this is related to a general interest in horror, which became a dominant children's genre in the 1990s, from the Point Horror series of Scholastic books to the Goosebumps series of the American R. L. Stine or the Spooksville books of Christopher Pike. Children have of course always been fascinated by horror, which can be a way of both exciting and overcoming their fears, but never so much as now has this fearful desire been so expressed and met: and nowhere but in England does it seem to have been so popularly received.[3]

A recurrent horror is the vampire: it is as though modern children no longer feel their identities so secure, but that they are now capable of leaching away into some more intense being and purpose than they possess. In Rosemary Hayes's *Dreamchild*, young Clare is taken over by the spirits of a family who lived there a century before, and brought to save a necklace from theft and give it to a museum: after that she is free and forgets the entire story. Nina in Annie Dalton's *Demon-Spawn* is possessed by the angry spirit of a dead woman, and led to reject her friend Carly, as the spirit herself wished she could once have done with her own sister. The music of the Hoarsemen in Annie Dalton's *The Alpha Box* is turning all people into robots with a death-wish. Ann Halam's novels all have girls' minds possessed: Jess in *The Haunting of Jessica Raven* has to work out the guilts of an unknown Frenchman, Maddy in *The Powerhouse* falls under the sway of an evil spirit, and Elinor in *Crying in the Dark* finds herself living out the last days of a miserable eighteenth-century serving girl in her own bedroom. So too in Catherine Fisher's *Belin's Hill* (1997) the Vaughan family have been at the mercy of the curse of an ancestral witch for almost five hundred years, while the boy-hero Huw falls under the power of a malignant pre-Christian spirit. In Robert Westall's *The Promise*, Bob's dead girlfriend Valerie has become a spiritual vampire; and his *Gulf* gives us a boy with an almost fatal propensity for being taken over by the minds of others, culminating in the Iraqi Gulf War soldier Latif. In Gillian Cross's *Pictures in the Dark*, people at school are in dread of the strange boy Peter's 'evil eye'; the same boy escapes his own mind by turning into a beast. Cross's continuing and popular 'Demon Headmaster' series, begun in 1982, portrays a whole school taken over and subjected to the will of an evil man with a lust for power. Frequently people become zombies, dehumanised automata: the French children in Halam's *The Haunting*, the dæmon-less children in Pullman's *Northern Lights*, Nina in Dalton's *Demon-Spawn*, the spirit-captured children in Cresswell's *Stonestruck*, Arabella in Pauline Fisk's *Midnight Blue* after she has been through the evil witch's mirror. In Cresswell's *Snatchers*, Ellie is turned into a ghost when her earlier baby self is stolen by a witch and taken to a man called the Boss.

The motif of theft is also a frequent one. Children are stolen in Cresswell's *Stonestruck*, and in *Snatchers* dreams are taken; a necklace, a circlet or an inheritance is purloined (Hayes's *Dreamchild*, Halam's *The Haunting of Jessica Raven* and *Crying in the Dark*). Friends are stolen in *Demon-Spawn* and Johnson's *The Creeper*; dreams in Dalton's *The Dream Snatcher*. Common, too, is a topic relatively new in twentieth-century children's fantasy: the ultimate theft that is death. In *The Haunting* and *Skellig* a brother and a baby are terminally ill; Robert Westall deals with a girlfriend's death in *The Promise*, and a soldier's in *Gulf*. This is part of a new frankness in children's literature generally – like the portrayal of the other half of the equation, sex: but it has a prominence that goes beyond that.

There is a recurrent sense of one's personal identity as something that can be drained, as though the walls between the self and the world are thin and permeable.[4] In such an environment it is difficult for 'character,' as such, to exist, and many of the children in these books are not strongly defined. They exist as fabrications, self-inventions, that can easily disintegrate. Of course, this may be true to the nature of children, who often have to 'make themselves up' to try out various selves, in order to find out who they are, and it has been the concern of 1990s children's fantasy to put us particularly close to them doing this. But the emphasis falls more on the void of nonentity into which they can fall back, imaged in all the monsters and terrors, than in the solid land of the 'true' self to which they may arrive. The lack of strong individuation in these fantasies is indicated by the way that it has here been possible to speak of them in groups rather more than singly.

Of this struggle to keep the self, the *Mennyms* books of Sylvia Waugh are perhaps a prolonged symbolic expression. In these books, we are presented with a family of human-sized cloth dolls, who are animated by the spirit of their dead maker, Aunt Kate, and live in her house in a quiet suburban cul-de-sac. They have been there for forty years, successfully avoiding suspicion from their neighbours. The five *Mennyms* books – *The Mennyms* (1993), *Mennyms in the Wilderness* (1994), *Mennyms Under Siege* (1995), *Mennyms Alone* (1996) and *Mennyms Alive* (1996) – describe a series of crises in the Mennyms' lives through which they are uprooted, ranging from a threatened motorway construction to their own temporary deaths. By the end their cunning and financial acumen have found them a new secluded home in the country, and covered their tracks completely.

All five novels are governed by the Mennyms' paranoia regarding contact with the human race, lest their fraudulent selves are exposed. They go walking and shopping only in heavy disguise or at night; they have only the briefest and most functional of interchanges with humans, and none at all (apart from the rebellious teenage 'daughter' Appleby) with their neighbours; they rarely answer the door, should anyone ever come, and on occasion they confine themselves to the house for long periods to evade any awakened interest in them. Part of Sylvia Waugh's skill lies in preventing us – at least at first – from asking awkward questions, such as how the Mennyms have avoided even nodding acquaintance with their neighbours over forty years, or why none of the neighbours have had children who might ask the Mennym children out to play, or how it is that the house has never had to be repaired, and the old twin-tub washing machine has continued indefatigably over all that time (*Siege*, 100).

Each book is also founded on a narrative of paranoia. In the first book the obstreperous Appleby fakes a series of letters from the supposed owner of the house, saying he will come to visit from Australia, and this causes a flurry throughout. In the second a pretend threat to Mennym security becomes a real one, in the shape of the planned motorway: here Aunt Kate intervenes to use a kindly human to help the Mennyms move to his house in the country and back when all is safe, after which he is made to forget everything. The Mennyms arouse the torpid interest of neighbours in the third book, and go to absurdly reclusive lengths to escape further notice, which provokes a further rebellion in Appleby, ending in her death. Death might seem to involve an exposure that Mennym self-effacement cannot defeat, but in the fourth book we find them preparing for their approaching demise by planning to 'disguise' themselves as dolls, rather than the supposedly human tenants of the house. In the fifth book, away from Brocklehurst Avenue, the true natures of the now revived Mennyms are discovered by their new owner and her nephew, but never revealed; and at the end, the Mennyms so conceal their escape, that no-one could trace them to their new house and their 'hard-won anonymity' (*Alive*, 200) – an anonymity they always had in reality. As in many other children's fantasies of this decade, fear of losing the self is a dominant motive – and yet the question remains, what self was there to lose?

The story is well sustained over the five books, though *The Mennyms* is probably the best and most witty. Waugh has a fine eye for the ordinary details of life that fill them; and these are further enlivened by the extraordinary individuals who are involved with them. Details abound of going out for walks and what clothes to wear; of 'meals'; of washing, drying and ironing; of paying bills and answering letters; of children's games and adults' hobbies; of looking after the baby, and many more domesticities. All these, and the vivid characters of the Mennyms, lend an air of immediacy to the books – though sometimes they are 'overstuffed' with them. Yet at the same time Waugh plays the seeming solidity of the Mennyms' domestic life against threats to it, whether from outside, in the form of a motorway or a nosy neighbour, or from their 'inside' in the form of Aunt Kate, who may remove their lives when she pleases.

While the story is not at all mocking in tone, it does have a certain satiric effect. The Mennyms' excessive privacy is far from making them stand out in their English suburban street, where neighbourly intercourse is rare, and each human family also keeps to itself. Of course, the Mennyms are different, for they have a terrible secret: but then many English people regard what they themselves are as a terrible secret, to be kept behind hedges and curtains. Then again, the Mennyms have as much life and character as any human family. Indeed, but for the fact that they are made of rags, one would think of them as a particularly personable family. Appleby, for instance, is a quintessentially rebellious teenager, while having her own unique ability at manipulating the world. Vinetta is a really lovable mother, the waspish Tulip a brilliant financial organiser as well as grandmother, the crusty and bedridden Sir Magnus a magnificent sage and leader. They are all like this only through the enlivening spirit of Aunt Kate, yet from time to time we have leisure to observe that a collection of dolls have as much life and character as humans – which of course breeds the other thought, that humans may have no more life in them than dolls. These are thoughts without edge however, more sardonic reflections rather than the flashings of the satiric axe. The theme does however relate directly to the thinness of human identity that we have seen in other children's fantasies of the 1990s.

This thinness also emerges from the Mennyms' attempts to copy human life. The spirit of the dead Aunt Kate that animates them (opposite to the vampirism of other fantasies of the decade) makes them want to behave like humans, so that they do a whole range of things that are unnecessary, while pretending that they are important. '"We pretend to live, and we live to pretend,"' says Sir Magnus (*Mennyms*, 141). The Mennyms need no food, yet they daily sit to imitation meals; no heat, nor light, yet they use both; no sleep, yet they retire to bed every night. They have no birth, no children; no real family, but they live as one; they do not grow, nor age, yet they all act their age and speak of what they will become. Even their emotions and characters are not their own, but are conferred on them by Aunt Kate, playing a large-scale game, or 'pretend,' with her dolls after her death. And we, as readers, have to play the game too, have willingly to 'suspend our disbelief' and pretend to grant the Mennyms life, if the fiction is to work. What we have is a simulacrum of a human family, each member imbued with a vivid character and feelings, and yet the whole structure depends on the whimsical animation of shapeless rags. Wider reflections concerning our own fashioning from dust are occasionally suggested, particularly when Mennym faith in a god beyond death traverses the same spiritual dilemmas we face before the end.[5] The life of the Mennyms books lies in the continual interplay between being and nothingness, between the Mennyms as alive and as mere things given life by another. But there remains hope in creation itself. Sir Magnus's '"We pretend to live"' might not mean just 'our life is a pretence,' but 'pretence gives us life.' To make games and stories like this one is in a sense to add to life. Certainly Sylvia Waugh's books add to our own sense of life.

The fantasies of the three remaining writers we shall deal with –William Mayne, Philip Pullman and J. K. Rowling – would all appear to go in the opposite direction to the paranoid, void-skirting idiom we have so far traced. Every one of them sets out to be a celebration of reality, a delight in being, without any sense of alloy. Where the other fantasies often involve contractions of purview, or are set within buildings, these are much more expansive, often involving travel outwards – out of a more secure self. Evil and darkness are now portrayed much more as being outside rather than potentially within. Yet these attempts at externalisation do not always succeed.

William Mayne's *Cuddy* (1994) is, in keeping with its decade, as close as it can be to the vision of a child. Here Mayne works further in the idiom of his *Kelpie* (1987) where Lucy ('light') sees the kelpie as the adults will not, because of her special 'angle of vision.' In the same way a group of modern Durham children meet St Cuthbert ('Cuddy') on the moor, and he tells them that he wants them to help him be buried on Farne Island, and not as he has been, in Durham Cathedral. Also in the story is the girl Ange's teddy bear Beowulf who, unknown to her, is the same bear that lived in Cuddy's time and ate the arm of the nun Elfrida. Ever since then Elfrida has been a part of the bear, and has continually tried to convert him. In part this strange book is a child's vision of reality, showing that it is only children who are open to the jumbled sense of this world, the adults about them being uncomprehending or sceptical. Only children can see the real bears in their teddies; only children have that light grasp of this world that makes them citizens of all times; it is only children to whom the dead might live again and ask favours. On the Durham moor the children shift easily between time present and time Anglo-Saxon, both in their own uncompartmentalised minds and in that Christian medium where all times come together. Beyond a hilltop the moor suddenly changes to a cliff, beneath which a black longship is beaching; and then a stone hut the children take refuge in has its wall broken down by the barrel of a tank gun controlled by an inexperienced Territorial soldier. There are to be no walls around the self in this novel. Meanwhile Beowulf and his interior companion Elfrida carry on their conversation. The text is a series of narrative hummocks, or a crevasse-filled glacier, opening and shutting at random: reality is not the single consistent plane we adults would make it, but exists, like children and Christians, on several levels at once.

> Instead of sky above, and earth below, there was a mixture, though not a muddle. Everything was clear, but out of order. The ground curved round overhead in a twisted ring that went over and under itself, a plait made of many strands of countryside and water, arranged in wandering loops and stitches, every way up but each right for itself, the same places in a different universe, and the sky between. (66)

The vision is also an incarnate one, the divine mixing with the mundane:

> The people below knelt. Many were in white. One stood beside a table, and another sprayed him with smoke from a golden bowl on a golden chain. The smell was like the strangest take-away, newly opened from an unknown country. (135)

Wonder and the matter-of-fact co-exist naturally, as they do for children. There is awe, but also a dash of vulgarity in the 'sprayed' and the 'smoke'; and again in the 'take-away,' which immediately switches again to the exotic and Traherne-ish 'opened from an unknown country.' So the saintly Elfrida is incarnate in the beastly bear, and both learn to share natures; so too St Cuthbert, who is also Cuddy, has to depend on a chance group of children to get him home. In this – difficult – book, Mayne comes his nearest to equating the child's vision with a potentially Christian one.

What happens in the book is that Mayne portrays the insecurities of the self as in other 1990s fantasies, but in a context that transforms them into a happy sharing of one's being. In a Christian context we are all parts of one another within the body of Christ and the community that is his Church, and the loss of oneself does not open on to the terrifying void threatened in other fantasies, but on to the love of God. *Cuddy* is a somewhat strange fantasy for Mayne to have written, since little in his earlier work suggests a Christian vision (though *It* portrays some of the conflicts of paganism with Christianity). But it does continue a theme which has been in his work from the first, and that is the truth of the vision of young children. From the determined belief in fairies of Mary in *A Grass Rope* (1955), through the transforming vision of *Kelpie* (1987) to the world-altering certainties of this novel, there is a fairly straight line. And it is this faith that keeps Mayne's books away from the darker views that his subject matter might otherwise have portended.

Such darker views are differently opposed in the fantasies of Philip Pullman and J. K. Rowling. Unlike all the other children's fantasies of the decade, these are set in fantasy worlds that have little relation to our own. Where the action of, say, Helen Cresswell's *Stonestruck* is set in wartime Wales, or that of David Almond's *Skellig* is located in a suburban garage, here we are in 'bubble' worlds that only magical gates from our world can reach. They are not even dreamt by children in this life, but are self-consistent worlds on their own. In such worlds one can ignore the problems of the everyday life of this one, and can present evils and difficulties of a more fantastic character to be surmounted. This is why these books stand on their own in their decade: they simply do not engage with it. The irony is that this has made them enormously popular. This does not mean they are not fine books, only that they are so within limits.

Within its alternative universe, Philip Pullman's 'His Dark Materials' trilogy – *Northern Lights* (1995), *The Subtle Knife* (1997) and *The Amber Spyglass* (2000) – presents a vision opposite to that of most 1990s children's fantasy: one in which identity expands and solidifies rather than thins and fades. This is a fantasy world in which being is portrayed as more real than nothingness, and as growing more so throughout the narrative. Indeed the basic theme of the trilogy is the wonder and preciousness of existence: and in its pursuance not only the forces of annihilation are overthrown, but the entire religious view of life that makes the next world matter more than this one.[6] In his fantasy world, Pullman has set out to portray a reality whose complexity may equal ours.

Pullman, in *Northern Lights* at least, shows himself a master of narrative. He gives us a finely-imagined world full of enigmatic adults seen from a child's standpoint. Here at least we have the 1990s child's eye view; and also the exposure of children to adult concerns. Whatever happens, we rarely in this book leave Lyra in her struggle to make sense of her world. Something great, exciting and terrible is going on, and we want to find it out. And it is found out in bits, the discovery of each of which whets the reader's appetite for more. The insatiability of the narrative matches that of the theme: there is a sense of appetite, of eating more and still more experience. Who is Lyra? What is the strange 'Dust' that her uncle Lord Asriel speaks of as entering the world in the Arctic regions? Why does the Master of Jordan College in Oxford want to poison Lord Asriel? Why are children disappearing? Piece by piece we begin to find out; but little about the Dust until the last: and then there is another surprise, whereby the story does not end, but opens another.[7]

The identity of any one thing keeps enlarging and becoming more complex – plots within larger plots, characters with larger and larger roles. This dilation is seen in the way the book continually upsets our assumptions about the nature of a thing. At the beginning of *Northern Lights* we are with a girl called Lyra who has a companion 'dæmon,' which we are inclined to think of as either a 'demon' in our sense, or else as her spirit-self: only gradually do we learn that such creatures are symbiotes, as much animals as spirit, and as much dependent as independent – though the boundaries are never defined. The scientist-explorer Lord Asriel who visits Jordan College is presented as Lyra's uncle, but later she finds out that he is her father, which creates further questions about his nature and motives in leaving her as a ward in Oxford. Meanwhile we believe that the book is set in some alternative version of our own world (à la Joan Aiken), but later we find out that we are not in our own universe but in another. Again, the world of the book, which at first is confined to Oxford and its visitors, becomes a wider one in which Tartars threaten the frontiers, and a theocracy obsessed by human sinfulness rules England. Our purview is made larger as we move with Lyra from Oxford to sophisticated London and thence to the wilderness of north 'Norroway.' The father towards whom Lyra directs her way throughout the story turns out to be a savage megalomaniac who rejects her, and is ready to kill her best friend Roger for his own ends. In this way our minds, like Lyra's, are gradually pushed more open to a sense of the complexity of 'reality' in the book.

This complexity is also seen in the way that we often have to hold two unreconciled things in our minds at once. Dæmons are mixtures of animal and spirit, humans a duality of man and dæmon. The world is a mixture of civilisation and barbarism. And it is a world at once scientifically advanced, and intellectually retarded by theocracy. An alethiometer is a scientific instrument for telling truth, and its levers are moved and read by the human spirit. The Dust that is leaking into the world from another universe is seen by the Church as something bad, a sign of sinfulness; but there is as much scope for Lyra's question at the end, "'What if it's really good ... [?]'" This merges into a view of reality as essentially dual,[8] and is part of a broad theme of each person's identity being far larger and more multiple than at first appears.

By contrast, being evil in the story involves simplifying reality, separating things from one another, refusing the new and the challenging. Asriel/Azrael is the name of the angel in Jewish and Mohammedan mythology who separates the soul from the body in death; 'coulter,' as in Mrs Coulter, Lyra's mother, derives from 'cutter.'[9] The Puritanical Church sees man as cut off from God through his fall: its theology has little place for the idea of God joined to sinful man in incarnation. The Church also sees the Dust as simply evil (on its reading of 'dust' in Genesis). It draws the fantastic conclusion that since the Dust attaches itself only to children past puberty, they might be kept perpetually innocent by severing them from their dæmons (which shift to a fixed rather than a changing form at puberty). Hence the building of a far-off northern research station to guillotine their dæmons from children, which in fact turns them to zombies and their dæmons to wraiths.

Lyra, by contrast, is portrayed as having the love that can bring people and worlds together. From the outset she has her friends among the street children of Oxford, and her whole mission to the north is based on love for others, not only for her father but for the children too. It is she too who helps the dispossessed fighting bear Iorek Byrnison regain his pride and then his kingdom, for no other motive than fellow-feeling. One meaning of her name 'Lyra' is the organ that joins the left and right hemispheres of the brain (*S.O.E.D.*) Her gaze is always outside her self, both towards others and to the growing wonder for her of the world. Her whole journey, which opens her purview from Oxford to London to the wild north and then a new world, mirrors the expansion of her own spirit; her very name 'Lyra' is also that of an ancient constellation of the sky, into which she finally passes. Lord Asriel ends with plans for making war, for furthering division: Lyra leaves to find the Dust and help her world with it.

A prominent theme in the book is the dehumanising of people, in the Church's negative view of humanity that brings about the mass-guillotining of children's dæmons from them. The clinical research station hangs over the story like a bloody horror. In this, and in the picture of the zombies the children become, Pullman is registering the influence on him, even within the precincts of a secondary world, of a motif we have seen prominent in other 1990s children's fantasies – that of terror at the draining of the self. It is a theme that is displayed again in the following books of the trilogy. It also expresses itself as a 'childist' hostility towards authority figures as potential menaces to freedom: Lyra's parents are failures and are later killed off, while the tyrannical Calvinist Church and heaven itself become enemies to be overthrown.

The next book, *The Subtle Knife*, is often a mirror image or inversion of the first. The book has a new hero, a boy from our world searching, as Lyra was in the first book, for his own father lost in the Arctic on Earth. The two, Lyra and Will Parry, meet in a world between theirs, called Cittàgazze, which is full of predatory 'Spectres' that drain the life from anyone past puberty, turning them into zombies. Like the strange Dust in Lyra's world, which in Will's world is seen as the invisible 'dark matter' making up most of the universe, the Spectres are attracted to mature consciousness: but they seek to destroy it, whereas the Dust was only drawn to it.

Like all the evil things in *Northern Lights*, the Spectres were produced by dividing created things, when certain over-curious philosophers in Cittàgazze first invented the Subtle Knife and then used it to cut into the smallest known particle of matter, wherein the spectres were sealed. They thus undid "'the bonds that held the smallest particles of matter'" (196) and caused an inverted 'Big Bang' in which the destroying Spectres burst forth from this pin-point to fill their universe. The Spectres proceeded to cut consciousness off from adult humans, by feeding on the Shadow or Dust particles that clustered round them. Just like the Church and the research station in *Northern Lights*, they split humans from their spirit selves: they simplify, and so reduce.

And as in *Northern Lights*, the point is the joining of things and, in that, love. Three worlds are linked and people from them meet; Will struggles towards his father, and joins forces with Lyra; Lyra's allies in her world seek to help her. More ambiguously, perhaps, many join Asriel's powers; but he is seen now in a more heroic role, mustering an army to overthrow the tyranny of God himself. The evil people in the Subtle Knife do not join forces, but use and 'undercut' one another, as Lyra's mother does Lord Boreal while both seek the Knife.

Yet at times the relative disunity of the second book, its continual flickering from one action and setting to another, tends to weaken this theme. Characterisation is too thin or clichéd to draw us in: Will has not a tenth of the personality Lyra had in *Northern Lights*, the witches who help Lyra are seen only in romantic terms as beautiful and dangerous, Lyra's friend Lee Scoresby the Texan is lean and hardbitten like a fantastical Clint Eastwood.[10] Settings are only sketched: we hardly have any clear sense of the Oxford of Will's world, or of Cittàgazze. While it is true that *The Subtle Knife* is not simply the personal quest that *Northern Lights* was, and that it has a much more epic and universal concern that needs a broad sweep of characters, it still lacks a heroic focus, and Pullman has used rather too many threads of narrative. To that one may add that there is far more explanation of the cosmos here: we are constantly being informed of the make-up of the multiverse, whereas in the previous books it had to be guessed and wondered at through hints. This is an ambitious book and often an exciting one, but it does not have the depth of *Northern Lights*.

The Amber Spyglass, which won Pullman a delayed Whitbread Award, has much of his original power. Proudly admitting in the Acknowledgements, 'I have stolen ideas from every book I have ever read,'[11] he harnesses among others C. S. Lewis, David Lindsay and Brian Aldiss to create a world of six-legged antelope creatures with trunks, who travel on wheels made out of giant spherical nuts, living in natural and supernatural symbiosis with huge trees, and in an atmosphere of golden spiritual Dust. He also gives us an amazing journey to the land of the dead, to meet the murdered boy Roger of *Northern Lights* again. At the same time, the characterisation and language come alive; the relationship of Lyra to Will is subtly developed; and in the first half the interweaving of four different threads of narrative, each told with economy and power, and each interrupted at just the right point of suspense, is as fine as in the first book. With its prodigal invention the book is a hymn in praise of creation.

The large idea of the book is that the Dust is draining out of the worlds because of the many holes the Subtle Knife has over time cut between them. Both a product of mature consciousness and attracted to it, the Dust is seen as continually re-energising life by its presence. The draining of this vitality is stopped only when Will and Lyra, from different universes, fall in love and come together. There is some scattered mention of their being a new Adam and Eve, but little is made of it. Love, viewed presumably as the highest form of consciousness, recovers for the world its mantle of Dust, but at the price of its own satisfaction, for what heals each world parts it from every other. This is the vision we may deduce from the book. And the trilogy as a whole can be seen as a gradual enlarging of consciousness as it moves further out into more worlds; and this is symbolised in the story itself, which is a progressive finding out about the Dust. When the consciousness of the characters has fully taken in what the Dust is, then the Dust may return.

But there are problems elsewhere in *The Amber Spyglass*. It is no surprise that Pullman delayed publication of the book until he had tied up the narrative threads, for the knots he has tied are somewhat hasty and loose. There are some difficulties in swallowing Mrs Coulter's sudden access of love for Lyra,[12] or the rewriting of her past actions to fit it. The war between Asriel and the kingdom of heaven is a noisy unvisualised affair ending in the extraordinary sexual duping of the heavenly leader Metatron. It is out of the way well before the end of the book, for it has become a sort of side-show. In the land of the dead the noxious harpies abruptly turn over a new leaf, and help the hordes of the dead back to the light where their elements can freely dissipate. And we suddenly learn that the action of the Subtle Knife means that Lyra and Will must live forever apart in once more separate universes: this, while it seems a gesture towards avoiding a facile happy ending, is certainly poignant, but it has not really been prepared for. And then, more than all this, the metaphysics of the trilogy, which promised so much, fades to a mutter, and the golden Dust that has been at the centre of the story, suggestive of a world of the spirit instinct in matter, shrinks to a mere terrestrial tonic.

But then, that had to be, given Pullman's now evident views. For, while he allows that there might be winged creatures called angels, and a land of the dead, he in the end takes a plainly materialist line. All things are ultimately physical, and are sustained and may be defeated by physical means. Even the consciousness to which the Dust is drawn is a sort of electrostatic blaze; and Dust is – dust. And life is really all that counts. Death is the horror, which is why the dead here must be brought back to mingle with the elemental stream of life. In the end there is only precious, precious life, on which the Dust is scattered like glitter: truly a philosophy for our times.

In *The Amber Spyglass* the threatened draining of life and identity, which in *Northern Lights* was directed at children, and in *The Subtle Knife* spread to adults via the Spectres, has now become world-destroying, in the shape of the golden, life-giving dust being drawn steadily to nothing. The prominence of this theme in Pullman's trilogy shows the power it exerts on the imaginations of 1990s children's fantasy writers generally, and the extent to which the desire to celebrate light, life and being is predicated on a potent sense of their opposites.

We end here with the first four *Harry Potter* books by J. K. Rowling, which have become as much phenomena as literature: *Harry Potter and the Philosopher's Stone* (1997), *Harry Potter and the Chamber of Secrets* (1998), *Harry Potter and the Prisoner of Azkaban* (1999) and *Harry Potter and the Goblet of Fire* (2000). Three more are in prospect, from a writer increasingly harried by her unprecedented fame: whether under such pressure she will be able to sustain the magic effect of the first four must be in question.

It would have been hard for anyone to predict great success for the first book when it came out. In an age when most British children (including J. K. Rowling herself) go to comprehensive schools, it celebrates the privileged lives of those at a boarding school; and at a time when most children are being educated against the class system, it presents as its hero a boy born with the wizard equivalent of a silver spoon in his mouth. It is certainly quaint to see the children of the world's Anglo-Saxon democracies queueing up in droves to buy a 1990s remaking of Greyfriars School or *Stalky & Co*. Adults in short trousers we might just understand – but cool children of an electronic age?

The first answer to this is that stories of boarding schools have been popular with children since they began with *Tom Brown's Schooldays* (1857): indeed the genre has just survived forty years of increasing irrelevance to the English social fabric. For there are many characters and stories that children hold on to whatever changes take place in the world outside, from Lord Snooty or Desperate Dan to the *William* books, Enid Blyton and *Biggles*. Younger children in particular like a world which is largely predictable, as real life often is not, and a system whose parameters are known – a feeling heightened in an age when family life is less secure. With a boarding school story, they have not only the routine of school itself, but the sense of a self-contained and organised community, where one's whole life is timetabled, one's place in terms both of house loyalty and school hierarchy settled, and one's values made clear.[13] In addition there is the pleasure of a closed society itself, not just from the friendships and the camaraderie of those bound by a shared predicament, but from the sense that all actions will be contained and completed rather than left dissipated or unresolved in the much less tidy or protected world outside. With such basic assurances, children can enjoy the wildest flights of imagination, the most peculiar characters or the most unexpected events as the icing on the basic sponge of their certainties.

At the level of the story itself, J. K. Rowling has shown why Harry could not have gone to a comprehensive school in any case; and she also largely removes the snob element of going to Hogwarts. Wizards have to go to private schools, because they live within a human or 'Muggle' state which does not know of their existence, never mind providing them with comprehensive education. (Harry is, as it were, going to a 'special aptitudes' school.) Further, school snobbery, such as it is, is assigned to the nasty boy Draco Malfoy, with his anti-Muggle racism. Many of the children at the school are of mixed race, with one parent a Muggle and the other a witch or wizard; the parents of one of Harry's friends, Hermione Granger, are both Muggles. Harry Potter's mother was a Muggle, and so was the evil Voldemort's father. Hogwarts is thus a multiracial society, more even than 1990s Britain outside it.

Nevertheless, going to Hogwarts is a privilege, and one the orphaned Harry feels keenly. And that is the point. For the *Harry Potter* books are about that side of fantasy all too easily condemned – wish-fulfilment, the heart of all fairy tales. Harry Potter, forced in childhood to live with his hideous bullying relatives the Dursleys, and then suddenly awarded a place at Hogwarts School for wizards, is the fairy tale drudge who wins the magical lottery.[14] From being the oppressed and ignored, Harry becomes the often feted cynosure. From being alone, he gains the huge new family of the school and the domestic family of the Weasleys, with whose children he becomes friends. From being without a purpose, his life is given structure and meaning. And he is the weedy and bespectacled child who becomes the sports star, the wizard Clark Kent who makes a Superkid. All this is avidly devoured by child and adult readers alike.

But there are other reasons for the huge success of the *Harry Potter* books. For, consider three of the other smash hits with children last century – the *William* stories, Enid Blyton's books, and the fantasies of Roald Dahl.[15] All of them can be enjoyed by children aged about 7–11, the so-called 'tweens,' who have reached the point where they can (if they will) read longer books by themselves, and have more leisure than they will have again till they retire. Comparatively few of the post-1945 children's fantasies we have looked at have younger children as their primary readers, and they thus miss a large reservoir of potential enthusiasts of particular avidity, and make their appeal to the more divided attention of older children. Further, they often require thought and sophistication to understand – in short, a certain amount of work, which most younger children do not often feel should be required of their amusements. Fine though many of these books are in literary terms, they are not always *easy*. And that, without implying any superficiality, is precisely what *Harry Potter* is. A stimulating narrative, broad-brush characters with whom we can identify, invention and humour, draw us in like bright lights to a circus of literary pleasures.

'Literary' is about right, because Rowling has all the skills that make popular literature popular. In particular she has the art that Enid Blyton has in overplus, of drawing the reader on, both by making him or her live through the characters and by the management of suspense. In *The Goblet of Fire* she makes the story grip from the first chapter with a picture of the horror Voldemort and his new threat to Harry Potter. But then, while this larger perspective is the continuous background excitement, for much of the book she draws us to the concerns of Harry and his friends, so that we are perpetually interested in what will happen to them next, however trivial-seeming the occasion. What will the Weasley boys make of fat Dudley Dursley? How will Harry and Ron become friends again? Will Hermione go to the dance with Harry? How will Harry defeat the Hungarian Horntail? These are not just narrative but psychological questions, because we see everything as Harry struggles with it. When he is to take on the dragon, he hears from his tent the successes of his competitors with theirs, so that when he stands up 'his legs seemed to be made of marshmallow,' and when he goes out we are with each panic-stricken step he takes, and we then ourselves feel the change of gear as his will takes over (309). Only by precisely yet intimately imagining the situation does Rowling bring it over so vividly, till it is like every other terrible demand we ourselves have faced and tried to surmount.

Another great appeal of Rowling's books to children is their use of magic, in a world slightly different from this one: magic, which in one way is the wild imagination actualised.[16] The fantasy world itself, of Hogwarts School for Wizards, is not a remote one, but is present within our own as a continuous alternative between platforms 9 and 10 at King's Cross Station. The school game of Quidditch is a sort of aerial American football. Becoming a wizard is made a learning process like becoming a scientist or a civil servant, with regular school exams and certificates such as OWLs or NEWTs. The children in the stories do much as other children – they eat, sleep, play tricks, make friends and enemies, sometimes learn, do sports and go home in the holidays – yet their whole learning is devoted to managing reality with magic; and their school subjects range from Defence Against the Dark Arts to Care of Magical Creatures. Instead of growing beans in Botany they grow mandrakes in Herbology; instead of learning maths they do Divination. This perpetual tension of like and unlike gives enduring energy to the books.

Beyond this, and aside from the unceasing threat of Voldemort, the books are a child's ideal world – a world of friends and fun, of strange games and adventures, of a turning year governed by the odd rituals and festivals of a country boarding school, of a life untroubled by the future. Each of the four books follows the same sequence, taking us from winter term through to summer, passing the mysteries of Hallowe'en and the intimate jollities of Christmas at school, moving from cold, sleety games fields and hot common-rooms, through the long, languid days of summer term, to the packed train to and back. Only with the Dursleys, those sad representatives of our Muggle world to whom he must return in the summer holidays, is Harry unhappy. But life at Hogwarts is often a kind of cornucopia, a steady rain of thrills, jokes, inventions, marvellous characters, feasts, victories and friendships falling on the stories, defeating, as much as the narratives themselves do, the dark and the hateful. It is not just Harry but the reader who shares in these things.

The structures of the books reflect this. In the first two books we find that the subjects of the Philosopher's Stone and the Chamber of Secrets edge into the narratives only half-way through; and in *The Goblet*, the Voldemort plot, though prepared in the first chapter, does not come into prominence till the last quarter of the book. Only in *The Prisoner* does the plot begin earlier. In *The Philosopher's Stone* this could be because much introduction is needed to Harry and the school first. But it is mainly because as each of the titles says, it is *Harry Potter and...*: in other words the stories are about him as a boy at a school for wizards as much as about him as a daring crimestopper. For much of the time the concern is, variously, with Harry's life with the Dursleys, his friendships with the Weasleys and Hermione, his school classes, his sports prowess, his school feasts and his holidays. Each book is longer than the last, *The Goblet* almost twice as long, to accommodate this expanding interest. And this is what draws the reader in, as much as any plots: the whole is sometimes like a fantastic 'soap.'

What particularly stand out in all the books are the inventiveness and the humour, as part of a general delight in being. In the first story there are an owl mail service, a bank run by goblins, the game of Quidditch, screaming books, talkative ghosts, a Mirror of Desire, several star-struck centaurs, and a series of bizarre obstacles to reaching the Philosopher's Stone, including a deadly logic puzzle and a room full of flying keys. This is matched by a large range of peculiar adult characters (the children are all 'normal'), strange classes and rituals. There is constant comedy in the interplay of the wizard world with the one we know. In the wizard shopping street Diagon Alley several boys are found gazing into a shop window at the latest sporting broomstick, the 'Nimbus Two Thousand' (56); the giant groundsman Hagrid has a dragon that continually bites his hand. In *The Chamber*, Harry's friend Ron has a backfiring wand, the ghost Nearly Headless Nick throws a Deathday Party, people escape from their portraits, and potted mandrakes grow from screaming babies to moody adolescents before being chopped up. The History of Magic class is taught by a ghost called Professor Binns who enters his classroom through the blackboard:

> Ancient and shrivelled, many people said he hadn't noticed he was dead. He had
> simply got up to teach one day and left his body behind him in an armchair
> in front of the staff room fire; his routine had not varied in the slightest since.
> (*Chamber*, 112–13)

Much though it may recall T. H. White or the schoolmasters of Mervyn Peake's *Gormenghast*, this is handled with appealing originality and poise.

Yet for all this happiness and delight Rowling is no sentimentalist. Harry's parents are dead, and his sense of loss is always there, and the school can only partly assuage it. At the school the enmity of the boy Draco Malfoy towards Harry is immovable, and the school house from which he comes, Slytherin, is filled with the malevolent, the envious and the bullying sides of the human character. (New arrivals at the school are sorted among four Houses according to their different natures.) In every book a plot aimed at Harry's destruction is set in motion by the evil and terrible wizard Voldemort from afar, and though these may be overcome, what Voldemort stands for is not. Even the terrible agents of the 'good,' the identity-draining Dementors, become a threat to him.[17] And the sludge-like loathing of the Dursleys for magic in general and for Harry Potter in particular, surrounds each story, to remind us that Harry's happiness can exist only in the wizard world, and not in the human one to which he also belongs. Whether he will ever be able to enter our world, is for future books to determine.

The theme of the satanic Voldemort and his continual pursuit of Harry continues the concern of 1990s children's fantasy with horror and paranoia.[18] In every book Harry is Voldemort's special target, working first through agents and then more nakedly. Yet he always operates through the school itself, suggesting that its happy nature is not so much inherent as founded on the continually active good will of those who run it, particularly its headmaster Albus Dumbledore. (Indeed, were we to read symbolically, the school might become a single fallen soul – Slytherin's crest is a snake – assaulted by the devil but upheld by choice and grace.) Voldemort is the other and dark face of the school, at which he was once a pupil called Tom Marvolo Riddle; and his name means 'death wish,' malign twin to the delight that elsewhere pervades the books. He is in a sense that side of Harry himself that is least sure of his identity and his hold on life in a world without family or more than term-time security; and we know that Voldemort himself was abandoned by his Muggle father in childhood when he found out that his wife was a witch. But he is also the alien, the monster Grendel outside the feast hall, the creature of night whose one thought is to "'let me rip you … let me tear you … let me kill you …'" (*Chamber*, 92). Voldemort is the culmination of the portrayals of malice and threat to identity in earlier 1990s fantasy, and unlike most of them, he is not yet finally defeated, despite Harry's continual victories over him.

However it must be said that sometimes the Voldemort plots are not perfectly handled. Most of them depend on surprise, which is always impressive, and certainly works very well in *The Chamber*, where the discovery that the serpentine basilisk lives in the school's plumbing is a marvellous blend of humour and horror. But the technique used in *The Philosopher's Stone*, of casting elaborate suspicion on the unpleasant master Snape, before finally producing the stammering and inoffensive-seeming Professor Quirrell as the true villain, is a somewhat clumsy device of the sort all too-often used in detective stories. The same thing happens in *The Prisoner*, where we variously suspect Professor Lupin or Sirius Black, before the apparent 'good guy' Professor Mad-Eye Moody is hauled forward. (In *The Prisoner* the plot is much more persuasive, yet the whole is curiously lifeless or shrill, certainly weaker than the other books.) In many of the books there is much revelation of 'What was really going on behind the scenes,' crammed into the last chapters, so that we get the whole story only when it is over. Without adequate preparation, the two levels of narrative, of school life and Voldemort, can produce too violent a jerk when brought together, as in *The Goblet* when, in the moment of his winning the Tri-Wizard Tournament, the victory goblet transports Harry to the lair of Voldemort, and suddenly we are in another plot, switched from a triumphal car to a plunging aircraft.

One of the differences between the *Harry Potter* books and Philip Pullman's 'His Dark Materials' trilogy lies in their lack of a rationale, a fabric of meaning into which events are fitted. Pullman's books are based on a continual finding out of more about how the universe works. But in the *Harry Potter* books we are given no scope to ask where wizards fit in the scheme of the world, or, say, to speculate that they represent the other side of the mind from the rational and empirical. They are, and that is enough. Indeed there is not much suggestion of a really alternative wizard society: Mr Weasley and others who work in the wizard ministry seem to devote their energies solely to the concealment of wizards' existence. Diagon Alley might suggest a commercial basis to their society, but since no wizard shops anywhere else, this remains undeveloped. And everything, including Voldemort, seems to be focused on Hogwarts: in some ways Voldemort is no more than an old boy with a grudge. There really is no wider frame. Indeed, whereas in Pullman's trilogy we explore ever outwards, into worlds beyond, in *Harry Potter* we go into a little world inside this one, reached only through platform 9¾ of King's Cross Station.

There is actually real scope for saying that the whole thing is a dream on Harry's part. What else might a lonely and miserable child do but imagine a world where he was the cynosure, the recipient of fabulous gifts, the success at games, the happy boy amongst friends? The whole introduction to the story, with the owls and cats gathering in Privet Drive around the house suggests the filming over of reality with dreams of magic. The idea of platform 9¾, the platform you sheerly imagine to be there in order to get there, is very much that of a dream. Even the Dursleys, so extremely imagined as to be grotesques, seem less realities than a child's exaggeration of unpleasantness to fantasy; and Voldemort is the other side of dream – nightmare. Thus, just as we go inside the world to Hogwarts, so we may also go inside Harry's mind for the whole fantasy. This would relate the Harry Potter books to other dream-fulfilment and nightmare children's fantasies of the 1990s, by Pauline Fisk, Ian McEwan, Jan Mark, Ann Halam, Helen Cresswell and Annie Dalton.

And everything comes in to Harry, in contrast to Pullman's Lyra, who has to journey away to find her happiness: the *Harry Potter* books are fundamentally centripetal rather than centrifugal. Things are done to Harry, from the bullying of the Dursleys to the transporting of him to Hogwarts or the plots of Voldemort: he himself actually initiates little, nor, unlike Lyra, does he set out with a purpose in view. The books are often framed round the idea of continuous gifts to him – magic, Hogwarts, friends, sporting success. And everything is a continual surprise. Such plans as there are in the books founder – particularly those of Voldemort. Time is comparatively suspended in the present, as in pastoral idyll; or it is cyclic, as in the school year. (Indeed, as pastoral idyll, and as series of fantastic 'treats,' the books look back to 1920s and 1930s children's fantasy.) There is little sense of the future, of what Harry will become or where things are tending, even allowing for the fact that the books change in character as he grows older. Indeed the very philosophy of the books seems to be to take things as they come. Harry is fundamentally easy-going and 'cool.' So far as acting against evil is concerned, he rather reacts as situations present themselves, or he is thrust into unforeseen situations and forced to think 'on the hoof' – as in *The Chamber*, when Dumbledore sends him into his own past to put things right. Symbolic of the whole is the game of Quidditch itself, where the golden Snitch materialises wherever it will, and the Seeker (Harry's position) has then to try to seize it before it disappears, and thus win the game.

There will be those with 'literary standards' who cannot accept the *Harry Potter* books as literature.[19] And certainly the books can be accused of being derivative,[20] of lacking discipline and structure, of presenting often simplified characters, of not being centrally concerned with moral or educative issues,[21] of not having a detailed relationship to our own world, of being wish-fulfilment rather than self-development, and so on. Some would add that they are badly written, but this is not so. Yet all these judgements would partly miss the point.

This is a different kind of literature. It expresses a child's ideal world and a child's way of seeing, because that is the unique ability J. K. Rowling has. Her books sometimes seem not so much written *for* children, in the sense of an adult writing about remembered childhood, as in a way *by* them: they are what Peter Hollindale would term 'childist.' Children's uncertainties, their fears, humour and loves, their jagged and often jumpy ways of seeing the world, their love both of security and adventure, their thrills at festivals, their games, this is the very grain of these books, all shot through with a wizardry which is here only ultimately that of Rowling herself. Indeed the very idiom of the books changes in parallel with Harry growing older. If we can see these books as part of the new mode of 1990s children's fantasy, written wholly from a child's point of view, then we will not try to put them beside those of say Philippa Pearce or C. S. Lewis, or ask them for conventional literary methods when those they use are real enough in their own terms.

It seems somehow fitting that our story should have ended with books which, while they often invite literary criticism, so turn it on its head.

8 CONCLUSION

Having looked across the whole range of English children's fantasies, we can more readily ask what they all have in common, and what is peculiarly English about them. These questions are now more answerable than may have seemed: despite their often sheer contrasts in character and their many sources, these stories are not merely a motley collection that just happens to have been written within the limits of one island, but already show a surprising number of similarities.

As we saw in the introduction, English children's fantasy has its sources in the particularly early and rapid English industrial revolution, and in the Romantic glorification of the imagination and the child. The ideas of the lost pastoral and of lost childhood fuse into one chord of longing for lost innocence, which expresses itself through worlds that rewrite actuality. But children's fantasy is rooted in England in another way also. By contrast with adult English fantasy, most of which comes from the South-east, around London, much children's fantasy is produced by writers from all over the country. These range from Beatrix Potter in the Lake District, William Mayne in Yorkshire, Alan Garner in Cheshire, Kenneth Grahame in the Thames Valley, Kipling in Sussex or Richard Adams in Wiltshire, to Susan Cooper in Cornwall, Buckinghamshire and Wales.

All these writers set their fantasy in the local environment, usually rural, but recently more urban, and often draw attention to special regional features. Kingsley celebrates the landscapes of both Yorkshire and Hampshire in *The Water-Babies*; William Mayne's characters are embedded in Yorkshire or Durham; Robert Westall sets us squarely in Tyneside, or among the Farne Islands, or in a Suffolk village; Penelope Lively brings to life Midlands England; Jill Paton Walsh portrays the old industrial landscapes of the Black Country. We have a crowd of voices from different soils and hills and woods, often strongly regional in bias, yet all together making up a picture of a whole country. In a sense these children's fantasies, like the pastoral poetry of Clough or Tennyson or Housman, take the English back to the country they have left long ago.

Of course not all English fantasies are so expressive of a landscape. Many, particularly comic fantasies, are written out of the sheer anarchic pleasure of creating one's *own* world. (It is a centrifugal impulse, often much wilder than that in adult fantasy.) From the mad realm of Thackeray's Paflagonia to the animal hotel of Doctor Dolittle, and from the rest-home for toys in Hundred Acre Wood to the suburban house of the giant Mennym dolls, each author remakes the world

CONCLUSION

as he or she chooses. Inventiveness, one of England's most marked characteristics, is at a premium. The sheer peculiarity of Nesbit's Psammead, Milne's Eeyore, or Dahl's Giant Peach, makes them stand out like violent splashes of colour. And the greatest inventiveness, as Tolkien says, lies in making them part of a fantastic world that works.[1] Lewis Carroll invents a Cheshire Cat, a White Rabbit, a Mad Hatter and a madder Queen of Hearts, and puts them all in a realm inside which they talk to one another, and are highly believable. C. S. Lewis finds the images of a lion, a witch and a wardrobe cohering into an amazing story, with its own strange laws; Diana Wynne Jones mystifies us with a town council made up of magic personages, until all falls into place when she explains everything as the computer creation of the apparently innocent child who has been telling us the story. The Mennyms have dedicated their whole lives to pretending that they are real people, which means that they are continually constructing fantasies such as 'eating' non-existent meals or going to bed when they need no sleep. The play-fulness, the skill in making a believable fantastic world out of the most diverse images, is a key part of much English children's fantasy – and fittingly, because play, and play with reality, is what children seem to understand with their own games of make-believe. The English, we may add, have always loved games: they invented a large number of them, even if they are now often more distinctive for losing them. And they have a passion for crosswords, in which nonsensical-seeming clues contain sense.

Such pyrotechnics are not often to be found in the fantasy of other countries, with the exception of Germany, in some of the stories of E. T. A. Hoffmann and Clemens Brentano, in *Struwwelpeter*, and in the postmodernist cornucopia of Michael Ende's *The Neverending Story* (1979). The Italian Carlo Collodi's *Pinoc-chio* (1883) is not so much about the marvel of a puppet coming to life, as about how a boy's rebellious nature is finally so reined in that he can turn from sym-bolic wood to flesh and blood. A like process, if in the reverse moral direction, is followed in Christine Nostlinger's *Conrad* (1975) where a perfect factory-made boy is finally made naughty and human. In Selma Lagerlöf's *The Wonderful Ad-ventures of Nils* (1906), the 'impossible', that is, a boy flying on a gander's back, is not really the main concern: rather it is the way his country, Sweden, is opened up to him as he flies. Antoine de Saint-Exupéry's *Le Petit Prince* (1945) is inter-ested in the wisdom to be gained from children, not in the marvel of the Prince flying to earth from his strange planet. The fantastic abruptnesses of several of these stories are more a means of changing our minds than of playing a game.

English children's fantasy delights in contrasts and juxtapositions – playing croquet with flamingoes as hammers and hedgehogs as balls, a toad in tweeds driving a car, an eighteenth-century landscape-garden irritably trying to throw off a twentieth-century housing development, a boy finding a dishevelled angel in his father's garage. Much nineteenth-century comic fantasy involves playing the traditional fairy tale against contemporary mores; and the more serious sort often works the other way round. Children's fantasy in the twentieth century is particularly fond of bringing different times together: children try to tell Julius Caesar how to steer a course at sea using a shilling compass (Nesbit), a boy travels back on a train to his babyhood (Richard Parker), a modern boy finds a Stone Age boy living happily in a nearby chalk-pit (Clive King). Then there are frequent interplays of the natural and the supernatural: naughty Prince Eigenwillig is hauled by his fairy godmother through a keyhole, bored young Griselda strikes up a friendship with a mechanical cuckoo, children find themselves involuntary participants in an old Welsh myth, a schoolboy discovers that he is the lord of the 'Old Ones,' another schoolboy is taken by the Yeti. ... English fantasy always goes for the shock, bouncing one context off another, then letting them communicate as best they can.

This interest in interplay is not so often seen in the children's fantasies of other countries, which tend to keep to one level of reality (Germany is here again sometimes an exception). Nils and the geese in Lagerlöf's story live in their own strange world, as do Astrid Lindgren's Moomins; no-one in *Pinocchio* is surprised at being addressed by a wooden puppet; and in Ursula Le Guin's 'Earthsea' books, the wizard Ged fits into a world run by magic. English children's fantasy tends rather to show magic entering the ordinary world or vice versa – though there are of course exceptions such as animal and sometimes toy or doll fantasy. The English predilection for putting opposites together often comes from their comic sense of disparity. It also expresses a strong native empiricism, a clear sense of boundaries. There are not many ambiguities in their fantasy, and few of the doubles or doppelgängers of the Scottish and European form. But the particular interest of the English in playing reality and the ordinary against magic shows in their equally strong contrary fascination with the supernatural, a fascination seen throughout their literature and philosophy.[2] The clash of the two in fantasy expresses this division, transformed to literary effect.

On the whole English children's fantasy, like the adult form, does not have dual reference, that is, it is not often symbolic or allegorical. C. S. Lewis, whose work comes near to this, claimed that in *The Lion, the Witch and the Wardrobe* he was writing not allegory but myth, by which he meant that his Narnian redemption may partake in the same divine truth as our own, but is particular to Narnia alone, and that Aslan is not a great lion who represents God, but a new and divine creature.[3] Tolkien opposed the idea of allegory in his work (as did George MacDonald)[4] though this has not stopped readers from tracing patterns of significance in *The Lord of the Rings*. There are occasions when what we are reading suggests another meaning at a different level, as with several fantasies of the 1970s, where the journeys can be as much in the mind as in the outer world; and there are a few allegorical fantasies such as *Animal Farm* (1945) and the *Pentecost* books of William Corbett. But generally, as the conjurer Paul Daniels used to put it, 'WYSIWYG' – 'What you see is what you get.'

This is again actually in contrast to some of the children's fantasy of other countries. For instance Russell Hoban's *The Mouse and his Child* (1967) is a satire on American consumerism, Christine Nostlinger's *Conrad* is a critique of social conformism and unregulated science, Hans Christian Andersen's *The Snow Queen* is a secret allegory of his own life; Pinocchio's story is an exposure of adult evils as much as of Pinocchio's own rascality; *The Wonderful Adventures of Nils* is a celebration of Sweden. All these stories involve moving in adult society, something English child protagonists do not often do. Indeed their central characters are often not children at all, but a young mouse, an elf (into which the boy in *The Adventures of Nils* is quickly turned), a darning needle, a wooden puppet, a factory-made boy, a wizard, a Moomin, an elephant (*Babar*) or a pig (E. B. White's *Charlotte's Web*). These books take us away from childhood itself into an adult world of problems and joys, pains and hidden meanings: they often begin with the main character leaving home, as when Nils flies away from his cold parents on a gander, Pinocchio disobeys his carpenter father and sets off to see the world or the Mouse and his Child are thrown out of the child's house when they are broken. For these books childhood is not so much a world on its own as it is for the English: they do not have quite the degree of the English sentiment about childhood, nor perhaps quite the (comparatively recent) English devotion to children and animals.

English children's fantasy does not on the whole follow this (fairy-tale) pattern of leaving home to seek one's fortune. There are exceptions such as Kingsley's *The Water-Babies* (but then Tom has no home, and is searching for one); Tolkien's *The Hobbit* and Dahl's *Charlie* and *James* (but both look to the European tradition to which Dahl half belonged); or *Watership Down* (but their old home is doomed, and they must find another). Much of the English children's fantasy of the entire period from 1870 to 1950 is about one's locality and what one finds there;[5] and if we think, say, of the *Green Knowe* books, *Tom's Midnight Garden*, *Earthfasts*, *The Owl Service*, *Charlotte Sometimes*, *The House in Norham Gardens*, the 'Dark is Rising' series, *Archer's Goon*, the *Mennyms* or the *Harry Potter* books, all of them deal with a child or children in one place. 'Home' is a very important place in English children's fantasy. Kingsley's Tom at last finds the way home, the Borrowers find a new home, Adams's rabbits a new warren. Home and security are central in *The Wind in the Willows*. Every creature in the *Pooh* books has its own house and home. Often home reveals secrets you never suspected, as in E. Nesbit's Arden books, or in the old wardrobe in the Professor's house in *The*

Lion, the Witch and the Wardrobe, or the depths within *Green Knowe*: home is the way into the self, and when you are most at home, you are most solidly 'there.'

The pattern is also one of return: the action often ends where it began, with Alice back on the bank, and the magic removed; things are put back where they belong, from a dispossessed prince (Thackeray) to a lost treasure (*The Hobbit*). In Vivien Alcock's *The Stonewalkers* the dreadful awakened statues are destroyed and Poppy goes home, now a better person; Penelope Farmer's Charlotte and Penn are back home again after being fifty years in the past and in the Castle of Bone; Mary Poppins departs once more. The frequent circularity of the narrative expresses a certain retentiveness, an expansion of the self rather than a transformation. Other countries' fantasies can be more open-ended. The Mouse and his Child walk off, now self-winding, into more and wider experience; Nils does not return home but goes on wandering; we are left to wonder what became of the Little Prince after his death; Pinocchio and Conrad have become fully human and 'self-wound,' ready for the world. *The Neverending Story* will be told anew by each future child who enters the world of Fantastica.

Victorian English children's fantasy took much from the Grimms, but one feature it and later fantasy omitted – the idea of magic as a gift with which to increase one's wealth and status. The idea of poor men marrying princesses is rarely to be found, either in invented English fantasy or indeed in many of the traditional English fairy tales, which often involve restoration of a status quo or the preservation of something (a lost sister recovered in 'Childe Rowland' and 'The Laidly Worm,' the hero kept alive in 'Jack and the Beanstalk,' 'Jack the Giant-killer' and, till the end, 'Tom Thumb'). Thackeray's Giglio and Rosalba are both restored to royalty; and the gifts of beautifying Rose and Ring prove vain in both senses. When in Jean Ingelow's *Mopsa the Fairy* Mopsa recovers her throne, she turns common Jack away, for she is pledged to a noble fairy.[6] E. Nesbit's children in *Five Children and It* may be given a wish a day, but they come to comic grief with every one they make. Lewis's children have to deal with Narnia by the light of their characters only. Lyra's truth-telling alethiometer, which seems at first so crucial to her journey in *Northern Lights*, turns out not to be needed, and she fails to save her friend Roger. Nor at the end is there material reward. Symbolic of the English mode is a hobbit who steals treasure for others; or another hobbit called Frodo who devotes his vast journey to the destruction of an immense magical gift. There are one or two apparent exceptions to this opposition to gifts or advantages – Susan Cooper's Will Stanton, who turns out to have the powers of an 'Old One,' and J. K. Rowling's Harry Potter, who has a genius as a wizard – but they use these powers to help others, not themselves. Susan Cooper, we might remark, introduced Will Stanton to her saga some years after she had removed to America, which has different ideas of advantages and their use; and

Harry Potter is only half-aware of his power, and circumvents problems mostly by wit and courage and with the help of his friends.

In American children's fantasy, by contrast, magical advantages and rewards are less disdained: this is a society more at ease with materialism and the idea of success. In Frank Baum's *The Wonderful Wizard of Oz* (1900) the characters set out to be given something by the Wonderful Wizard: the Tin Woodman wants a heart, the Scarecrow wants brains, the Lion courage; and Dorothy only wants to go home to Kansas. Dorothy has the magic slippers of the Witch of the West which give them all instant passage. By searching for their dream, they find it, for the first three have the qualities they are searching for by the time they reach the Emerald City, and Dorothy's journey has in a sense already taken her home. In Russell Hoban's *The Mouse and his Child*, the mice finally become self-winding and free. American children's fantasy can have a dream, a (magic) talent, a quest to a goal, and success, in a way that its English cousin does not. The predominant English stress, throughout the two hundred years of its children's fantasy, is on good conduct and self-control, where the American one is rather more on doing well in the world and utilising one's nature to the full.[7] In *Charlotte's Web*, the old spider spins words out of her web in the pig-pen so that the farmer will attribute them to Wilbur the pig, and not want to kill and eat him: in the end Wilbur's little goes so long a way that he is awarded a medal as a wonder pig at a fair. (Dick King-Smith parodies this in *The Sheep-Pig*.) In Ursula Le Guin's *A Wizard of Earthsea* (1968), Ged learns how to develop his talent fully and is able to save the world with it. Americans are far happier with the hero figure and the Superman, where the English are more self-deprecating.

So much for the distinctive character of English children's fantasy as a whole. But it also develops as well as standing still, and its Englishness is also to be seen in its changes. For English children's fantasy as we have now seen it has its own individual cultural history: a history outlined in the way the fantasies group themselves into varyingly-sized periods, each with a common idea or concern. These periods, from the Victorian to the 1990s, tell a story of the slow liberation of children's fantasy from adult control. Yet at the same time there are ways in which it repeats itself.

So far as liberation is concerned, it can be put this way. At first more or less controlled by the adult desire to educate children, usually morally, children's fantasy after about 1890 begins to suffer from the opposite line of interference, which now glorifies childhood, and makes the fantasy world a playground for adult nostalgia or, later, whimsy. But since 1950, children's fantasy has shown increasing attempts at sympathy with 'the condition of being a child,' while often trying to help 'the child' grow out of it. This sympathy has now developed to the point where the supposed child's voice and values alone are to be heard in the telling. The possible effects of this upon old 'literary' standards of what a children's book should be have been shown – fractured narratives, unedited material, idiomatic immediacy: but the example of the multi-worlds and realities of 1980s fantasy should teach us that this need not be decline, but can herald a new form of literature with its own rules. Whether it is more a 'children's' literature is another matter. Getting on one's hands and knees and trying to talk 'child-ese' was something the Edwardians also tried, if with far less empathy.

As for repetition, we find that many of the concerns of Victorian children's fantasy, and the whole pattern of such fantasy's early development to 1950, are recapitulated in the fantasy of the last five decades. For instance, the early Victorian concern with morality and responsibility reappears in children's fantasy of the 1950s, which is preoccupied with the idea of growth and 'becoming.' Then again, from 1950 to 1970 we find an emphasis on realism in children's fantasy, a closeness to human and everyday experience, which repeats the impulse of writers of the 1870s and early 1880s, from George MacDonald to Lucy Lane Clifford. And the tension between the educative and imaginative impulses in Victorian children's fantasy, or between control and freedom, is partly mirrored in the increasing struggle in the 1960s and 1970s to keep children's fantasy connected to old values in the face of growing rebellious imaginative forces. More broadly, the change from the relatively controlled children's fantasy of the Victorian period to the indulgent fantasy of 1900 to 1950 parallels that from the frequently earnest children's fantasy of 1950–1980 to the relativist and 'child'-centred fantasy of the 1980s and 1990s.

Nevertheless there remains one salient difference between now and then. The children's fantasy of 1900 to 1950 might often be set in a delightful world of childhood, where nasty morals, like nasty medicine, were kept well away; but that did not stop the morals being there in the wings. The Bright Young Things of the 1920s might challenge morals, but that did not make them go away: they only returned in new and suburban strength in the 1930s. The whole period from 1900 to 1950 contrived to make its children's fantasy a sort of Switzerland, a morally neutral enclave. But since 1950 it has not just been a case of rebelling against morals and authority, it has been a case of removing them altogether, until by the end of the 1970s we find that old values, the security of tradition, and authority figures, have all become deracinated. The process continues in the undermining of 'reality,' considered as something objectively 'there,' outside the self, in the multiverse fantasy of the 1980s. The children's fantasy of the 1990s, outwardly similar to that of 1900–1950 in its deference to 'the child,' is also sheerly different from it, in that where the earlier fantasy frolicked in a happy enclosure of adult assurance, the present mode is exposed to an annihilating gale of fears. The insecurity felt by the children of 1970s fantasy has in the 1990s become a defi-

CONCLUSION

nite threat from figures of menace, many of them linked to death and the devil – predatory ghosts, child-vampires and monstrous parents and guardians, not to mention a more fantastic ménage of devils, witches and wizards. Children begin to be pursued, and there are many scenes of darkness and night, filled with horror: fear of exposure and paranoia abound. The object in these fantasies becomes getting clear of an affliction, whereas in earlier stories it was a case of solving a problem, exploring time or rebelling against authority: it is enough now to return to normal. There is a sense of things being out of control, added to by the fact that the 'supernatural' is not now part of any scheme, moral, educational or comic, but is simply a random irruption of malignity.

Another development over the history of English children's fantasy is a gradual advance, up to the 1990s, in the ages of the child characters, in parallel with both a shift from a child-centred to a youth-centred culture, and the extension of the school leaving age. Children are under ten in a fair amount of Victorian fantasy, are around ten to twelve in much fantasy from 1900 to the 1960s; from when, for three decades, many children are teenagers, and some of them almost school-leavers. This goes together with the fact that whereas up to 1950 most English children's fantasy could be enjoyed by almost all children of reading age – even if there might be parts that were beyond them – after that time the readership becomes increasingly confined to teenagers. Few, for instance, could appreciate William Mayne without some years of reading; few could understand *Tom's Midnight Garden* or *The Owl Service* or *The Wind Eye* without some experience of life. There is often the sense – without this implying any devaluation – that children's fantasy has been for a number of writers an alternative to writing an adult novel. This has meant that there has been a great deal of maturity and vision present in these books, much more certainly than in the pre-war decades, but it has left younger readers with rather scant material in the mainstream fantasy tradition. This is more striking when we recall just how much fantasy was for younger children in the 1920s and 1930s, and how Victorian fantasies had something to offer all ages, from the knockabout comedy in Thackeray or the funny water creatures in Kingsley, to the chess game in *Through the Looking-Glass* or the discussions on death in MacDonald's *At the Back of the North Wind*. Only in the 1990s have we seen a change back to more fantasy for younger children, as in Annie Dalton's *Demon Spawn* and *The Dream Snatcher*, Helen Cresswell's *Stonestruck*, *The Watchers* and *Snatchers*, the *Harry Potter* books, or Pete Johnson's *The Creeper*.

One other change in English children's fantasy is in the use of magic. It is fair to say that in most Victorian fantasy (with the signal exception of the *Alice* books) there is someone in charge of administering it – from Lady Abracadabra in Paget's *The Hope of the Katzekopfs* or Fairy Blackstick in Thackeray's *The Rose and the Ring*, to Mrs Molesworth's Cuckoo or E. Nesbit's Psammead, Phoenix and

Mouldiwarps. If no particular personage is present, then the magic may often act by rules of moral or comic justice, again supposing a system of control, as in the punishment of the children in Lucy Lane Clifford's 'The New Mother.' Starting with E. Nesbit, however, magic begins to be seen as an anarchic force in its own right, which just appears and happens to you irrespective of any moral scheme, and this notion persists in children's fantasy till the 1950s. Then the sense of a 'larger scheme' returns briefly, in C. S. Lewis's Narnia books, Theresa Whistler's *The River Boy*, Catherine Storr's *Marianne Dreams* and Arthur Calder-Marshall's *The Fair to Middling*, where we feel that the fantastic events are governed by some further spiritual realm. Since then, magic has been seen as the projection of the unconscious, an accident, or a particular individual's power, and the old patterns have gradually gone. Now the power of magic may be challenged, as in Garner's *The Owl Service* or Robert Westall's novels. Susan Cooper's 'The Dark is Rising' series accomplishes the opposite of its purpose in demonstrating through its failure the present irrelevance of metaphysics. In the 1980s the supernatural or magical often becomes identified with no more than the powers of nature – as in the witches and technological priestesses of Susan Price, Ann Halam and Monica Furlong, or in the magical-natural Yeti of Michael Morpurgo, or in the rain-maker of Jan Mark's *Aquarius*. In the 1990s we find that magic is often an affliction to be removed or a threat to be escaped.

Children's fantasy has an obvious function in giving young people the pleasures of wish-fulfilment and the free imagination, while reminding them of the broad patterns of behaviour that have guided humanity to its best achievements. But since 1950, in becoming steadily more involved with 'the actual lives of children,' their fantasy has not only achieved a psychological and moral complexity it did not previously possess, but it has also lost certainty. The years from 1950–2000, which in the wider world see a gradual loss both of fixed values and of a sense of social identity, have in English children's fantasy now brought us to the often frightened, insecure child that is their product. It is not altogether surprising that children should have turned with one voice to a writer whose fantasies of school life are founded on a social structure and values no longer to be found in the outside world.

What then of the future? The current forty year-old mania for youth is part of our faith-shorn fear of age and death – of which also in one sense children's fantasy is itself a product. And now, it has even been argued, both children's fantasy and childhood itself are on the way out.[8] Curiously, in the decades to come it may be the old themselves who become the new power-class in England, holding as they increasingly do the money, the power, and the greater numbers. They also now possess the leisure that once belonged to childhood, and for which an increasingly work-driven society longs. One might speculate that retirement, especially if death is further postponed or blunted, could become the new desirable age, and we could find a new genre in which people yearned for the future rather than the past, for the bowling green rather than the sand-pit. In such a world children would move from the centre to the margins of attention; and what English children's fantasy there was would drop from its present favoured position with the English reading public, and become no more important to them than Shakespeare.

NOTES

1 INTRODUCTION

1. Robert Bloomfield, *The History of Little Davy's New Hat*, vii.
2. Jack Zipes, *Sticks and Stones: The Troublesome Success of Children's Literature from Slovenly Peter to Harry Potter*, 73.
3. Jacqueline Rose, *The Case of Peter Pan: or, The Impossibility of Children's Fiction*; Karen Lesnik-Oberstein, *Children's Literature: Criticism and the Fictional Child* .
4. Peter Hollindale, *Signs of Childness in Children's Books*, 70.
5. See also Perry Nodelman, *The Pleasures of Children's Literature*, 80–6; and 166, where he suggests that 'a vision of childhood as simple and pure might be an attempt by adults to colonize children, and persuade them they are more innocent than we secretly believe they actually are.'
6. Rose, *The Case of Peter Pan*, 12; Lesnik-Oberstein, *Children's Literature*, 161, 180.
7. Macdonald, 'The Fantastic Imagination,' in *A Dish of Orts: Chiefly Papers on the Imagination, and on Shakspere*, 317.
8. Pullman, cited in Robert McCrum, 'The World of Books,' 14. Pullman goes on: '"When you say, 'This book is for children,' what you are really saying is, 'This book is not for grown-ups.' ... But I don't care who's in my audience – all I care is that there should be as many of them as possible.'" However, as Peter Hollindale points out in *Signs of Childness in Children's Books*, many authors, while insisting that they do not write for children, still say that they write for the child in themselves (74).
9. See also Zipes, *Sticks and Stones*, 40, citing Philippe Ariès and others.
10. Hume, *Fantasy and Mimesis: Responses to Reality in Western Literature*, 21.
11. For a fuller examination of the terms, see Hollindale, *Signs of Childness*, 23–32.
12. *Observer* (25 June 2000), 1–2 (news item by Amelia Hill), citing the Children of the Nineties study directed by Professor Jean Golding at Bristol University's Institute of Child Health.
13. See also Hollindale, *Signs of Childness*, 57–9, 86–7 (also citing others) on the present-day disjunction of the generations.
14. What these writers (and one might add George MacDonald's *At the Back of the North Wind* (1871)) do is promote poor children out of their class: they

do not deal with the problems of the poor themselves. I therefore disagree here with Humphrey Carpenter, *Secret Gardens: The Golden Age of Children's Literature from Alice's Adventures in Wonderland to Winnie-the-Pooh* , 128, who sees a middle-class fantasy for children as beginning only with E. Nesbit.

15. Also observed by Carpenter, 16.
16. Reynolds, *Children's Literature in the 1890s and the 1990s*, 13–16, 27.
17. Ibid., 13, 18, 24.
18. See also Manlove, *The Fantasy Literature of England*, 10–14.
19. For a full account of the different approaches, see *Understanding Children's Literature*, ed. Peter Hunt.
20. See also Hollindale, *Signs of Childness*, 68–9, lamenting the removal of certainty, continuity and identity from children's literature by the approaches of literary theory.
21. Maria Nikolajeva, *The Magic Code: The Use of Magical Patterns in Fantasy for Children*, 117–19.

2 VICTORIAN CHILDREN'S FANTASY

1. See Manlove, *The Fantasy Literature of England*, 33–6.
2. Compare Roger B. Henkle, *Comedy and Culture: England 1820–1900*, 122: 'The phenomenal world exploded in Dickens's generation; the pulse of life quickened.'
3. See e.g. Jeremy Maas, 'Fairy Painters,' *Victorian Painters*, ch. x; Michael Booth, ed., *English Plays of the Nineteenth Century*, vol. V: *Pantomimes, Extravaganzas and Burlesques*; Nicola Bown, *Fairies in Nineteenth-Century Art and Literature*.
4. Compare Jackie Wullschläger, *Inventing Wonderland: The Lives and Fantasies of Lewis Carroll, Edward Lear, J. M. Barrie, Kenneth Grahame and A. A. Milne*, 101: 'The fairy tale shaped the Victorian novel so definitively that adult fiction became in a sense children's fiction – a natural development in a culture which made much of children.' See also e.g. Harry Stone, *Dickens and the Invisible World*.
5. Gillian Avery, *Nineteenth Century Children, Heroes and Heroines in English Children's Stories 1780–1900*, chs 2, 6; *From Instruction to Delight: An Anthology of Children's Literature to 1850*, ed. Patricia Demers and Gordon Moyles ; Mary V. Jackson, *Engines of Instruction, Mischief and Magic: Children's Literature in England from its Beginnings to 1839*; Peter Hunt, *Children's Literature, An Illustrated History*, chs 3,4,6.
6. John Ashton, *Chapbooks of the Eighteenth Century*.
7. Alan Richardson, 'Wordsworth, Fairy Tales and the Politics of Children's

Reading,' in *Romanticism and Children's Literature in Nineteenth-Century England*, ed. James Holt McGavran, 34–53, esp. 37–40. Samuel F. Pickering, *Moral Instruction and Fiction for Children 1749–1820*, ch. 1, 'Allegory and Eastern Tale,' points out the extensive use of orientalised romance for both moral instruction and entertainment in the eighteenth century (Johnson's *Rasselas* (1759) being a prime example).

8. On this 'genre,' see Karen Patricia Smith, *The Fabulous Realm: A Literary-Historical Approach to British Fantasy, 1780–1990*, ch. 4.

9. Fielding, *The Governess*, 68; see also 179.

10. First separately published as *Hop o' My Thumb* (1853), *Jack and the Bean-Stalk* (1854), *Cinderella* (1854) and *Puss in Boots* (1864).

11. Henkle, *Comedy and Culture*, 51, speaking of the changing character of 1830s English comedy, sees also a rebellion at growing 'respectability' and convention in society: 'comedic romances of adventure appeared that dreamed aloud the inchoate emotions of rebellion against the ordered, banal life that was steadily encroaching. A form of middle-class myth took shape that sustained the possibilities of freedom of action. The "green world" of the English countryside swelled again in the nostalgic imagination.' See also 55; and 17–19, where comic anarchy in Thackeray, Dickens and Carroll is discussed.

12. Dickens, 'Frauds on the Fairies,' 97–100. For the others, see Coleridge, letters of 9 and 16 October 1797, in *The Collected Letters of Samuel Taylor Coleridge*, ed. E. L. Griggs, I, 347, 354; Lamb, letter to Coleridge of 23 October 1802, in *The Letters of Charles and Mary Lamb*, ed. E. V. Lucas, I, 326; and *Quarterly Review*, LXXIV (1844), 8–9, 21–2.

13. Edgar Taylor, tr. and ed., *German Popular Stories* (C. Baldwin, 1823), iv.

14. In *The Doctor*, vol. IV (1837), ch. CXXIX. There is an earlier and different MS version of 'The Story of the Three Bears' in poetic form by Eleanor Mure (1831) repr. by Oxford University Press in 1967. Southey speaks of the tale as an old one in his introduction (316).

15. Paget, *The Hope of the Katzekopfs*, 204.

16. Parts of Keary's 'Mrs Calkill's Wonderful House' look to the Other-end-of-Nowhere section of *The Water-Babies*, and Ingelow's *Mopsa* clearly follows on from *Alice*. *Alice* itself must owe something to Kingsley's example, though John Goldthwaite's idea that it closely remodels *The Water-Babies* is pressed too hard to be more than occasionally convincing (*The Natural History of Make-Believe: A Guide to the Principal Works of Britain, Europe, and America*, 89–122). An argument that *Mopsa* is closely linked to George MacDonald's *At the Back of the North Wind* (first serialised in *Good Words for the Young*, Nov. 1868–Oct. 1869) is advanced by U. C. Knoepflmacher,

Ventures into Childland: Victorians, Fairy Tales, and Femininity, 281–3, 287–90, 302–6, 309–10, but since Ingelow's book was published on June 5th, 1869 (*Athenæum*) and therefore could not have been finished till early 1869, this argument seems insecure.

17. Carpenter, *Secret Gardens: The Golden Age of Children's Literature from Alice's Adventures in Wonderland to Winnie-the-Pooh*, 11.

18. First published in MacDonald, *Dealings with the Fairies*.

19. In Ewing, *Lob Lie-by-the-Fire, or, The Luck of Lingborough and Other Tales* .

20. *Charles Kingsley, His Letters and Memories of His Life*, ed. Frances E. Kingsley, II, 39.

21. Carroll declared, '"Alice" and the "Looking-Glass" are made up almost wholly of bits and scraps, single ideas which came of themselves' (extract from 'Alice on the Stage' (1887), repr. in Lewis Carroll, *Alice in Wonderland: Authoritative Texts…, Backgrounds, Essays in Criticism*, ed. Donald J. Gray, 281.

22. C. N. Manlove, *Modern Fantasy: Five Studies*, 46–7.

23. Henri F. Ellenberger, *The Discovery of the Unconscious: The History and Evolution of Dynamic Psychiatry*, ch. 5, esp. 303–9, describing three major European dream theorists of the 1860s.

24. Catherine A. Bernard, 'Dickens and Victorian Dream Theory,' in *Victorian Science and Victorian Values*, ed. James Paradis and Thomas Postlewait, 197–216.

25. Probably derived from Annie Keary's 'Gladhome' and 'Mrs Calkill's Wonderful House'.

26. First published in Knatchbull-Hugessen, *Moonshine, Fairy Stories*.

27. First published in Clifford, *Anyhow Stories, Moral and Otherwise* (Macmillan, 1882).

28. Geoffrey Rowell, *Hell and the Victorians: A Study of the Nineteenth Century Theological Controversies Concerning Eternal Punishment and the Future Life*; Michael Wheeler, *Heaven, Hell, and the Victorians*.

29. *The Water-Babies*, 94–5, 244–5. See also *Charles Kingsley: His Letters and Memories of His Life*, ed. Frances E. Kingsley, II, 143–4 (letter of 12 October 1862).

30. Manlove, *Modern Fantasy*, 17, 38–53.

31. Carroll wrote, 'I can guarantee that the [*Alice*] books have no religious teaching whatever in them – in fact, they do not teach anything at all' (letter of 18 August 1884, repr. in *The Selected Letters of Lewis Carroll*, ed. Morton N. Cohen, 137).

32. See Carpenter, *Secret Gardens*, 64–8; and Goldthwaite, *The Natural History of Make-Believe*, 155–8, who views Carroll as a blasphemer by literary necessity, since a work such as *Alice* demands a relativist approach to

truth (Goldthwaite sees Carroll as trying to rectify or 'unwrite' this in his subsequent fantasy).

33. *Selected Letters*, 194 (letter of 31 March 1890).
34. See on this Kirstin Drottner, *English Children and their Magazines 1751–1945*, 68–70.
35. Janet Oppenheim, *The Other World: Spiritualism and Psychical Research in England 1850–1914*.
36. George MacDonald, *Lilith: A Romance*, 350.
37. George MacDonald, *The Princess and the Goblin and The Princess and Curdie*, ed. Roderick McGillis, 209.
38. J. R. R. Tolkien, 'On Fairy-Stories,' in *Tree and Leaf*, 59.
39. First book publication of 'Con and the Little People' was in Molesworth, *Tell Me a Story* (Macmillan, 1875).
40. The first two stories were first published in book form in Ewing, *The Brownies and Other Tales* (Bell, 1870); 'Benjy' in *Lob Lie-by-the-Fire*.
41. For a more favourable view, attempting to tie these tales to themes of gender he traces elsewhere in Ewing's fantasy, see Knoepflmacher, *Ventures into Childland*, 390–7.
42. These three collections are themselves collected in Mary De Morgan, *The Necklace of Princess Fiorimonde and Other Stories*, ed. R. L. Green (Gollancz, 1963) – the text used here.
43. 'The Story of Vain Lamorna,' 'Siegfried and Handa,' 'The Hair Tree' (all 1877), 'The Wanderings of Arasmon,' 'The Pedlar's Pack,' 'The Wise Princess' (all 1880).
44. 'The Seeds of Love' (1877), 'The Wanderings of Arasmon,' 'The Heart of Princess Joan' (1877).
45. First published in Clifford, *The Last Touches and Other Stories* (A. & C. Black, 1892), and repr. in *Victorian Fairy Tales*, ed. Jack Zipes.
46. For an excellent account of the autistic behaviour in the story, based on personal experience of an autistic child, see Charlotte Moore, 'Mind the Gap,' *Guardian G2*, 22 May 2002, 11.
47. Lang, *The Blue Fairy Book* (Longmans, Green, 1889), introd., xi.
48. Thus Wilde's 'The Remarkable Rocket' looks to Andersen's 'The Darning Needle'; 'The Devoted Friend' to 'Great Claus and Little Claus'; and 'The Nightingale and the Rose' to 'The Nightingale' – though here Wilde may also be indebted to Mary De Morgan's 'The Toy Princess.'
49. Wilde, *Complete Works*, ed. Vyvyan Holland, 1092. Jack Zipes, who in *Fairy Tales and the Art of Subversion*, 113–21, sees Wilde's fairy tales as vehicles of social protest, rather misreads this essay (p. 115), and takes Wilde's part-intention in the tales for his whole achievement.

50. Quoted in *The Oxford Companion to Children's Literature*, ed. Carpenter and Pritchard, 238.
51. Carpenter, *Secret Gardens*, 151; see also 18–19, and Kimberley Reynolds, *Children's Literature in the 1890s and the 1990s*, 1–27, esp. 13–17.
52. Quoted in *Victorian Fairy Tales*, ed. Michael Hearn, introd., xxvi.
53. First published in Anstey, *The Talking Horse and Other Tales* (Smith, Elder, 1892).
54. First published in Anstey, *The Talking Horse*.
55. *Beyond the Looking Glass: Extraordinary Works of Fairy Tale and Fantasy, Novels and Stories from the Victorian Era*, ed. Jonathan Cott, 216.
56. *Victorian Fairy Tales*, ed. Zipes, 359–60.

3 THE LONG IDYLL: 1900–1950

1. Goldthwaite, *The Natural History of Make-Believe*, 311, puts it more fatalistically: 'We are all of us engaged in a comically lamentable business; our fate is to keep putting ourselves at risk and to come home again and again, like Brer Fox [of the *Uncle Remus* stories], "wid a spell er de dry grins"'. This is what she [Beatrix Potter] knew and what she told in tale after tale.'
2. On *Peter Pan* see Manlove, *Scottish Fantasy Literature: A Critical Survey*, 143–52.
3. Nesbit, *Wings and the Child, or, The Building of Magic Cities*, 20.
4. See e.g. 'Fortunatus Rex & Co.' and 'The Sums That Came Right,' in E. Nesbit, *Nine Unlikely Tales* (Fisher Unwin, 1901).
5. 'The Island of the Nine Whirlpools' in Nesbit, *The Book of Dragons* (Harper, 1900); and 'Melisande: or, Long and Short Division,' in *Nine Unlikely Tales*.
6. See e.g. 'The Princess and the Hedge-Pig' and 'Belinda and Bellamant,' in Nesbit, *The Magic World* (Macmillan, 1912).
7. On this see Manlove, *The Impulse of Fantasy Literature*, ch.4: 'The Union of Opposites in Fantasy: E. Nesbit.'
8. Nesbit, *The Story of the Amulet*, 52.
9. This itself is an enlarged version of an original short story in *Nine Unlikely Tales* – 'The Town in the Library in the Town in the Library.' E. M. Forster much admired it.
10. Kuznets, *When Toys Come Alive: Narratives of Animation, Metamorphosis, and Development*, 130–5.
11. J. M. S. Tompkins, *The Art of Rudyard Kipling*, 75.
12. Goldthwaite, 324, sees the method as deriving from the *Uncle Remus* stories (1880–1904).

13. Compare however Elliott Gose, *Mere Creatures: A Study of Modern Fantasy Tales for Children*, 17–28, describing the *Just So Stories* as creating a mythic world of their own, in which Darwin's ideas are reshaped to suit.

14. The word 'wanderlust' originates from the Edwardian period (*S.O.E.D.*).

15. Grahame, 'The Reluctant Dragon,' *Dream Days*, 174.

16. Carpenter, *Secret Gardens*, 117, relates the tension between these two impulses more to Grahame's own nature.

17. Tolkien, 'On Fairy-Stories,' 40; on dragons, see 39–40.

18. On which see e.g. Stephen Kern, *The Culture of Time and Space 1880–1918* .

19. See e.g. Marcus Crouch, *Treasure Seekers and Borrowers, Children's Books in Britain 1900–1960*, 39–42, 50–1.

20. Carpenter, *Secret Gardens*, 170.

21. Nicola Bown, *Fairies in Nineteenth-Century Art and Literature*, 183–7.

22. On 1920s fantasy and fairy books, see Manlove. *The Fantasy Literature of England*, 95–7, 102–4. On the artists, see Brigid Peppin, *Fantasy: The Golden Age of Fantastic Illustration*; Alison Packer, Stella Beddoe and Lianne Jarrett, ed. *Fairies in Legend and the Arts*; and on individual artists, *Kay Nielsen*, introd. Keith Nicholsen; Marcie Muir, *The Fairy World of Ida Rentoul Outhwaite*; James Hamilton, *Arthur Rackham*; Jane Laing, *Cicely Mary Barker and Her Art*. Much of 1920s fairy illustration is however derivative whimsy.

23. Farjeon wrote a sequel specifically for children in 1937, *Martin Pippin in the Daisy Field*, which is actually weaker than the first, being rather forced and fey.

24. A typical Romantic passage, in which love is described as 'a shoal of nameless longings,' is at p.40.

25. Theresa Whistler, *Imagination of the Heart: The Life of Walter de la Mare*, 69, 131–2, 256, 291.

26. Respectively, first published in de la Mare, *The Riddle and Other Stories* (Selwyn and Blount, 1923); *Two Tales* ('The Bookman's Journal Office' [1925]); *The Connoisseur* (William Collins, 1925); *On the Edge* (Faber and Faber, 1930); and *The Wind Blows Over* (Faber and Faber, [1936]).

27. Whistler, *Imagination of the Heart*, 167.

28. It has also been seen as a boy's consolation for loneliness in his home life, by Peter Hollindale, 'John Masefield,' *Children's Literature in Education* 23, 193–4.

29. Tolkien, 'On Fairy-Stories,' 52.

30. See also Manlove, *The Fantasy Literature of England*, 103–4.

31. Carpenter, *Secret Gardens*, 203–9, sees the *Pooh* books as a rejection of idyll in a portrait of social egotism.

32. Ibid., 210; see also 190.

33. This could have been the source for the animation of the random objects on the boys' bedroom floor in Diana Wynne Jones's *The Ogre Downstairs* (1974).
34. The first significant appearance of the scarecrow in children's fantasy is in L. Frank Baum's *The Wonderful Wizard of Oz* (New York, 1900).
35. Farjeon, *Sam Pig Goes to Market*, 69–88.
36. Almost certainly derived from Jean de Brunhoff's *Babar the Elephant*, first translated as *The Story of Babar, The Little Elephant*, in 1934, and followed by four more Babar books to 1939.
37. White probably got the idea of transformation to animals from Masefield's *The Box of Delights*, ch.4, where Herne the Hunter turns Kay into a stag, a wild duck and a fish: Masefield's books are actually a prime source for *The Sword in the Stone*. It may be that Masefield himself got the idea from Mark Lemon's *Tinykin's Transformations* (1869), in which the little boy hero is turned by Titania into a bird, a fish, a deer and then a mole. But then all of them are ultimately indebted to the transformations of fairy tale.
38. Thus *The Hobbit* also starts with a party in the Shire, Gandalf describes some of the journey ahead, and a reluctant hobbit sets out in a company. Then there is a journey through a mine, temporary absence of Gandalf, a stop at Elrond's hall, attack by wargs, constant threats from trolls (as the Nazgûl), salvation through eagles, meeting with Beorn (compare the Ents), attack by giant spiders, visit to a circular town (Lake Town, Minas Tirith), Bilbo's journey to meet the dragon alone and his return, the evil hypnotism of the treasure (as with the Ring), and a great closing battle. The point has been made before, by Paul H. Kocher, *Master of Middle-earth: The Achievement of J. R. R. Tolkien*, 30.
39. This goose flight is probably indebted to Selma Lagerlof's *The Wonderful Adventures of Nils* (1906; trans. 1907).
40. And Watkins-Pitchford may well have derived this idea of small men in a boat from Masefield's *The Midnight Folk*, 147–53.
41. Interviewed by Emma Fisher, for Justin Wintle and Emma Fisher, *The Pied Pipers: Interviews with the Influential Creators of Children's Literature*, Godden remarked, "'I like miniature things altogether, miniature boats and model trains, anything like that'" (293).
42. See *Chosen for Children, An account of the books which have been awarded the Library Association Carnegie Medal, 1936–1975*, ed. Marcus Crouch and Alec Ellis, 37–9.
43. See his *The Age of Scandal* (1950) and *The Scandalmonger* (1952).
44. As he may well have owed the titles in the Faun Tumnus's bookcase in *The Lion*, ch.2, to those in the Lord Salmon's bookcases in *The Stream That Stood*

Still, 89; and the idea of better and better Narnias at the end of *The Last Battle* (1956) to the more perfect country at the end of *The Tree That Sat Down*, 178–92.

45. Nearest is Kingsley, who in *The Water-Babies* celebrates the divinely-fuelled machines of nature in his great and small fairies.

46. She said in an interview, "'This lack of response, being brought up abroad, I find absolutely devastating in England. They don't react. You mustn't talk, you mustn't cry, you mustn't mention this or that – I find it very difficult'" (Wintle and Fisher, *The Pied Pipers*, 290).

47. Margaret and Michael Rustin, in *Narratives of Love and Loss: Studies in Modern Children's Fiction*, 84–91, argue that the doll characters are to be seen 'as representations of the emotional development of the relationships between Emily and Charlotte, and also their feelings about the adults who appear, and as delineations of different aspects of the character of the children' (86). See also Kuznets, *When Toys Come Alive*, 111–15.

48. These are *Impunity Jane* (1955), *The Fairy Doll* (1956), *The Story of Holly and Ivy* (1959) and *Candy Floss* (1960); also in *The Mousewife* (1951). The doll stories were later collected as *Four Dolls* (Macmillan, 1983).

4 INTO A NEW WORLD: 1950–1970

1. Alec Ellis, *A History of Children's Reading and Literature*, 205–14.

2. This point is also made by Carpenter, *Secret Gardens*, 216–20.

3. Lewis, *De Descriptione Temporum* (1955).

4. And also of the long winter freeze of 1947–8 when the book was being written.

5. Lewis, *That Hideous Strength: A Modern Fairy-Tale for Grown-Ups* (John Lane the Bodley Head, 1945), ch.14, title.

6. Lewis, *Perelandra*, 115, 247; *Miracles*, 135–40, 161 n., 191–92.

7. In his 'Sometimes Fairy Stories May Say Best What's to be Said' (1956), Lewis says how he realised that fairy tales could convey Christian truths without appearing to do so, and thus avoid the paralysing effect of the traditional imagery on the sensibility.

8. Boston, *The Children of Green Knowe*, 14–15.

9. Compare Margaret Meek, 'The Critic Entering the Author's World,' in Margaret Meek, et al., *The Cool Web: The Pattern of Children's Reading*, 327: 'If one stands outside the enchanted garden one could find the whole experience precious in the extreme and too rare to be of more than limited significance, or, more simply, irrelevant, if not odd.' However Meek finds herself drawn in by 'the spellbinding quality of the writing' (ibid.).

10. See also Hollindale, *Signs of Childness*, 89–91.

11. This interest is seen also in contemporary science fiction, in Arthur C. Clarke's *Childhood's End* (1953) and John Wyndham's *The Chrysalids* (1955) and *The Midwich Cuckoos* (1956): there was a fascination with the mind and its powers in the 1950s, largely because of the veneration for science.

12. Storr, 'Fear and Evil in Children's books,' 34–5.

13. Nevertheless, while Storr insists on the need for control, organisation and coherence in art, she maintains that 'as a writer I rely enormously on the unconscious' ('Why Write? Why Write for Children?,' 29).

14. Judith Barker, *The Brontës*, 156.

15. Somerville, *The Rise and Fall of Childhood*, ch.20, pp. 228–42.

16. On Garner's debts to Jungian thought, see Neil Philip, *A Fine Anger: A Critical Introduction to the Work of Alan Garner* , esp. 150.

17. Garner sees myth as 'a recycling of energy. Myth is a very condensed form of experience – it is very highly worked material. It has passed through unknown individual subconsciousnesses, until it has become almost pure energy' (Wintle and Fisher, *The Pied Pipers*, 229).

18. Philip, *A Fine Anger*, 56–62.

19. John Ezard, 'Dahl beats all competitors to collect honour as nation's favourite author' (*Guardian*, 10 March 2000, 5). This was the result of a poll of 40,000 people for World Book Day: Dahl had 4.5 per cent of the vote, and next was J. K. Rowling with 3.5 per cent – putting two writers of children's fantasy at the head of national popularity.

20. Though Dahl may well owe something here to the magic-carpet travels in J. B. S. Haldane's *My Friend Mr Leakey*, with its similarly wild adventures and abrupt transitions.

21. For a sometimes penetrating, sometimes ludicrous account of this story, see Mark I. West, 'Regression and Fragmentation of the Self in *James and the Giant Peach*,' 219–25.

22. Whether he is actually a boy or a man is indeterminate (8).

23. *A Castle of Bone* is itself pilfered by Lynne Reid Banks for the magic cupboard in her *Indian Trilogy* (1981–9).

24. Compare the questions raised by Hugh Crago, 'Penelope Farmer's Novels,' *Signal* 17 (May, 1975), 84. Farmer herself admits that she was poor at making connections, and was happier working with a language of only partly-understood symbols, which took their place in a mythic narrative that might order experience but never defined or explained it (Farmer, 'Discovering the Pattern,' in *The Thorny Paradise*, ed. E. Blishen, 103–7; and 'On the Effects of Collecting Myth for Children and Others,' 176–85). However both Crago, 83–90, and Margaret P. Esmonds, 'Narrative Methods in Penelope Farmer's

A Castle of Bone,' 171–9, esp. 178, question her success and her consistency in writing such myths, and in making them understandable to children.

25. *Earthfasts* has two sequels, *Cradlefasts* (1995) and *Candlefasts* (2000); the first is a realistic, and sentimental, continuation of the characters' lives, and the second is a sentimental and fantastic one. *Candlefasts* is actually still mainly about the human society, with the fantastic as a backdrop: the focus is on the growth of the new child Lyddy, and on whether farmer Frank and his wife Eileen will lose their home, Swang Farm, when the lease is up. The fantastic in the form of the moving Jingle Stones and journeys to the past through them, is not much of concern for itself, but only insofar as people get lost through the Stones, or a stray child from the past is brought into the present and eventually adopted when the portal on time finally closes.

26. Aiken writes of going 'just a step beyond the ordinary' in 'On Imagination,' in *Innocence and Experience: Essays and Conversations on Children's Literature*, ed. Barbara Harrison and Gregory Maguire, 58: 'Imagination does not have to deal with the supernatural; imaginative use of everyday material is just as valuable, if not more so.' (She cites as an example thinking up forty different uses for a tea-pot.) Aiken values the exercise of the imagination for its own sake rather than for any vision that comes through it.

27. On her pleasure in imagining herself into others' skins, see her remarks on *The Moon in the Cloud* in *Chosen for Children*, ed. Crouch and Ellis, 148.

28. Garfield sees himself as involved in this identity-shifting: 'I need all the trappings of illusion. I need to efface myself before I can be myself. I need to go away into another age before I can act out my fantasies'; and 'The question of identity … is obviously one that fascinates [me]' (*The Thorny Paradise*, 84; *The Pied Pipers*, 196)

5 REBELLION AND REACTION: THE 1970s

1. In this sense it seems mistaken to maintain that the other world exists *only* as a symbolic commentary on this one, as do Swinfen, *In Defence of Fantasy*, 64–7, and Alison Lurie, *Don't Tell the Grown-Ups: The Subversive Power of Children's Literature*, 186–8.

2. As Cresswell says in 'Ancient and Modern and Incorrigibly Plural,' in *The Thorny Paradise*, 111–12.

3. As does *The Bongleweed*, 170. See also *The Thorny Paradise*, 115, 116.

4. Anne Merrick, '"The Nightwatchmen" [sic] and "Charlie and the Chocolate Factory" as books to be read to children,' 24, also speaks of Cresswell's 'inner fantasy or world of the imagination,' contrasting it with Roald Dahl's more externalised fantasy.

5. Compare Cresswell in *The Thorny Paradise*, 110: 'I find the present technocracy alien and humanly barren, and ... I do not believe in the one-sided development of rationality at the expense of every other aspect of human experience.'

6. However Adams detested the idea of a book only for children: see his 'Some Ingredients of *Watership Down*,' in *The Thorny Paradise*, 163.

7. As a boy Adams particularly appreciated the stories of Ernest Thompson Seton, because 'He didn't dodge danger, fear, bloodshed and death. ... If the physical truth is cruel and terrible, be a man and say so ... and you may help your reader more than you know' (ibid., 166).

8. Adams says he took Fiver from Umanodda in de la Mare's *The Three Mulla-Mulgars*, his favourite book (ibid., 168).

9. Most suggested journey analogies are with Virgil's *Aeneid*, but as a Christian Adams would have been at least as likely to use the biblical story of the flight from Egypt. Here we have Fiver's premonitions of approaching disaster (like those of Joseph's dreams); a god, via the stories of El-ahrairah, continually provides the rabbits with spiritual sustenance and advice; a water barrier is crossed; a sign in the sky in the shape of the gull Kehaar shows the way; and a rival people in the promised land is overthrown in battle. The *Aeneid* analogy is compromised by the fact that the rabbit hero is not an Aeneas but a Ulysses the trickster, and by the absence of a Dido.

10. Possibly Parker got his idea of the ancient train at the unmarked platform from the strange night train that travels, unseen and unknown to timetables, in Helen Cresswell's *The Night-Watchmen*.

11. See her 'Children and Memory,' 400–7, esp. 404: 'In my own books, I have been concerned with the themes of continuity and memory.' In her non-fictional prose Lively speaks more morally of the sense of historical continuity being derived from our knowledge of the past rather than from the past coming to us supernaturally: but the fantastic vision is not a mere image of the other, and within the books, especially *The House in Norham Gardens* and *A Stitch in Time*, it has the weight of sober conviction.

12. This story is probably indebted to David Severn's *Drumbeats* (1953), the tale of a similarly stolen sacred drum which reveals a will of its own.

13. On the importance of place to Lively, see 'Children and Memory' 400–1, and 'Bones in the Sand,' in *Innocence and Experience*, ed. Harrison and Maguire, 16, 20.

14. This may well have come from the similar sense in Thomas Hardy's *A Pair of Blue Eyes* (1873), ch. 22, where Knight, clinging for his life to the rock slope above a sheer precipice, finds gazing into his face the eyes of an aeons-dead trilobite.

15. The Maria / Harriet relation is not unlike that of Jane Austen's Emma and Harriet.
16. For an excellent account of the changing perspectives, human and temporal, in the story, see John Stephens, *Language and Ideology in Children's Fiction*, 213–19.
17. See 'Children and Memory,' 403–7.
18. Where for instance in *The Driftway* the symbol of the fog and its clearance at the end reflects the gradual clearing of young Paul's mind, or the motif of clocks in *The House in Norham Gardens* mirrors the theme of time's changes and mortality, in *A Stitch in Time* we find a more submerged and subtle symbolism, which adds meaning rather than simply underlining it. The drawing room of Mrs Shand, landlady of the cottage, contains numerous grandfather clocks, all of which indicate different times, because they were allowed to run down variously at the death of Mrs Shand's husband. This suggests both the dislocation of spirit in Mrs Shand's refusal of temporal process (like Dickens's Miss Havisham) and Maria's own uncertain grasp of the past. Similar is the country house fair, or 'Fayre,' where everyone has dressed themselves up in 'historical' clothes from every period, all of them a medley of inaccuracies. Yet at the same time the chaos of the clocks and the (happy) confusion of the Fayre, which everybody enjoys, tells us that Maria's ordered and controlled modern life must be broken up.
19. Cooper, 'Newbery Award Acceptance Address,' 363ff.
20. See also Neil Philip, 'Fantasy: Double Cream or Instant Whip?,' 83, 87–8; David Rees, *What Do Draculas Do?: Essays on Contemporary Writers of Fiction for Children and Young Adults*, 175.
21. See also Rees, 181–2.
22. Cf. Gillian Spraggs, 'A Lawless World: The Fantasy Novels of Susan Cooper,' 23–31.
23. E. Nesbit also uses this trick in her story 'The Blue Mountain' (1900) about a city of ants (*Nine Unlikely Tales*, 1901).
24. The last in *The Time of the Ghost* (1981).
25. Respectively in her *Five Children and It*, 'The Princess and the Hedge-Pig' and 'Septimus Septimusson,' the latter two being from *The Magic World* (1912).
26. In *The Crown of Dalemark* (1993).
27. It seems a pity that Westall has so often been accused of being 'macho' and violent in his fiction, when he shows the limitations of these characteristics. See also Peter Hollindale, 'Westall's Kingdom,' 151–3.
28. See Jill Paton Walsh, 'The Writers in the Writer: A Reply to Hugh Crago,' 3–11.

6 PLAYING WITH REALITY: THE 1980s

1. Geoff Moss, 'Metafiction, Illustration, and the Poetics of Children's Literature' and 'My Teddy Bear Can Fly: Postmodernizing the picture book,' in *Literature for Children: Contemporary Criticism*, ed. Peter Hunt, 44–66, traces such postmodernist writing in books of 1975–1990 for younger children. On adult postmodernist fantasy see Manlove, *The Fantasy Literature of England*, 159–65.

2. This is different from Joan Aiken's alternative worlds in the Dido Twite series, in that it involves not just one alteration of historical fact (the Jacobites having succeeded instead of the Hanoverians) but a totally new ontology based on magic.

3. This situation is not unlike that in Iain Banks's *The Bridge* (1984).

4. Judging by local (Edinburgh) library borrowings.

5. On which see Manlove, *The Fantasy Literature of England*, 59–60.

6. John Stephens, *Language and Ideology in Children's Fiction*, 272–7. Stephens sees Jones as playing a linguistic and ontological game in this novel, whereby the relation between signifiers and signifieds, names and things, is continually slipping, and we are left to decipher the hidden true links for ourselves.

7. The story also recalls that of Meredith's *The Shaving of Shagpat* (1856).

8. To which famous U.S. children's fantasy King-Smith is indebted, and which he is also probably parodying – for *Charlotte's Web* is a much more serious and instructive book. See also p. 198 below.

9. This cupboard has obvious affinities with the one in Penelope Farmer's *A Castle of Bone*.

10. There is a swindling tyrant of the same name in Angela Carter's *The Passion of New Eve* (1977).

11. This character is strongly reminiscent of the inspired Irishman Finn in Helen Cresswell's *The Winter of the Birds* (1975).

12. And yet may be real: in the medieval culture to which Merlin looks, dreams were seen as capable of being visions of truth.

13. Stephens, *Language and Ideology*, 113, writes: 'while *Merlin Dreams* may create, as the dust jacket claims, "a remarkable world of medieval fantasy," its first moves are to strip away the easy associations and assumptions of medievalism and to signal that a different kind of intertextuality is in operation.'

14. This is reminiscent of the repulsive father and the monster the son mentally makes of him in William Mayne's *A Game of Dark*; and also of the unpleasant stepfather in Diana Wynne Jones's *The Ogre Downstairs*, and the monstrous creations of his step-children upstairs.

15. *The Stonewalkers* has its probable source in the myth of Pygmalion, in which the sculptor's statue of Venus came to life; and the story of Frankie in *The Monster Garden* is partly reflected in the myth of Prometheus.

16. A book for younger children that is in complete and comic contrast to this is Anne Fine's *Bill's New Frock* (1989), in which a little boy one day wakes up to find that he is a girl, though still with his character as a boy, and is sent to school by his mother in a pink frock. There he tries to behave as Bill the boy, but finds himself continually frustrated by people treating him as a girl. The story certainly makes a comic object-lesson, and suggests that seeing things from the point of view of the opposite sex is a good thing, especially when that sex is portrayed as so much the better behaved. But the moral is only lightly touched. Nor does Bill really see things from a girl's point of view since, being half still a boy and rebellious, he finds girlhood much more painful than it is.

7 FRIGHTENED OF THE DARK: THE 1990s

1. The beginnings of 'I' narration in realistic children's fiction are only slightly earlier: see Barbara Wall, *The Narrator's Voice: The Dilemma of Children's Fiction*, ch.14, 246–57; and Andrea Schwenke Wyile, 'Expanding the View of First-Person Narration,' 185 and ff.

2. This title recalls Helen Cresswell's *Snatchers*, also of 1998: the idea of having something of oneself taken away runs right through 1990s fantasy.

3. Michael Wilson, 'The Point of Horror: The Relationship between Teenage Popular Fiction and the Oral Repertoire,' 2. In a recent book, *Frightening Fiction*, Kimberley Reynolds and Kevin McCarron have attempted to find explanations for the current vogue of the American 'Goosebumps' or 'Point Horror' series. The main argument is that these books are designed to raise fears and then quell them, so that young readers' sense of the terrifying character of life is both imaged and overcome, thus producing a feeling of release and integration. Reynolds writes, 'This may be a conscious strategy for reassuring and empowering children at a time when British culture has a highly developed sense of the possible range of dangers to children' (op. cit., 3). McCarron sees horror fiction as overcoming the one horror children cannot bear, chaos and confusion: by establishing clear rules and norms, and stark distinctions between black and white, such fantasy endorses reason and civilisation. This sort of reassurance and moral polarisation may be found in these American horror fictions, but this seems less the case with the English variety we have been considering, where the horror is a figure of something

as much in the child characters themselves as coming from outside, and where the resolutions are often so late and tacked on (as, say, in *Midnight Blue, Pictures in the Dark* or *Mennyms Alive*) as never quite to cancel the very real sense of paranoia and dread of dissolution they have evoked. Nor are these English fantasies geared to the psychic needs of a child audience in the way that Reynolds portrays the Point Horror and other 'genre' books: 'writers, editors and publishers have identified and succeeded in satisfying a taste among young people for narratives which evoke, but then generally dispel, bizarre, frightening and/or inexplicable events' (ibid.). The English books are more individual, and more referrable back to the visions of their writers, who are of course not children but adults who were children twenty or more years ago. To explain horror and paranoia solely in terms of the child readership seems a mistake. And equally, to explain them benignly, as serving a civilising and empowering function, seems only one side of the truth.

4. This theme was partly anticipated in the late 1970s, in Robert Westall's *The Watch House* and Jill Paton Walsh's *A Chance Child* (both 1979). Previously, in the fantasy of Penelope Farmer or Penelope Lively, identity was unstable rather than insubstantial. But already William Mayne is registering a change in *It* (1975), where the alien creature inhabits Alice's mind and directs her; and Mayne follows this in the 1980s with the shimmering worlds of 'Boy to Island' and *Kelpie* (1987). As usual, Mayne anticipates later trends.

5. See *The Mennyms*, 168; *Siege*, 93; *Alone*, 205; *Alive*, 140.

6. Pullman has a particular dislike for C. S. Lewis's vision of this in the Narnia books. On his theme of wonder at this world, see Millicent Lenz, 'Philip Pullman,' in Peter Hunt and Millicent Lenz, *Alternative Worlds in Fantasy Fiction: Ursula Le Guin, Terry Pratchett, Philip Pullman and others*, 135–7, 161–2.

7. Pullman said his central aim in the trilogy was to catch his readers up into the story and make them want to go on and find out more ('Book Club,' BBC Radio 4, 12 May 2000). He consistently rates narrative as the highest of the arts of a writer.

8. Though not Manichean: see Lenz, 'Philip Pullman,' 157–72. Blake is one of Pullman's favourite authors, largely for his dialectical vision. Julia Briggs has called the trilogy 'a Blakean rereading of *Paradise Lost*' ('Fighting the forces of evil,' 21).

9. *The Oxford Companion to English Literature*, ed. Paul Harvey, 3rd ed., 53; *S.O.E.D.*

10. Lenz, 'Philip Pullman,' 125, makes it rather Lee Van Cleef, who co-starred with Eastwood in 'spaghetti' westerns.

11. On Pullman's sources, particularly Margaret Cavendish's *The Blazing World* (1666), see Manlove, *The Fantasy Literature of England*, 188. The main authors Pullman himself names are, first, Homer, then Milton and Blake; then Swift and Dickens (Kate Kellaway, 'A wizard with worlds,' *Observer Review*, 22 October 2000, 11). But one can add Joan Aiken's Dido Twite as a possible model for Lyra.

12. At which Mrs Coulter is herself surprised (426–7).

13. Julia Eccleshare, *A Guide to the Harry Potter Novels*, 49, also offers this explanation. See also 37–42, 47–8.

14. See also Eccleshare, *Guide*, 16–17, making the 'Cinderella' connection also.

15. Eccleshare, *Guide*, 11–12, 33–7, also likens Rowland's popularity to that of Blyton and Dahl.

16. Compare Elizabeth D. Schafer, *Exploring Harry Potter*, 206, identifying the magic of the Stone in the *Harry Potter* world with the imagination.

17. Margaret and Michael Rustin, *Narratives of Love and Loss: Studies in Modern Children's Fiction*, 282, point out that their use of the Dementors with their 'means of terror not so far from Voldemort's own' deeply compromises the older generation of the wizards.

18. Jack Zipes, *Sticks and Stones*, 181, asks whether the Harry Potter books attract children because they mirror the paranoid world of pervasive evil and threat children themselves inhabit.

19. Nicholas Tucker, 'The Rise and Rise of Harry Potter,' 221–34, wrestles conscientiously with this issue; so does Cedric Cullingford in relation to popular literature as a whole, in *Children's Literature and its Effects: The Formative Years*. Jack Zipes, however, says 'it is difficult to accept them as literature *per se*' (*Sticks and Stones*, 170), criticising them for repetitive plots, stereotypical characters and chauvinist attitudes (170–9).

20. It can be argued that the wizard school idea is heavily indebted to similar schools in T. H. White's *The Sword in the Stone*, Ursula Le Guin's *A Wizard of Earthsea* (1968), Diana Wynne Jones's *Charmed Life* and *The Lives of Christopher Chant*, or Terry Pratchett's *The Light Fantastic* (1986); that the children are from school stories and the masters from Mervyn Peake's *Gormenghast* (1950); and that the plots are from the techniques of detective stories, such as Colin Dexter's Inspector Morse books, where only partially adequate explanations of what really happened are provided in a clutch at the end. A primary source, for the ideas of the magic King's Cross platform, the hideous Dursleys with their gross son Dudley and the search by magician messengers for the neglected wonder-orphan lodged with them, is Eva Ibbotson's *The Secret of Platform 13* (1994).

21. Though Elizabeth Schafer finds them full of moral teaching (op. cit.).

8 CONCLUSION

1. Tolkien, *Tree and Leaf,* 43–50.
2. On literature, see Manlove, *The Fantasy Literature of England.* Medieval, Renaissance and eighteenth-century English philosophy is continually bound up with the supernatural, whether in supporting or opposing it. Victorian philosophy is preoccupied with the metaphysical consequences of Darwinism, and then embraces idealism, a position that lasts some way into the twentieth century.
3. Lewis, *Letters to Children*, ed. Lyle W. Dorsett and Marjorie Lamp Mead, 44–5: 'I did not say to myself "Let us represent Jesus as He really is in our world by a Lion in Narnia": I said "Let us *suppose* that there were a land like Narnia and that the Son of God, as He became a Man in our world, became a lion there, and then imagine what would happen' (letter of 29 May 1954). See also 52–3, 93.
4. Tolkien, *The Lord of the Rings,* I, 6, 7; MacDonald, *A Dish of Orts,* 317–22.
5. It is possible that the vogue of the adventure story drew off the impulse to travel far in English children's fantasy.
6. Aidan Chambers sees English children's fantasy as class-based in a way that American fantasy is not (*Booktalk: Occasional Writing on Literature and Children,* 77–83. This may be true up to about 1975, when English children's fantasy was distinctively middle-class in its characters and attitudes, but it has since then been increasingly socially inclusive.
7. Compare Nodelman, *The Pleasures of Children's Literature,* 119: 'The characters in many American children's novels take it for granted that anyone, no matter how humble, can improve his or her lot in life and achieve a dream. That basic, unquestioned premise defines them as Americans. It is not shared so unquestioningly, however, by the British ... who tend to be content with the way things are.'
8. Jerry Griswold, 'The Disappearance of Children's Literature (or Children's Literature as Nostalgia) in the United States in the Late Twentieth Century,' in *Reflections of Change: Children's Literature Since 1945,* ed. Sandra L. Beckett, 35–41, citing also Neil Postman, *The Disappearance of Childhood* (1982) and Marie Winn, *Children Without Childhood* (1983).

BIBLIOGRAPHY

Note: Place of publication is London unless indicated otherwise.

1. Texts Used

Adams, Richard. *The Plague Dogs* (Penguin, 1978)
    Shardik (Penguin, 1974)
    Watership Down (Puffin, 1973)
Abbott, Edwin A. *Flatland: A Romance of Many Dimensions* (Oxford: Blackwell, 1962)
Aiken, Joan. *Black Hearts in Battersea* (Puffin, 1968)
    The Cuckoo Tree (Puffin, 1973)
    Night Birds on Nantucket (Random House, Red Fox, 1993)
    The Shadow Guests (Puffin, 1982)
    The Stolen Lake (Random House, Red Fox, 1993)
    The Whispering Mountain (Puffin, 1970)
    The Wolves of Willoughby Chase (Puffin, 1968)
Aikin, Lucy. *Poetry for Children*, 2nd ed. (R. Phillips, 1803)
Alcock, Vivien. *The Monster Garden* (Reed, Mammoth, 1996)
    Singer to the Sea God (Methuen, 1992)
    The Stonewalkers (Reed, Mammoth, 1991)
Almond, David. *Skellig* (Hodder, 1998)
A.L.O.E. 'A Lady of England' (Charlotte Maria Tucker). *Fairy Know-a-Bit, or A Nut Shell of Knowledge* (T. Nelson, 1866)
Andersen, Hans Christian. *The Complete Illustrated Stories* (Reed, Chancellor Press, 1983)
Anstey, F. [Thomas Anstey Guthrie]. *The Talking Horse and Other Tales* (Smith, Elder, 1892)
Arthur, Ruth. *The Whistling Boy* (Collins, Armada, 1973)
Auerbach, Nina, and U. C. Knoepflmacher, ed *Forbidden Journeys: Fairy Tales and Fantasies by Victorian Women Writers* (Chicago: University of Chicago Press, 1992)
Awdry, Rev. W. *Thomas the Tank Engine: The Complete Collection* (Heinemann, 1996)
Banks, Lynne Reid. *The Indian Trilogy* (Collins, 1993)
Barrie, Sir James. *The Plays of J. M. Barrie* (Hodder and Stoughton, 1928)
Baum, L. Frank. *The Wonderful Wizard of Oz* (Dent, Dutton, 1965)

B.B. [Denis Watkins Pitchford]. *The Little Grey Men* (Puffin, 1962)

Belloc, Hilaire. *Selected Cautionary Verses* (Puffin, 1950)

Beresford, Elizabeth. *The Wombles* (Ernest Benn, 1968)

Bianco, Marjorie. *The Velveteen Rabbit* (Reed, Mammoth, 1992)

Bloomfield, Robert. *The History of Little Davy's New Hat*, 2nd ed. (Darton, Harvey and Darton, 1817)

Boston, Lucy. *The Children of Green Knowe* (Puffin, 1975)
>   *The Chimneys of Green Knowe* (Puffin, 1976)
>   *An Enemy at Green Knowe* (Puffin, 1977)
>   *The River at Green Knowe* (Puffin, 1976)
>   *The Stones of Green Knowe* (Puffin, 1979)
>   *A Stranger at Green Knowe* (Puffin, 1977)

Boumphrey, Esther. *The Hoojibahs* (Oxford University Press, 1929)

Brown, Maggie. *Wanted – A King, or How Merle Set the Nursery Rhymes to Rights* (1890) repr. in Cott, ed., *Beyond the Looking-Glass*

Browne, Frances. *Granny's Wonderful Chair* (Puffin, 1985)

Browning, Robert. 'The Pied Piper of Hamelin,' repr. in Hearn, ed. *The Victorian Fairy Tale Book*

Buchan, John. *The Magic Walking-Stick* (Edinburgh: Canongate 1985)

Calder-Marshall, Arthur. *The Fair to Middling* (Hart-Davis, 1959)

Carroll, Lewis [C.L.Dodgson]. *The Annotated Alice: Alice's Adventures in Wonderland and Through the Looking-Glass*, introd. Martin Gardner (Penguin, 1970)
>   *Sylvie and Bruno* (Macmillan, 1889)

Clarke, Pauline. *The Twelve and the Genii* (Puffin, 1977)

Clifford, Lucy Lane. *Anyhow Stories, Moral and Otherwise; and Wooden Tony, An Anyhow Story*, introd. Alison Lurie (New York: Garland, 1977)

Collodi, Carlo [Carlo Lorenzini]. *The Adventures of Pinocchio*, trans. Irene R. Gibbons (Blackie, 1965)

Cooper, Susan. *The Dark is Rising* (Puffin, 1976)
>   *Greenwitch* (Puffin, 1977)
>   *The Grey King* (Puffin, 1977)
>   *Over Sea, Over Stone* (Puffin, 1968)
>   *Seaward* (Puffin, 1985)
>   *Silver on the Tree* (Puffin, 1985)

Coppard, A. E. *Pink Furniture: A Tale for Lovely Children with Noble Natures* (Cape, 1930)

Corbett, William J. *The Song of Pentecost* (Puffin, 1984)
>   *Pentecost and the Chosen One* (Methuen, 1984)
>   *Pentecost of Lickey Top* (Reed, Mammoth, 1995)

BIBLIOGRAPHY

Corkran, Alice. *Down the Snow Stairs: or, From Good-Night to Good Morning* (Blackie, n.d.)

Cott, Jonathan, ed. *Beyond the Looking-Glass: Extraordinary Works of Fairy Tale and Fantasy* (Hart-Davis, MacGibbon, 1974)

Cresswell, Helen. *The Bongleweed* (Puffin, 1981)

        Moondial (Puffin, 1988)

        The Night-Watchmen (Puffin, 1988)

        The Outlanders (Faber, 1970)

        The Piemakers (Puffin, 1976)

        The Secret World of Polly Flint (Puffin, 1983)

        Snatchers (Hodder, 1998)

        Stonestruck (Puffin, 1996)

        Up the Pier (Faber, 1989)

        The Watchers (Puffin, 1992)

        The Winter of the Birds (Puffin, 1979)

Cross, Gillian. *Pictures in the Dark* (Puffin, 1998)

Cruikshank, George. *The Fairy Library* (Bell and Daldy, [1870])

Dahl, Roald. *The BFG* (Puffin, 1984)

        Charlie and the Chocolate Factory (Puffin, 1973)

        Charlie and the Great Glass Elevator (Puffin, 1995)

        James and the Giant Peach (Puffin, 1973)

        Matilda (Puffin, 1989)

        The Witches (Puffin, 1989)

Dalton, Annie. *The Alpha Box* (Reed, Mammoth, 1992)

        Demon Spawn (Puffin, 1993)

        The Dream Snatcher (Reed, Mammoth, 1998)

        Out of the Ordinary (Reed, Mammoth, 1996)

Davies, Andrew. *Conrad's War* (Scholastic, 1993)

de Brunhoff, Jean. *The Story of Babar, The Little Elephant* (Methuen Children's Books, 1955)

de la Mare, Walter. *Broomsticks and Other Tales* (Constable, 1925)

        The Lord Fish (Faber, [1933])

        The Three Royal Monkeys [*The Three Mulla-Mulgars*] (Robin Clark, 1993)

de Larrabeiti, Michael. *The Borribles* (New York: Ace Fantasy, 1979)

        The Borribles Go for Broke (New York: Ace Fantasy, 1982)

De Morgan, Mary. *The Necklace of Princess Fiorimonde and Other Stories*, ed. R. L. Green (Gollancz, 1963)

Dickens, Charles. *A Christmas Carol* (Puffin, 1984)

        'The Magic Fish-Bone,' in Hearn, ed. *The Victorian Fairy Tale Book*

BIBLIOGRAPHY

Dickinson, Peter. *The Blue Hawk* (New York: Ballantine, 1977)
> *The Changes Trilogy* (Puffin, 1985)
> *Merlin Dreams* (Heinemann, 1996)

Dickinson, William Croft. *Borrobil* (Puffin, 1964)

Elias, Edith L. *Periwinkle's Island* (W. & R. Chambers, 1919)

Ende, Michael. *The Neverending Story*, trans. Ralph Manheim (Penguin, Roc, 1991)

Ewing, Juliana Horatia. *The Brownies and Other Tales* (Dent, 1954)
> *Lob Lie-by-the-Fire, or The Luck of Lingborough and Other Tales* (Bell, 1874)
> *Old-Fashioned Fairy Tales* (S.P.C.K. [1882])

Farjeon, Eleanor. *Martin Pippin in the Apple Orchard* (Collins, 1921)
> *Martin Pippin in the Daisy Field* (Michael Joseph, [1937])
> *Sam Pig Goes to Market* (Faber and Faber, 1941)

Farmer, Penelope. *A Castle of Bone* (Puffin, 1962)
> *Charlotte Sometimes* (Bodley Head, 1992)
> *Emma in Winter* (Chatto and Windus, 1966)
> *The Magic Stone* (Chatto and Windus, 1964)
> *The Summer Birds* (Bodley Head, 1985)
> *William and Mary* (Chatto and Windus, 1974)

Farrow, G. E. *The Wallypug of Why*, new ed. (Henry Frowde and Hodder and Stoughton, n.d.)

Fielding, Sarah. *The Governess, or Little Female Academy* (Oxford University Press, 1968)

Fine, Anne. *Bill's New Frock* (Methuen, 1989)

Fisher, Catherine. *Belin's Hill* (Bodley Head, 1998)

Fisk, Pauline. *Midnight Blue* (Oxford: Lion, 1990)

Fraser, Ronald. *Flower Phantoms* (Cape, 1926)

Furlong, Monica. *Juniper* (Transworld, 1992)
> *Wise Child* (New York: Knopf, 1987)

Gardam, Jane. *Through the Dolls' House Door* (Franklin Watts, Julia Macrae Books, 1987)

Garfield, Leon. *The Ghost Downstairs* (Penguin, Kestrel, 1972)
> *Mr Corbett's Ghost* (Puffin, 1971)

Garner, Alan. *Elidor* (Puffin, 1967)
> *The Moon of Gomrath* (Puffin, 1965)
> *The Owl Service* (Penguin, Peacock, 1969)
> *Red Shift* (Fontana, Flamingo, 1985)
> *The Weirdstone of Brisingamen* (Puffin, 1963)

Garnett, David. *Lady into Fox and A Man in the Zoo* (Hogarth Press, 1985)

Gatty, Margaret. *The Fairy Godmothers and Other Tales* (George Bell, 1851)

Godden, Rumer. *Four Dolls* (Macmillan, 1993)
  The Mousewife (Macmillan, 1983)
  Tottie, The Story of a Dolls' House (Puffin, 1983)
Goudge, Elizabeth. *The Little White Horse* (Oxford: Lion, 1988)
  Smoky-House (Hodder and Stoughton, 1974)
Grahame, Kenneth. 'The Reluctant Dragon', in *Dream Days* (Nelson, n.d.)
  The Golden Age (John Lane, 1896)
  The Wind in the Willows (Methuen, 1926)
Grimm, J. and W. *The Complete Grimms' Fairy Tales* (Routledge, 1975)
Halam, Ann [Gwyneth Jones]. *Crying in the Dark* (Orion, 1998)
  Daymaker (Puffin, 1989)
  The Haunting of Jessica Raven (Orion, 1994)
  The Powerhouse (Orion, 1997)
  The Skybreaker (Puffin, 1990)
  Transformations (Puffin, 1990)
Haldane, J. B. S. *My Friend Mr Leakey* (Puffin, 1971)
Harris, Rosemary. *Bright and Morning Star* (Puffin, 1978)
  The Moon in the Cloud (Faber, 1989)
  The Shadow on the Sun (Puffin, 1989)
Hayes, Rosemary. *Dreamchild* (Puffin, 1992)
Hearn, Michael Patrick, ed. *The Victorian Fairy Tale Book* (Edinburgh: Canongate, 1990)
Hoban, Russell. *The Mouse and His Child* (Puffin, 1976)
Hoffman, Heinrich. *Struwwelpeter* (Pan, Piccolo, 1972)
Horowitz, Anthony. *The Devil's Door-bell* (Patrick Hardy, 1983)
  The Night of the Scorpion (Patrick Hardy, 1985)
  The Silver Citadel (Methuen, 1987)
Housman, Laurence. *A Doorway in Fairyland* (Cape, 1922)
  Moonshine and Clover (Cape, 1922)
Hudson, W. H. *A Little Boy Lost* (Duckworth, 1905)
Hughes, Richard. *A High Wind in Jamaica* (Triad, Panther, 1976)
Hunter, Norman. *The Incredible Adventures of Professor Branestawm* (Bodley Head, 1965)
Ibbotson, Eva. *The Secret of Platform 13* (Pan Macmillan, 1994)
Ingelow, Jean. *Mopsa the Fairy*, repr, in Auerbach and Knoepflmacher, ed. *Forbidden Journeys*
Jacobs, Joseph, ed. *English Fairy Tales* (Puffin, 1970)
Jansson, Tove. *Finn Family Moomintroll*, trans. Elizabeth Potch (Puffin, 1961)
Jerrold, Douglas. *Works*, 5 vols. (Bradbury, Agnew, [1869?])
Johnson, Pete. *The Creeper* (Transworld, Corgi, 2000)

BIBLIOGRAPHY

Jones, Diana Wynne. *Archer's Goon* (Methuen, 1986)
    Black Maria (Methuen, 1991)
    Cart and Cwidder (Macmillan, 1975)
    Castle in the Air (Reed, Mammoth, 1991)
    Charmed Life (Puffin, 1979)
    The Crown of Dalemark (New York: Greenwillow, 1995)
    Dark Lord of Derkholm (New York: Greenwillow, 1998)
    Deep Secret (Gollancz, 1997)
    Dogsbody (Reed, Mammoth, 1993)
    Drowned Ammet (New York: Beech Tree, 1995)
    Eight Days of Luke (Puffin, 1977)
    Fire and Hemlock (Reed, Mammoth, 1993)
    Hexwood (Reed, Mammoth, 1993)
    The Homeward Bounders (Reed, Mammoth, 1993)
    Howl's Moving Castle (Methuen, 1986)
    The Lives of Christopher Chant (Methuen, 1988)
    The Magicians of Caprona (Reed, Mammoth, 1992)
    The Ogre Downstairs (Macmillan, 1996)
    Power of Three (Macmillan, 1996)
    The Spellcoats (New York: Beech Tree, 1995)
    A Sudden Wild Magic (Cassell, 1996)
    A Tale of Time City (Reed, Times-Mandarin, 1990)
    The Time of the Ghost (Macmillan, 1996)
    Witch Week (Reed, Mammoth, 1993)
Keary, Annie. *Little Wanderlin, and Other Fairy Tales* (Macmillan, 1873)
Kennemore, Tim. *Changing Times* (Faber, 1984)
King, Clive. *Stig of the Dump* (Puffin, 1993)
King-Smith, Dick. *Daggie Dogfoot* (Puffin, 1982)
    Harry's Mad (Puffin, 1986)
    The Sheep-Pig (Puffin, 1985)
Kingsley, Charles. *The Water-Babies: A Fairy Tale for a Land-Baby* (Macmillan, 1864)
Kipling, Rudyard. *The Jungle Book* (Macmillan, 1894)
    Just So Stories (Macmillan, 1902)
    Puck of Pook's Hill (Pan, Piccolo, 1975)
    Rewards and Fairies (Pan, Piccolo, 1975)
    The Second Jungle Book (Macmillan, 1950)
Kirby, Mary, and Elizabeth Kirby. *The Talking Bird, or, The Little Girl Who Knew What Was Going To Happen* (Grant and Griffith, 1856)
Knatchbull-Hugessen, Edward. *Moonshine, Fairy Stories* (Macmillan, 1871)

BIBLIOGRAPHY

Lagerlöf, Selma. *The Wonderful Adventures of Nils*, trans. and ed. Velma Swanston Howard (New York: Dover, 1995)

Lambourne, John. *The Kingdom That Was* (Murray, 1931)

Lang, Andrew. *The Gold of Fairnilee* (Bristol: J. W. Arrowsmith, 1888)

    Prince Prigio (Bristol: J. W. Arrowsmith, 1889)

    Prince Ricardo of Pantouflia (Bristol: J. W. Arrowsmith, 1893)

Lear, Edward. *The Complete Nonsense*, ed. Holbrook Jackson (Faber, 1947)

Le Guin, Ursula K. *A Wizard of Earthsea* (Puffin, 1971)

Lemon, Mark. *The Enchanted Doll* (Alexander Moring, the de la More Press, 1903)

    Tinykin's Transformations, repr. in Cott, *Beyond the Looking-Glass*

Lewis, C. S. *The Great Divorce* (Bles, 1946)

    The Horse and His Boy (Puffin, 1965)

    The Last Battle (Puffin, 1964)

    The Lion, the Witch and the Wardrobe (Puffin, 1959)

    The Magician's Nephew (Puffin, 1963)

    Perelandra (John Lane, The Bodley Head, 1943)

    Prince Caspian (Puffin, 1962)

    The Silver Chair (Puffin, 1965)

    That Hideous Strength (John Lane the Bodley Head, 1945)

    The Voyage of the 'Dawn Treader' (Puffin, 1965)

Lewis, Hilda. *The Ship That Flew* (Oxford: Oxford University Press, 1998)

Linklater, Eric. *The Pirates in the Deep Green Sea* (Macmillan, 1949)

    The Wind on the Moon (Puffin, 1972)

Lively, Penelope. *Astercote* (Reed, Mammoth, 1996)

    The Driftway (Reed, Mammoth, 1993)

    The Ghost of Thomas Kempe (Puffin, 1984)

    Going Back (Puffin, 1986)

    The House in Norham Gardens (Reed, Mammoth, 1994)

    The Revenge of Samuel Stokes (Puffin, 1983)

    A Stitch in Time (Reed, Mammoth, 1994)

    The Whispering Knights (Reed, Mammoth, 1995)

    The Wild Hunt of Hagworthy (Puffin, 1984)

Lofting, Hugh. *Doctor Dolittle and the Secret Lake* (Cape, 1949)

    Doctor Dolittle in the Moon (Cape, 1929)

    Doctor Dolittle's Caravan (Cape, 1927)

    Doctor Dolittle's Circus (Cape, 1925)

    Doctor Dolittle's Garden (Cape, 1928)

    Doctor Dolittle's Post Office (Cape, 1924)

    Doctor Dolittle's Return (Cape, 1933)

BIBLIOGRAPHY

Doctor Dolittle's Zoo (Cape, 1926)

The Story of Doctor Dolittle (Cape, 1922)

The Voyages of Doctor Dolittle (Cape, 1923)

Lurie, Alison, ed. *The Oxford Book of Modern Fairy Tales* (Oxford: Oxford University Press, 1993)

MacDonald, George. *At the Back of the North Wind* (Dent, 1956)

The Light Princess and Other Tales, ed. R. L. Green (Gollancz, 1961)

Phantastes and Lilith (Gollancz, 1962)

The Princess and the Goblin and The Princess and Curdie, ed. Roderick McGillis (Oxford: Oxford University Press, 1990)

[*The Wise Woman*] *The Lost Princess: A Double Story* (Dent, 1965)

Mark, Jan. *Aquarius* (Penguin, Kestrel, 1982)

They Do Things Differently There (Random House, 1996)

Masefield, John. *The Box of Delights* (Collins, 1984)

The Midnight Folk (Reprint Society, 1959)

Mayne, William. *Antar and the Eagles* (Walker, 1990)

The Battlefield (Hamish Hamilton, 1967)

'Boy to Island,' *All the King's Men* (Cape, 1982)

Candlefasts (Hodder, 2000)

Cradlefasts (Hodder, 1995)

Cuddy (Random House, 1994)

Earthfasts (Arrow, 1990)

A Game of Dark (Hamish Hamilton, 1971)

A Grass Rope (Oxford University Press, 1972)

It (Puffin, 1980)

Kelpie (Puffin, 1989)

Over the Hills and Far Away (Hodder, 1997)

A Swarm in May (Hodder, 1997)

A Year and a Day (Hamish Hamilton, 1976)

McCaughrean, Geraldine. *A Pack of Lies* (Puffin, 1995)

McEwan, Ian. *The Daydreamer* (Random House, 1995)

Milne, A. A. *The House at Pooh Corner* (Methuen, 1965)

When We Were Very Young (Methuen, 1965)

Winnie-the-Pooh (Methuen, 1965)

Molesworth, Mary Louisa. *Christmas Tree Land* (Macmillan, 1981)

The Cuckoo Clock (Macmillan, 1938)

The Tapestry Room (Macmillan, 1879)

Tell Me a Story (Macmillan, 1891)

Morpurgo, Michael. *King of the Cloud Forests* (Reed, Mammoth, 1997)

Morris, William. 'Lindenborg Pool,' *The Early Romances of William Morris* (Dent, 1973)

Mulock, Dinah [afterwards Craik]. *The Adventures of a Brownie* (N.Y.: Harper, n.d.)

      The Little Lame Prince and his Travelling Cloak, repr. in Hearn, ed. *The Victorian Fairy Tale Book*

Murray, Violet. *The Rule of the Beasts* (Stanley Paul, 1925)

Nesbit, E[dith]. *The Book of Dragons* (T. Fisher Unwin, 1900)

      The Enchanted Castle (Puffin, 1979)

      Five Children and It (Puffin, 1959)

      Harding's Luck (T. Fisher Unwin, 1923)

      The House of Arden (T. Fisher Unwin, 1908)

      The Magic City (Macmillan, 1980)

      The Magic World (Benn, 1959)

      Nine Unlikely Tales (Benn, 1960)

      The Phoenix and the Carpet (Benn, 1956)

      The Story of the Amulet (Puffin, 1959)

      Wings and the Child, or The Building of Magic Cities (Hodder and Stoughton, 1913)

Nichols, Beverly. *The Mountain of Magic* (Collins, 1975)

      The Stream That Stood Still (Collins, 1975)

      The Tree That Sat Down (Collins, 1975)

Norton, Mary. *The Borrowers* (Puffin, 1958)

      The Borrowers Afield (Puffin, 1960)

      Bedknob and Broomstick (Puffin, 1970)

      The Borrowers Afloat (Puffin, 1970)

      The Borrowers Aloft (Puffin, 1970)

Nostlinger, Christine. *Conrad, the Factory-Made Boy*, trans. Anthea Bell (Heinemann, 1986)

Orwell, George. *Animal Farm* (Penguin, 1951)

Outhwaite, Ida Rentoul, and Grenbry Outhwaite. *The Enchanted Forest* (A. & C. Black, 1921)

Paget, Francis E. *The Hope of the Katzekopfs: or, The Sorrows of Selfishness, A Fairy Tale*, 2nd ed. (Joseph Masters, 1847)

Parker, Richard. *The Old Powder Line* (Gollancz, 1971)

Parry, Edward Abbott. *Butterscotia; or, A Cheap Trip to Fairy Land* (Heinemann, 1927)

      Katawampus. Its Treatment and Cure, and The First Book of Krab (Heinemann, 1927)

BIBLIOGRAPHY

Pearce, Philippa. *Tom's Midnight Garden* (Puffin, 1976)
Potter, Beatrix. *The Complete Tales* (Penguin, Frederick Warne, 1997)
Price, Susan. *The Ghost Drum* (Faber, 1989)
    Ghost Song (Faber, 1992)
Pullman, Philip. *Northern Lights* (Scholastic, 1996)
    The Subtle Knife (Scholastic, 1997)
    The Amber Spyglass (Scholastic, David Fickling, 2000)
Robinson, Joan G. *When Marnie Was There* (Collins, 1971)
Rossetti, Christina. 'Goblin Market' (1862)
    Speaking Likenesses (Macmillan, 1874)
Rowling, J. K. *Harry Potter and the Philosopher's Stone* (Bloomsbury, 1997)
    Harry Potter and the Chamber of Secrets (Bloomsbury, 1998)
    Harry Potter and the Prisoner of Azkaban (Bloomsbury, 1999)
    Harry Potter and the Goblet of Fire (Bloomsbury, 2000)
Rushdie, Salman. *Haroun and the Sea of Stories* (Penguin and Granta, 1991)
Ruskin, John. *The King of the Golden River*, repr. in Zipes, ed. *Victorian Fairy Tales*
Saint-Exupéry, Antoine de. *The Little Prince*, trans. Katherine Woods (Penguin, 1962)
Sharp, Evelyn. *All the Way to Fairyland, Fairy Stories* (John Lane, 1898)
    Wymps and Other Fairy Tales (John Lane, 1897)
Sinclair, Elizabeth. 'Uncle David's Nonsensical Story of Giants and Fairies' (*Holiday House*, 1839), repr. in Zipes, ed. *Victorian Fairy Tales*
Sleigh, Barbara. *Carbonel* (Puffin, 1961)
    The Kingdom of Carbonel (Puffin, 1971)
Smith, E. A. Wyke. *The Marvellous Land of Snergs* (Ernest Benn, 1927)
Southey, Robert. 'The Story of the Three Bears,' *The Doctor*, vol. IV [1837], ch. CXXIX
Storr, Catherine. *The Castle Boy* (Faber, 1983)
    Marianne Dreams (Puffin, 1964)
Tarn, W. W. *The Treasure of the Isle of Mist* (Oxford University Press, 1959)
Thackeray, W. M. *The Rose and the Ring* (Puffin, 1964)
Todd, Barbara Euphan. *Worzel Gummidge* (Puffin, 1941)
Tolkien, J. R. R. *The Hobbit* (Allen and Unwin, 1951)
    The Lord of the Rings (Allen and Unwin, 1968)
    'On Fairy-Stories', *Tree and Leaf* (Allen and Unwin, 1964)
Tozer, Kathleen. *Here Comes Mumfie* (John Murray, 1947)
    The Wanderings of Mumfie (John Murray, 1945)
Travers, P. L. *Mary Poppins* (HarperCollins, 1998)
    Mary Poppins Comes Back (HarperCollins, 1998)

       Mary Poppins Opens the Door (HarperCollins, 1998)

Uttley, Alison. *Little Grey Rabbit's Birthday* (Collins, 1978)

       Sam Pig Goes to Market (Faber, 1941)

       A Traveller in Time (Puffin, 1977)

Walker, Kenneth M., and Geoffrey M. Boumphrey. *The Log of the Ark* (Constable, 1923)

Walpole, Horace. *Hieroglyphic Tales* (San Francisco: Mercury House, 1993)

Walsh, Jill Paton. *A Chance Child* (Puffin, 1985)

Waugh, Sylvia. *The Mennyms* (Random House, 1994)

       Mennyms Alive (Random House, 1997)

       Mennyms Alone (Random House, 1997)

       Mennyms Under Siege (Random House, 1996)

       Mennyms in the Wilderness (Random House, 1996)

Wesley, Mary. *Haphazard House* (Dent, 1993)

Westall, Robert. *Devil on the Road* (Macmillan, 1996)

       Gulf (Reed, Mammoth, 1993)

       The Promise (Walton-on-Thames: Nelson, 1992)

       The Scarecrows (Puffin, 1983)

       The Watch House (Macmillan, 1995)

       The Wind Eye (Pan Macmillan, 1992)

Whistler, Theresa. *Imagination of the Heart: The Life of Walter de la Mare* (Duckworth,1993)

       The River Boy (Hart-Davis, 1955)

White, E. B. *Charlotte's Web* (Puffin, 1963)

White, T. H. *Mistress Masham's Repose* (New York: G. P. Putnam's, 1946)

       The Sword in the Stone (Collins, 1938)

Wilde, Nicholas. *Into the Dark* (HarperCollins, 1989)

Wilde, Oscar. *The Happy Prince and Other Stories* (Puffin, 1962)

Williams, Ursula Moray. *Adventures of the Little Wooden Horse* (Puffin, 1959)

Wiseman, David. *The Fate of Jeremy Visick* (Puffin, 1984)

Zipes, Jack, ed. *Victorian Fairy Tales: The Revolt of the Fairies and Elves* (Routledge, 1991)

2. Secondary Sources

Adams, Richard. 'Some Ingredients of *Watership Down*'. In Blishen, ed. *The Thorny Paradise*

Aiken, Joan. 'On Imagination'. In Harrison and Maguire, ed. *Innocence and Experience*

Ashton, John. *Chapbooks of the Eighteenth Century* (Skoob, 1997)

BIBLIOGRAPHY

Auerbach, Nina, and U. C. Knoepflmacher, ed. *Forbidden Journeys: Fairy Tales and Fantasies by Victorian Women Writers* (Chicago: University of Chicago Press, 1992)

Avery, Gillian, with Angela Bull. *Nineteenth Century Children: Heroes and Heroines in English Children's Stories 1780–1900* (Hodder and Stoughton, 1965)

Avery, Gillian, and Julia Briggs, ed. *Children and their Books: A Celebration of the Work of Iona and Peter Opie* (Oxford: Oxford University Press, 1989)

Barker, Judith. *The Brontës* (Weidenfeld and Nicolson, 1994)

Barrett, Frank. *Where Was Wonderland?: A Traveller's Guide to the Settings of Classic Children's Books* (Hamlyn, 1997)

Bernard, Catherine A. 'Dickens and Victorian Dream Theory'. In Paradis, James, and Thomas Postlewait, ed. *Victorian Science and Victorian Values* (New Brunswick, N.J.: Rutgers University Press, 1985)

Blishen, Edward, ed. *The Thorny Paradise: Writers on Writing for Children* (Penguin, Kestrel, 1975)

Bloomfield, Robert. *The History of Little Davy's New Hat*, 2nd ed. (Darton, Harvey and Darton, 1817)

Booth, Michael, ed. *English Plays of the Nineteenth Century*. Vol. V, *Pantomimes, Extravaganzas and Burlesques* (Oxford: Clarendon Press, 1976)

Bown, Nicola. *Fairies in Nineteenth-Century Art and Literature* (Cambridge: Cambridge University Press, 2001)

Bratton, J. S. *The Impact of Victorian Children's Fiction* (Croom Helm, 1981)

Briggs, Julia. *A Woman of Passion: The Life of E. Nesbit 1858–1924* (Hutchinson, 1987)

———. 'Fighting the forces of evil'. *Times Literary Supplement* (22 December 2000), 21

Carpenter, Humphrey, and Mari Prichard, ed. *The Oxford Companion to Children's Literature* (Oxford: Oxford University Press, 1984)

———. *Secret Gardens: The Golden Age of Children's Literature from Alice's Adventures in Wonderland to Winnie-the-Pooh* (Boston, MA: Houghton Mifflin, 1985)

Carroll, Lewis [C. L. Dodgson]. *The Selected Letters of Lewis Carroll*, ed. Morton N. Cohen, 2nd ed. (Macmillan, 1989)

———. 'Alice on the Stage' (1887), repr. in Donald J. Gray, ed. *Lewis Carroll, Alice in Wonderland: Authoritative Texts . . . , Backgrounds, Essays in Criticism*, 2nd ed. (New York: W.W. Norton, 1992)

Cavendish, Margaret. *The Blazing World and Other Writings*, ed. Kate Lilley (Harmonsworth: Penguin, 1994)

Chambers, Aidan. *Booktalk: Occasional Writing on Literature and Children* (Stroud: Thimble Press, 1995)

Cooper, Susan. 'Newbery Award Acceptance Address'. *Horn Book Magazine* 52 (August 1976)

Cott, Jonathan, ed. *Beyond the Looking Glass: Extraordinary Works of Fairy Tale and Fantasy, Novels and Stories from the Victorian Era* (Hart-Davis, MacGibbon, 1974)

Crago, Hugh. 'Penelope Farmer's Novels'. *Signal* 17 (May, 1975)

Cresswell, Helen. 'Ancient and Modern and Incorrigibly Plural'. In Blishen, ed., *The Thorny Paradise*

Crouch, Marcus. *Treasure Seekers and Borrowers, Children's Books in Britain 1900–1960* (Library Association, 1962)

————. *The Nesbit Tradition: The Children's Novel in England 1945–1970* (Benn, 1972)

————, and Alec Ellis, ed. *Chosen for Children, An account of the books which have been awarded the Library Association Carnegie Medal 1936–1975* (Library Association, 1977)

Cullingford, Cedric. *Children's Literature and its Effects: The Formative Years* (Cassell, 1998)

Cunningham, Hugh. *Children and Childhood in Western Society since 1500* (Longman, 1995)

Darton, F. J. Harvey. *Children's Books in England: Five Centuries of Social Life*, 3rd ed., rev. Brian Alderson (Cambridge: Cambridge University Press, 1982)

Demers, Patricia, and G. Moyles, ed. *From Instruction to Delight: An Anthology of Children's Literature to 1850* (Toronto: Oxford University Press, 1982)

Dickens, Charles. 'Frauds on the Fairies'. *Household Words* VIII, 184 (1 October 1843)

Drottner, Kirstin. *English Children and their Magazines 1751–1945* (New Haven: Yale University Press, 1988)

Eccleshare, Julia. *A Guide to the Harry Potter Novels* (Continuum, 2002)

Egoff, Sheila. *Worlds Within: Children's Fantasy from the Middle Ages to Today* (Chicago: American Library Association, 1988)

————, G. T. Stubbs, and L. F. Ashley. *Only Connect: Readings on Children's Literature* (Toronto: Oxford University Press, 1980)

Ellenberger, Henri F. *The Discovery of the Unconscious: The History and Evolution of Dynamic Psychiatry* (HarperCollins, Fontana, 1994)

Ellis, Alec. *A History of Children's Reading and Literature* (Oxford: Pergamon, 1968)

Esmonds, Margaret P. 'Narrative Methods in Penelope Farmer's *A Castle of Bone*'. *Children's Literature in Education* 14, 3 (Autumn, 1983)

Ezard, John. 'Dahl beats all competitors to collect honour as nation's favourite author'. *Guardian* (10 March 2000), 5

BIBLIOGRAPHY

Farmer, Penelope. 'On the Effects of Collecting Myth for Children and Others'. *Children's Literature in Education* 8, 4 (Winter, 1977)

———. 'Discovering the Pattern'. In Blishen, ed. *The Thorny Paradise*

Fisher, Margery. *Intent Upon Reading: A Critical Appraisal of Modern Fiction for Children*, rev. ed. (Leicester: Brockhampton Press, 1964)

Frey, Charles, and John Griffith. *The Literary Heritage of Childhood: An Appraisal of Children's Classics in the Western Tradition* (New York: Greenwood, 1987)

Goldthwaite, John. *The Natural History of Make-Believe: A Guide to the Principal Works of Britain, Europe, and America* (New York: Oxford University Press, 1996)

Gose, Elliott. *Mere Creatures: A Study of Modern Fantasy Tales for Children* (Toronto: University of Toronto Press, 1988)

Griggs, E. L., ed. *The Collected Letters of Samuel Taylor Coleridge*, 6 vols. (Oxford: Clarendon Press, 1956–71)

Griswold, Jerry. 'The Disappearance of Children's Literature (or Children's Literature as Nostalgia) in the United States in the Late Twentieth Century'. In Sandra L. Beckett, ed. *Reflections of Change: Children's Literature Since 1945* (Westport, CT: Greenwood, 1997)

Hamilton, James. *Arthur Rackham* (Pavilion, 1990)

Hardy, Thomas. *A Pair of Blue Eyes* (Macmillan, 1975))

Harrison, Barbara, and Gregory Maguire, ed. *Innocence and Experience: Essays and Conversations on Children's Literature* (New York: Lothrop, Lee and Shepard, 1987)

Hearn, Michael Patrick, ed. *Victorian Fairy Tales* (Edinburgh: Canongate, 1988)

Henkle, Roger B. *Comedy and Culture: England 1820–1900* (Princeton, N.J.: Princeton University Press, 1980)

Hollindale, Peter. 'John Masefield'. *Children's Literature in Education* 23 (1976)

———. *Ideology and the Children's Book* (Stroud: Thimble Press, 1988)

———. 'Westall's Kingdom'. *Children's Literature in Education* 25 (1994)

———. *Signs of Childness in Children's Books* (Stroud: Thimble Press, 1997)

Hume, Kathryn. *Fantasy and Mimesis: Responses to Reality in Western Literature* (N.Y.: Methuen, 1984)

Hunt, Peter. *An Introduction to Children's Literature* (Oxford: Oxford University Press, 1994)

———. *Children's Literature, An Illustrated History* (Oxford: Oxford University Press, 1995)

———, ed. *International Companion Encyclopedia of Children's Literature* (Routledge, 1996)

———, ed. *Understanding Children's Literature* (Routledge, 1999)

BIBLIOGRAPHY

Jackson, Mary V. *Engines of Instruction, Mischief and Magic: Children's Literature in England from its Beginnings to 1839* (Lincoln, Nebraska: University of Nebraska Press, 1989)

Jones, Diana Wynne. *The Tough Guide to Fantasyland* (New York: Daw, 1996)

Kellaway, Kate. 'A Wizard with Worlds'. *Observer Review* (22 October 2000), 11

Kern, Stephen. *The Culture of Time and Space 1880–1918* (Cambridge, MA: Harvard University Press, 1983)

Kingsley, Charles. *Madam How and Lady Why* (Macmillan, 1869)

Kingsley, Frances E., ed. *Charles Kingsley, His Letters and Memories of His Life*, 11th ed., 2 vols (Kegan Paul, 1878)

Knoepflmacher, U. C. *Ventures into Childland: Victorians, Fairy Tales, and Femininity* (Chicago: University of Chicago Press, 1998)

Knowles, Murray, and Kirsten Malmkjær. *Language and Control in Children's Literature* (Routledge, 1996)

Kocher, Paul H. *Master of Middle-earth: The Achievement of J.R.R. Tolkien* (Thames and Hudson, 1972)

Kuznets, Lois. *When Toys Come Alive: Narratives of Animation, Metamorphosis, and Development* (New Haven: Yale University Press, 1994)

Laing, Jane. *Cicely Mary Barker and Her Art* (Frederick Warne, 1995)

Lang, Andrew. *The Blue Fairy Book* (Longmans, Green, 1889)

Lenz, Millicent. 'Philip Pullman'. In Hunt, Peter and Millicent Lenz. *Alternative Worlds in Fantasy Fiction: Ursula Le Guin, Terry Pratchett, Philip Pullman and others* (Continuum, 2001)

Lesnik-Oberstein, Karen. *Children's Literature: Criticism and the Fictional Child* (Oxford: Clarendon Press, 1994)

Lewis, C. S. *Perelandra* (John Lane the Bodley Head, 1943)

———. *Miracles: A Preliminary Study* (Bles, 1947).

———. *De Descriptione Temporum* (1955). Repr. in *They Asked for a Paper: Papers and Addresses* (Bles, 1962)

———. 'Sometimes Fairy Stories May Say Best What's to be Said' (1956). Repr. in *Of Other Worlds: Essays and Stories*, ed. Walter Hooper (Bles, 1966)

———. *Letters to Children*, ed. Lyle W. Dorsett and Marjorie Lamp Mead (Collins, 1985)

Lively, Penelope. 'Children and Memory'. *Horn Book Magazine* 49 (Aug., 1973)

———. 'Bones in the Sand', in Harrison and Maguire, ed. *Innocence and Experience*

Lucas, E. V., ed. *The Letters of Charles and Mary Lamb*, 3 vols. (Dent and Methuen, 1935)

BIBLIOGRAPHY

Lurie, Alison. *Don't Tell the Grown-Ups: The Subversive Power of Children's Literature* (New York: Little, Brown, 1990)

Lynn, Ruth Nadelman. *Fantasy Literature for Children and Young Adults: An Annotated Bibliography*, 4th ed. (New Providence, NJ: R.R.Bowker, 1995)

Maas, Jeremy. 'Fairy Painters', *Victorian Painters* (Barrie and Rockcliffe, Cresset Press, 1969)

MacDonald, George. 'The Fantastic Imagination', *A Dish of Orts: Chiefly Papers on the Imagination, and on Shakspere* (Sampson Low Marston, 1893)

———. *Lilith: A Romance* (Chatto and Windus, 1895)

———. *The Princess and the Goblin and The Princess and Curdie*, ed. Roderick McGillis (Oxford: Oxford University Press, 1990)

Manlove, Colin N. *Modern Fantasy: Five Studies* (Cambridge: Cambridge University Press, 1975)

———. 'The Union of Opposites in Fantasy: E. Nesbit', *The Impulse of Fantasy Literature* (Macmillan, 1983)

———. *Scottish Fantasy Literature: A Critical Survey* (Edinburgh: Canongate Academic, 1994)

———. *The Fantasy Literature of England* (Macmillan, 1999)

McCrum, Robert, 'The World of Books'. *Observer Review* (22 Oct., 2000), 14

McGavran, James Holt, Jr., ed. *Romanticism and Children's Literature in Nineteenth-Century England* (Athens, GA: University of Georgia Press, 1991)

McGillis, Roderick. *The Nimble Reader: Literary Theory and Children's Literature* (New York: Twayne, 1996)

Meek, Margaret, Aidan Warlow, and Griselda Barton. *The Cool Web: The Pattern of Children's Reading* (Bodley Head, 1977)

Merrick, Anne. '"The Nightwatchmen" [sic] and "Charlie and the Chocolate Factory" as books to be read to children'. *Children's Literature in Education* 16 (Spring, 1975)

Moore, Charlotte. 'Mind the Gap'. *Guardian G2* (22 May 2002), 1

Moss, Geoff. 'Metafiction, Illustration, and the Poetics of Children's Literature' and 'My Teddy Bear Can Fly: Postmodernizing the picture book'. In *Literature for Children: Contemporary Criticism*, ed. Peter Hunt (Routledge, 1992)

Muir, Marcie. *The Fairy World of Ida Rentoul Outhwaite* (A. & C.Black, 1986)

Mure, Eleanor. *The Story of The Three Bears metrically related, with illustrations locating it at Cecil Lodge in 1831* (Oxford University Press [1967])

Myers, Mitzi. 'Romancing the Moral Tale: Maria Edgeworth and the Problematics of Pedagogy'. In McGavran, ed. *Romanticism and Children's Literature*

Nesbit, Edith. *Wings and the Child, or, The Building of Magic Cities* (Hodder & Stoughton, 1913)

Nicholsen, Keith. *Kay Nielsen* (Hodder & Stoughton, 1975)

Nikolajeva, Maria. *The Magic Code: The Use of Magical Patterns in Fantasy for Children* (Stockholm: Almqvist and Wicksell International, c. 1988)

———. *Children's Literature Comes of Age: Towards a New Aesthetic* (New York: Garland, 1996)

Nodelman, Perry. *The Pleasures of Children's Literature*, 2nd ed. (New York: Longmans, 1996)

Observer (25 June 2000), 1–2 [news item by Amelia Hill]

Oppenheim, Janet. *The Other World: Spiritualism and Psychical Research in England 1850–1914* (Cambridge: Cambridge University Press, 1985)

Packer, Alison, Stella Beddoe, and Lianne Jarrett. *Fairies in Legend & the Arts* (Cameron and Tayleur, in association with David and Charles, 1980)

Paul, Lissa. *Reading Otherways* (Stroud: Thimble Press, 1998)

Peppin, Brigid. *Fantasy: The Golden Age of Fantastic Illustration* (New York: New American Library, 1975)

Philip, Neil. 'Fantasy: Double Cream or Instant Whip?' *Signal* 35 (May 1981)

———. *A Fine Anger: A Critical Introduction to the Work of Alan Garner* (Collins, 1981)

Phillips, Robert, ed. *Aspects of Alice: Lewis Carroll's Dreamchild as seen through the Critics' Looking-Glasses 1865–1971* (Penguin, 1974)

Pickering, Samuel F. *Moral Instruction and Fiction for Children 1749–1820* (Athens, GA: University of Georgia Press, 1993)

Rees, David. *What Do Draculas Do?: Essays on Contemporary Writers of Fiction for Children and Young Adults* (Metuchen, N.J.: Scarecrow Press, 1990)

Reynolds, Kimberley. *Children's Literature in the 1890s and the 1990s* (Plymouth: Northcote House, 1994)

———, and Kevin McCarron. *Frightening Fiction* (Continuum, 2002)

Richardson, Alan. 'Wordsworth, Fairy Tales and the Politics of Children's Reading'. In McGavran, ed., *Romanticism and Children's Literature*

[Rigby, Elizabeth]. *Quarterly Review* LXXIV (1844), 1–40 [article on children's literature]

Rose, Jacqueline. *The Case of Peter Pan: or, The Impossibility of Children's Fiction* (Macmillan, 1984)

Rowell, Geoffrey. *Hell and the Victorians: A Study of the Nineteenth Century Theological Controversies Concerning Eternal Punishment and the Future Life* (Oxford: Clarendon Press, 1974)

Rustin, Margaret, and Michael Rustin. *Narratives of Love and Loss: Studies in Modern Children's Fiction* , rev. ed. (Karnac, 2001)

Salway, Lance, ed. *A Peculiar Gift: Nineteenth Century Writings on Books for Children* (Penguin, Kestrel, 1976)

Schafer, Elizabeth D. *Exploring Harry Potter* (Ebury Press, 2000)

Sherwood, Mary Martha. *The Governess, or The Little Female Academy* (Wellington, Salop: F. Houlston, 1820)

Smith, Patricia. *The Fabulous Realm: A Literary-Historical Approach to British Fantasy 1780–1990* (Metuchen, NJ: Scarecrow Press, 1993)

Somerville, C. John. *The Rise and Fall of Childhood* (Beverly Hills, CA: Sage, c. 1982)

Spock, Benjamin M. *Baby and Child Care* (Bodley Head, 1955)

Spraggs, Gillian. 'A Lawless World: The Fantasy Novels of Susan Cooper'. *Use of English* 33 (1982)

Spufford, Francis. *The Child that Books Built: A Memoir of Childhood and Reading* (Faber, 2002)

Stephens, John. *Language and Ideology in Children's Fiction* (Longman, 1992)

Stone, Harry. *Dickens and the Invisible World* (Macmillan, 1979)

Storr, Catherine. 'Fear and Evil in Children's Books'. *Children's Literature in Education* 2 (1970)

———. 'Why Write? Why Write for Children?'. In Blishen, ed. *The Thorny Paradise*

Swinfen, Ann. *In Defence of Fantasy: A Study of the Genre in English and American Literature since 1945* (Routledge, 1984)

Taylor, Edgar, tr. and ed. *German Popular Stories*, 2 vols. (C. Baldwin, 1823, 1826)

Tolkien, J. R. R. 'On Fairy-Stories', *Tree and Leaf* (Allen and Unwin, 1964)

Tompkins, J. M. S. *The Art of Rudyard Kipling* (Methuen, 1959)

Townsend, John Rowe. *Written for Children: An Outline of English-language Children's Literature*, rev. ed. (Penguin, Kestrel, 1983)

Tucker, Nicholas. *The Child and the Book: A Psychological and Literary Exploration* (Cambridge: Cambridge University Press, 1981)

———. 'The Rise and Rise of Harry Potter'. *Children's Literature in Education* 30, 4 (1999)

Wall, Barbara. *The Narrator's Voice: The Dilemma of Children's Fiction* (Macmillan, 1991)

Walsh, Jill Paton. 'The Writers in the Writer: A Reply to Hugh Crago'. *Signal* 40 (January 1983)

Watson, Victor, ed. *The Cambridge Guide to Children's Literature* (Cambridge: Cambridge University Press, 2001)

West, Mark I. 'Regression and Fragmentation of the Self in *James and the Giant Peach*', *Children's Literature in Education* 16, 4 (Winter, 1985)

Wheeler, Michael. *Heaven, Hell, and the Victorians* (Cambridge: Cambridge University Press, 1990)

BIBLIOGRAPHY

Whistler, Theresa. *Imagination of the Heart: The Life of Walter de la Mare* (Duckworth, 1993)

Wilde, Oscar. *Complete Works*, ed. Vyvyan Holland (Collins, 1966)

Wilson, Michael. 'The Point of Horror: The Relationship between Teenage Popular Fiction and the Oral Repertoire'. *Children's Literature in Education* 31, 1 (2000)

Wintle, Justin, and Emma Fisher. *The Pied Pipers: Interviews with the Influential Creators of Children's Literature* (Paddington Press, 1974)

Wullschläger, Jackie. *Inventing Wonderland: The Lives and Fantasies of Lewis Carroll, Edward Lear, J.M.Barrie, Kenneth Grahame and A. A. Milne* (Methuen, 1995)

Wyile, Andrea Schwenke. 'Expanding the View of First-Person Narration', *Children's Literature in Education* 30, 3 (1999)

Zipes, Jack, ed. *Victorian Fairy Tales: The Revolt of the Fairies and Elves* (Routledge, 1987)

———. *Fairy Tales and the Art of Subversion: The Classical Genre for Children and the Progress of Civilisation* (Routledge, 1988)

———, ed. *The Oxford Companion to Fairy Tales: The Western Fairy Tale Tradition from Medieval to Modern* (Oxford: Oxford University Press, 2000)

———. *Sticks and Stones: The Troublesome Success of Children's Literature from Slovenly Peter to Harry Potter* (Routledge, 2001)

INDEX

INDEX

Printed in the United States
16699LVS00004B/310-318